THIRTY
—BEFORE—
THIRTY

30 Q&As From Around The World On Life, Love, Travel

GRISELDA BENAVIDES

Thirty Before Thirty
By Griselda Benavides

Copyright © 2018 by Griselda Benavides

All rights reserved. This book or any portion thereof may not be reproduced or used in any manner whatsoever without the express written permission of the author.

Printed in the United States of America

First Printing, 2018

ISBN-13: 978-0-692-15691-9

www.griseldabenavides.com

Disclaimer:

The information/advice provided in this book is for entertainment and/or informational purposes only and shouldn't be seen as a supplement and/or replacement for medical, legal, tax, emotional advice, or other types of advice. No liability is assumed for losses or damages due to the information provided. You are responsible for your own choices, actions, and results. You should consult medical, legal, tax, emotional and all other type of advice, needed, from a qualified/trained professional.

Opinionated content in this book doesn't reflect the opinions of the author.

Names, characters, places, and incidents, brands, are mentioned by the participants of this book for testimonial purposes.

Participants of this book have authorized their approval and/or personal consent to be in this book. It was an at-will consent. They are aware they are not contributors of this book but only participants/and or interviewees. They are aware edits to their content had to be made. No liability is assumed for losses or damages due to the information provided.

Parent/guardian consent has been given for child/minor participant. They have authorized their approval and/or personal consent to be in this book. It was an at-will consent. They are aware they are not contributors of this book but only participants/and or interviewees. They are aware edits to their content had to be made. No liability is assumed for losses or damages due to the information provided.

The editor and everyone else who provided a service for this book are aware they are not contributors of this book but solely providers of a service of which they were employed for. Their employment was at-will. They understand the author of this book owns all rights to this book, that includes, Copyright, ISBN and everything else relating to this book.

Although the author and publisher have made every effort to ensure that the information in this book was correct at press time, the author and publisher do not assume and hereby disclaim any liability to any party for any loss, damage, or disruption caused by errors or omissions, whether such errors or omissions result from negligence, accident, or any other cause.

TABLE OF CONTENTS

Introduction 5
Jóse Hernàndez 9
Nadia Adose 22
Enrique A. Gutierrez 27
Christina McFaul 40
Andrea Maradiaga 50
Baoyiruole 60
Angie C. Seagren 69
Mario Alberto Guzman Jaime 75
Michele and Keith Green 87
Yasmin Siqueira Dahás 98
Sonia Masters 104
Chato 116
Polen Pulluoğlu 136
Rodrigo Navarro-Ramirez, M.D., M.S 143
Ruth and Marco Argueta 161
Stefhania Mejia 165
Gloria Barrera 177
Ginamarie and Annamarie Russo 187
Angie and Jorge Garcia 193
Marisol Ugues 199
Alexandar Yu 204
Araceli Torres Padilla 209
Tina Carstensen 215
Jorge Moto 231
Ariyanna O'Neal 248
Melina Chavez Bobadilla 251
Linda Neel 258
Carlos Ibarra 264
Lupe Carrillo 274
Staff Sergeant Nelson Benavides, Staff Sergeant
Jeeandy Morales, Staff Sergeant Joseph Nino 290
Acknowledgments 330
Q&A Session Between You and I 337

With special dedication to my favorite storytellers and lifelong best friends, my mom, and dad! I love you!

To Betty, Lis, Nelson, Lorena, and Shannon.

To Olivia, Stella, and Mailah.

To everyone who has touched my life in a greater way than they might have ever imagined.

Florentino Nava Arias

Saint Joachim Catholic Church

Jose Corona and Margarita Rodriguez.

My doggies in doggie heaven, Kobe, and Snoopy.

To my friends and family who share their story in this book.

Matthew 6:25-34

INTRODUCTION

I grew up around stories, and I never knew there were any such stories as those that could be told in a minute or so. All of the stories that I heard were long and full of details. The year, the clothing and everything else was included, and no detail was ever forgotten. Those stories made me feel as if I was there.

I guess I can say its a family thing, predominantly from my father, Adrian. Some, I can imagine, find his stories and responses overly detailed, perhaps even boring and unnecessary. His doctor, for example, might be one of those. After all, he only has a certain time allocated for each one of his patients. Although I am sure that for Adrian, he reserves extra time.

"Have you had any trouble sleeping lately?"

"Lately no, but when I was kid in (insert date), and I was sleeping under the trees of my family's cornfields, and I was all alone there, as an 8-year-old boy, sometimes, I would. Oh, and…"

"Mr. Benavides, but currently, do you have any issues sleeping?"

"Oh, currently?"

And before any other question can remind my father of something else, the question is quickly closed for discussion.

However, for me, his stories have an entirely different effect. They are the ones that have uplifted me when I have needed it most, and it's my father's stories that have allowed me to feel brave when I have needed to. They've inspired me to live a life full of adventure, and most importantly, Adrian's stories are what I believe have been the connecting force of our solid father-daughter relationship. His stories allow me to feel as if we have always been together and as if there has never been a gap between us in our lives.

Like the times he's told me about herding the cattle of his family and, after doing so, sleeping under the stars, late into the night, alone as an 8-year-old boy, surrounded by watermelon, corn, or whatever the fruit or vegetable of the season was of his family's farmland in Jalisco, Mexico. I've always felt that I, too, was there.

Or his time in Corcoran.

And my mother, she's no exception to storytelling. She's used her stories in a very creative way, to discipline through them and teach, without making it obvious.

There is the time she told about her first time in Mexico City. She described how excited she was to come across the word "spaghetti" on the menu where she would be having dinner. She was delighted in imagining how tasteful the spaghetti would be that she decided she would order it. The full plate of spaghetti ended up falling on her lap. The entire plate…which she remembers caused a huge mess, a big commotion and the plate was so hot that when it fell on her lap, it almost burnt her.

The advice that was offered through that story was to never order anything complicated to eat while on an important dinner with strangers—that includes first dates.

It was no surprise to me that I would want to spend the entire year before my 30th birthday to consist of stories. It was then that I decided I would combine my love for stories, writing and listening as I heard friends from all over the world tell me their very own stories.

Thirty Before Thirty is exactly that, a collection of interviews that I conducted the entire year prior to turning 30 and even upon turning 30. I asked about life, love, and travel. The interviews were either conducted in person, via phone, or through email. My goal was to not be pretentious, I felt that as a writer, it was my responsibility to showcase the most profound of stories, not the most famous, the saddest, or solely of the elite. I felt that I had to introduce new stories that have the possibility of bringing positive changes to our lives. I decided that I wanted this to be a Q&A because what can be simpler than asking a question and hearing the answer?

I want this book to be a book that you can open and read a little bit of, and then go back to it but, in the process, be completely transformed through the advice of each one of the participants. I want this book to capture your attention far beyond the length of it and for it to be a call to action for all of the topics discussed. I also really want to bring positivity to this age and, ultimately, to every age.

The wonderful irony of this experience was that I thought this was going to be easy, and way easier than my first book, *A Plenitude of Heartbeats*. But this actually resulted in the hardest project of my life. I often heard my inner voice laughing at me and saying, "And you thought this was going to be easy," in a fancy English accent. But the irony is that right when I felt like I couldn't continue, I would conduct an interview, and what was meant to ideally inspire you, the reader, actually was inspiring me and motivating me to continue. One of my favorite pieces of advice that I heard was from Carlos Ibarra. He said: "In all seriousness, goals are tough, and they take work."

...I also kept reminding myself of what Chato said: "Don't worry about putting this on the third floor, worry about putting it on the first step, and then the second, and so on."

And lastly, I thought about, you, about how much I want you to read what everyone who shared their story in this book has to say about life, love and travel. Just thinking that they might actually change your life for the better makes everything worth it!!

From my entire heart,

Griselda Benavides

JÓSE HERNÀNDEZ

CALIFORNIA, USA

I told my sister I was going to be interviewing you today, and as I was reading her all of your accomplishments she interrupted me and said, "Oh, I know. He's the best."

I think there are a lot of us that feel that way about you.

You're a Grammy-nominated artist, founder of the first all-girl mariachi band. And of course the founder of Mariachi Sol de Mexico and… of the Mariachi Heritage Society. You're an entrepreneur, husband, and father.

You're also a 5th-generation mariachi singer.

I read you started singing at around 3 or 4-years-old.

Does that mean, you always knew what you would do in life?

Was it always clear you would be a musician?

Thank you!

Yes, there was never a plan to do anything else. I think the genes are very strong in my family. All of my nieces and nephews are musicians. They don't make a living from it, but they all sing very well.

We've been *very, very* blessed.

My family has been doing this for many generations.

How was life around the past generations of musicians in your life?

Were they always singing?

And if so, how did that influence you?

Not so much singing at home. As far as my father and my brothers, I would hear them practice their instruments right before a show. But they were always working together, so they didn't really play at home together. Unless it was a rehearsal (or something like that) for a big show they were doing.

I used to sit with my father when my brothers were on TV from Mexico City, backstage. I would look at my dads face; he looked *so* proud.

I think that sort of drove me to want to do it, too.

I know you were born in Mexicali (Baja California, Mexico) but its interesting to me that you and your family are so connected to the culture of Jalisco. For example, mariachi music comes from the state of Jalisco (Mexico), and you and your family happen to be huge icons in the mariachi music industry.

You also have a couple of Jalisco themed songs.

Did your family perhaps relocate from Jalisco to Mexicali?

Yes, they did.

My dad's side of the family is from a little ranch called, La Cofradía, that's in the *Municipio de* Tuxcueca which is where Lake Chapala is—Tuxcueca is directly across from Lake Chapala. My dad is from that little town, and that's where he grew up.

His father used to play, his grandfather and grandmother also used to play.

My mom is from a town called, Teocuitatlá, Jalisco. She was born there but raised in Pueblo Nuevo, Jalisco; it used to be called, Concepción de Buenos Aires.

My dad fell in love with my mom, when they were very young.

They were around 16-years-old.

They ended up moving with the families and getting married. She had her first child at 16-and-a-half (my oldest brother). They moved to Chapala, Jalisco and that is where my brothers were born.

At about 3-years-old you moved from Mexicali to California.

Do you remember the move?

If so, how was the transition and change like?

"When I came to California?"

No, I don't remember. I was 3-and-a-half-years-old, I was still very young.

What I do remember, a little bit of is when we were at our house in East Los Angeles. We were living at the Maravilla Housing Projects. I remember my dad would always say, "Don't go outside, it's dangerous," (laughs).

My dad was always working, and my older brothers were pretty much always working. My two older sisters, my brother Jesus, who plays the guitar with me (still) would be at home.

How was the mariachi music scene in California when you were growing up there?

Well, it was sort of scarce. The most famous place was called, *El Milion Dolar*, the Million Dollar Theater, which was on 3rd and Broadway (I think). The Million Dollar was where all the artists would sing at like, Javier Solis, Jose Alfredo Jimenez...

I grew up going there a lot.

I remember going with my father and hearing them backup all of those great artists, it was amazing.

If we examined your life closely and all of your accomplishments like, Mariachi Sol de Mexico, Mariachi Reyna de Los Angeles, the Mariachi Heritage Society, being nominated for the Grammy's.

Opening your restaurant, being a husband and a father.

We could possibly determine you had everything so figured out. And even though I am sure everything you have accomplished hasn't been easy—you have made it seem like it has. It seems as if everything has flowed so seamlessly and perfectly for you.

What do you think?

Did you have everything figured out?

I always knew because I played with my family.

By that time, by the time, I was out of high school, they were very well-connected in the industry. All the people from the radio knew who they were. And the people from local television did as well. They helped start channel 34 (KMEX). They also did the grand opening for them—that's how far back we go.

When they did the grand opening for *El Mercadito* in East Los Angeles, in 1968 or something like that, I was a kid, and I remember being there for that. There are a lot of things that are pretty neat, it just seemed so natural to me, growing up with my family being musicians.

Where do you stand in the sibling order?

I am the youngest; I am the youngest of 8.

I have two older sisters that were born before me, then my brother Jesus, then Humberto, Crescencio, Antonio, and Pedro.

You have managed to have a very solid musical career but also a very solid marriage. I looked at your timeline, and it seems like you married

before everything had really started for you. Before creating your mariachi groups, before purchasing your restaurant, before starting your foundation...etc.

When did you meet your wife...do you remember that day?

If so, where was it and what did you think of her when you first met her?

It was strange because I was hanging out with my older brothers at a very young age and they lived "the life," (laughs). They were around a lot of parties—you could imagine the 60's—it was incredible. And my dad raised us very, *very*, macho, very *al estilo* Jalisco. *La mujer esta en la casa*, and we are the providers, type of mentality.

It was crazy—it was a huge learning experience.

I met my wife right after high school. I didn't really have a girlfriend in high school; it was very hard for me to understand high school girls because I was always hanging around older women with my brothers. And I was playing sort of professionally at 15, 16-years-old. So, when I first saw my wife, it was sort of hard.

We had a family restaurant in Montebello.

When I saw my wife, she stood out because she was blonde—she has blonde hair and blue eyes. She was around my age when we met, she told me she was 21, but I didn't believe her. I saw her on my day off—on a Monday night at the restaurant. On that night we had another group of ours fill in for us.

She was there dining at the restaurant.

A lot of the women that went to the restaurant went to see the group, the musicians in the group were very young, and they were good-looking guys. It was one of the top groups in the entire country. We were, very, *very* sociable, especially with the people that went to go see us perform. So, we had a lot of friends.

When I saw her, I walked over to her and said, "Hi."

And after that, I sang her a song—I still remember singing her a song. After that night she came back a couple of weeks later. I really, *really* liked her...a lot. She came back with her aunt, and I sat down and held her hand—walked her to her car. After that, she kept coming back every week or every two weeks.

I eventually met her parents.

My dad never, ever, let me move out of the house to have an apartment with another guy. He would always say, "*No, no, el dia que tu te vayas es para casarte. Aqui no vas andar trayendole la ropa sucia a tu mama* (laughs)."

The group you are describing was that Mariachi Sol de Mexico?

No, Los Galleros. It was my older brothers group. Los Galleros is a group that he and my father formed in 1967 or 1968—something like that.

Shortly after marrying Teresa, you purchased your restaurant *Cielito Lindo*.

Can you tell me more about, how that happened?

I left my brothers group when I was 22-years-old because I wanted to finish music school.

He told me, "*Para que vas a la escuela? Vas a ser mariachi.*"

I have always wanted to dedicate myself to music because I knew how talented my brothers were. And I wanted to continue with the tradition, but I wanted to prepare myself for it, that was something my brother didn't understand.

I had to leave the group, and right after leaving, I created my own group. I started working on weekends in Whittier (by a little restaurant in Whittier).

When I recorded my first album with my group, Juan Gabriel heard it and asked me to record for him. And an album for Aida Cuevas—she really liked how I played the trumpet—she knew I had a lot of ideas and that I was an arranger.

Juan Gabriel asked me to do his next album, too.

I started making a lot of money as an arranger, and I was already out of music school. I invested my money in properties; I ended up selling my properties when I was 25-years-old and buying my restaurant.

I also put Teresa through school.

When I finished school, I asked her what she wanted to do. She told me, she wouldn't mind being a nurse. She became an RN and practiced (I think) for about a year and then she started helping me at the restaurant.

How was that feeling like, when Juan Gabriel contacted you?

He was at that moment one of the best in the Spanish music industry and now a legend.

And you were so young, how did you feel?

"You know what?"

My friend called me; he was helping arrange the first record for Aida Cuevas. My friend is an arranging icon, Rigoberto Alfaro. He was a very, very, *very*, well-respected arranger and producer in Mexico. He asked me to play the trumpet for Juan Gabriel. He had to go back to Mexico, so he left me in charge. And Juan and I hit it off. He felt very comfortable working with me. So, he asked me to work with him.

It felt pretty cool because it was Juan Gabriel. He was right on top of his game.

I thought, "Oh, what a great opportunity."

I have seen you perform numerous times and I love it, as I have told you before Mariachi Sol de Mexico is my favorite. But I have also seen Reyna de Los Angeles, and I am amazed at what they do and how they look on stage.

Why did you decide to create Reyna de Los Angeles, the first all-girl mariachi group?

Well in 1991, I started my foundation, the Mariachi Heritage Society because we were doing really good with my business. I felt that I needed to—and—should help my community.

I formed my foundation, and we started teaching at the Los Angeles Music and Arts school in East Los Angeles. We had about 40 or 35 students, half of them were little girls. The little boys would say, "I want to play with Mariachi Sol de Mexico, one day." But the little girls had no role models. There were no female groups that were well-known, maybe certain groups, little groups but there were none that were well-known nationwide. To be honest, hardly even in Mexico.

I asked one of my friends to make some phone calls for me; I wanted to create a female group.

We put the group together, and I told them,"You are going to be a symbol here, you are the first ones at this level. We have to be impeccable. You have to wear clean boots. Your hair has to be pulled-back. Look beautiful. We have to give the best image that we can."

It was awesome, they got so much notoriety.

Don Francisco featured us in his program, and all that stuff was pretty neat.

They got the ball rolling when it came to an all-female group. I think that when they saw Reyna (Mariachi Reyna de Los Angeles), other females felt like they could do that too. Which is pretty cool—also pretty strong.

When Selena recorded with mariachi, she recorded with me.

We also started the Mariachi Festival in Las Vegas, Nevada, one at the Hollywood Bowl and another one in Albuquerque, New Mexico. I had all the connections, and I knew that I could make a very successful group.

Have any of your daughters been members of Reyna de Los Angeles?

My oldest daughter Karina used to play with Reyna de Los Angeles. She played with them for about a year and a half and then she finished college—right now she is working with a real estate company—I think that is what it is.

All of them sing.

Melody is a singer and songwriter, she is 26 and graduated from NYU.

I've heard a lot of ways people accomplish a dream. Some sit down and write down each step that their dreams require. Others are spiritual about it and pray. Some do both.

You have accomplished a lot of your dreams and therefore are the perfect person to ask—when attempting to achieve a dream what is the first step you take is?

And how do you proceed?

I think that in the 90's when everything sort of took off, the restaurant and everything else—I loved playing there at the restaurant and I am still there once in a while—my group still plays there. But I wanted to take it up a notch. I wanted Sol to be heard in concert halls where people could connect with us and be drawn to listen to us.

I did pray about it.

I asked God to open doors for me, and that's when the festivals started, I look back at my life, and that's a big part of it. Ever since then, it's been growing, growing...and growing...

And in the entertainment industry it's hard to have a perfect family life, there are always struggles, but my family has always been very, *very* strong.

I have spoken to many people who have told me about the worst job they have ever had and how that actually pushed them harder towards their dreams. It seems like you have never had a bad job since you described your family has opened a lot of doors for you.

But has there been a moment that has stood out to you, that has pushed you to work harder?

Perhaps even forced you to take a risk?

With me, I have always done what I love to do and never considered it, working. Working with family is the best, that's where I wanted to stay my whole life. But it didn't work out, it didn't work out with my older brother, and I had to leave.

There are egos involved in this kind of business. It was very uncomfortable, very emotional for me and being the youngest I would get really emotional. I would get really hurt. My older brothers didn't understand that, they were raised by my grandparents and they had a different way of seeing life. My two sisters, my brother Jesus and I—we see life differently. For me, sharing mariachi music is great and to be able to teach it, as well.

I taught at Cal Poly Pomona (California State Polytechnic University, Pomona) when I was 21, 22-years-old—I used to teach a night class there.

And my brothers and other mariachi directors didn't understand why I did that. "Why are you sharing your knowledge? Why are you doing that?

You're creating your own competition, they're going to drive down the prize," they would say.

And I never saw it like that.

You happen to be a father, and as you mentioned earlier, you have a very strong family.

What advice do you give your children about life?

When you have kids, you want to give them what you didn't have.

We never really had a lot of materialistic stuff when we were young. My dad was a musician—a struggling musician. My mom helped him out and worked at the sweatshops in Downtown Los Angeles, sometimes, or by picking grapes in Delano.

So, when you never see, "the good life," you don't know what you're missing (laughs).

"Right?"

I try to tell my kids that they're growing up with everything. They don't see me as much, but every time I do see them, I just tell them they need to put their passion into life. I wish that they would take over, one day (of what I leave for them). I think they know the business good enough that they'll be able to sustain it.

Although this book is intended for everyone, the theme of it is 30. What stage of your life were you in at 30?

I was married, I moved in with my wife, right out of high school. We started living together in February (3 months after we met) and eventually we got married.

I was 30-years-old in 1988, at that age, I had already recorded with different artists and at 30 I also had my restaurant.

Do you have any advice for those of us turning 30 this year?

My goodness, it's just so different.

What they called the "American Dream," before when I was younger, it was still achievable. I bought my first house for $54,000 as a musician—as a mariachi. Now its very rare that a mariachi could buy his own home, it's very difficult.

Now you really have to focus on education.

I think music education, for those that like mariachi. Its great for them to have their degree, they can teach mariachi music because that's what they love and they can play on weekends. Some of the guys in my group have their degree and their master's degree.

It's pretty neat to see that, also in Reynas.

Anything else you want to add?

Be very proud of who you are and don't just go along just because its good to go along with it (laughs).

Be who you are and if you have questions, don't be afraid to investigate (laughs), there are always two sides to every story.

I'll tell you this, when I was a kid, it used to sort of hurt me to be called a "beaner." And to be called, "this and that," because we were Mexican-American. We weren't illegal, we were legally living in the US, during that time it was so easy, I think in 1 week, my father immigrated us here—legally. He was sponsored through the restaurant he worked for. But still, we were looked upon as 'beaners," even among Mexican-Americans.

Growing up, that's what I saw and heard. My dad didn't like it. "*No te juntes con ellos. No te juntes con aquellos,*" he would say.

I don't know if you know about that, at your age. A lot of young people don't know that, and it's sad. But now you're also taught this in college. It's different. Now you are taught Chicano studies—and you're taught bilingual education. But in the 60's, it was different.

My dad just taught us to believe in what we do.

And my way of showing how proud I was of my heritage was to excel, always in music and in sports. I used to do that when I was a kid. Maybe that's why I am really involved in education, in teaching about mariachi music and about my culture. I love to see kids who are proud of who they are. And now when I see mariachi programs in schools, it makes me feel *so* proud.

We need to be around people, who need to be educated on what we do. I felt very uncomfortable living in Newport Beach when I moved here. The realtor selling the home I bought in Lido Island asked my realtor what I did for a living.

When my realtor responded by saying, "He's a mariachi."

The man asked him, "Oh, really? Does he stroll around any restaurants around here?"

My realtor told him that I owned a restaurant and performed all over the world.

We cannot close the doors on ourselves. We have to go places that put us in uncomfortable situations like that one. We can go and show them the beauty of our culture. There are a lot of people who don't know about our culture, and we perceive them as racists but it's not that they're racists, it just that they're ignorant to the facts (laughs).

We can teach them and inform them.

Thank you!!

NADIA ADOSE

DUBAI, UNITED ARAB EMIRATES

You were born in Ethiopia and have lived in Canada, France, Mexico and in Dubai, with such a diverse and exotic background, what can you tell us about life?

Well, I am not sure, if I have figured out everything about life yet but so far I have learned a few things about life to be true, it doesn't matter what your plan is, life and the universe have its own plan for each one of us.

I have met people from various sociocultural backgrounds, economical backgrounds, and intellectual backgrounds, they all tell similar stories, they started somewhere to get somewhere, and they ended up somewhere else.

I also think, life is very dynamic and can be unpredictable at times, what matters is how we deal with the challenges and the rewards associated with those changes.

What about humanity, do you think we are more alike than we think we are?

Well, humanity is a different story, as a human being we can be as kind and sympathetic as one can imagine but we can also be as ignorant, as unsympathetic and as cruel as unimaginable.

I have traveled and lived in a few continents, to my surprise, we are so much alike but different at the same time. We all have the same basic needs:

air, water, food, shelter, some form of security, some form of social interaction and ethical guidance (whether we call it religion, or personal values). But we all perceive the world very differently, our ability to see beyond our differences; whether it's a socioeconomic difference, religious difference, cultural difference, or racial difference is very limited.

Out of the places where you have lived, besides your home country, of course, where have you felt the most incorporated and welcomed in?

With a risk of it sounding like I am pleasing you, the one place I felt the most incorporated and welcomed was in Guadalajara, Mexico. It was also where I learned the pleasures of a simple life, and where I learned to find pleasure in things, and its where I never felt like an outsider.

What has been your favorite part about the places where you have lived?

My favorite part about Canada is that no matter where you come from, or who you are it is a place where you can grow and change for the better.

My favorite part about France is, it is a place that has incorporated the old, and the new. The lifestyle is quite relaxed and you can easily travel and enjoy the various regions, and what it has to offer. The country is very diverse, in geography, scenery, food, and in culture.

My favorite part about Mexico is the lifestyle, the weather, the food, the culture, the friends that I made along the way. And most of all the people's ability to open themselves and accept people...

My favorite part about Dubai is the diverse environment; people are from all over the world. You can live the kind of life you wish to live, you can meet people from all over the world, and you can enjoy new things all of the time...as long as you can keep up.

You're the first person that I have ever met from Ethiopia; it was so intriguing for me to know you are from there. Tell me more about Ethiopia.

Ethiopia is very different from any place where I have ever been, period.

It's the only African nation that was never colonized, it is a collection of various kingdoms that were made into one country.

Each region has its own distinct language, culture, and geographic setting. In total, there are over 80 different languages spoken, and there are over 40 diverse cultures. We have our own letters, numbers, and calendar (we are currently in the year 2010).

People are respectful, trusting and generous to a fault. I think everyone should visit Ethiopia at least once in their life.

Aside from having lived in so many different places, another interesting fact about you is that you were in the military when you lived in Canada. How was that experience like?

Yes, I was in the Army and it was very hard, it was emotionally hard. Especially, when you are a woman who is dark-skinned of African descent, and you are a Muslim who is in the Canadian Army.

When did you realize you wanted to become a soldier?

When a recruiter came to my high school and told me all of the fun things I would be doing if I joined the Army.

The next thing I knew was that I was at the basic training course and doing drill.

You have been brave in many moments of your life, is that something that has come naturally to you?

I suppose. I don't know if I can say it has come naturally, but I have never been able to back down from any challenges.

You are a practicing Muslim, and you are a woman, there are a lot of assumptions that come with those two words. Is there anything, you want to tell us about that combination?

I am not sure what I can say about that, as Ethiopian's we are brought up in a diverse religious environment, we have Muslim's, Christian's and Jewish

Ethiopian's. But religion had never been a point of discussion until I moved to North America.

Personally, I strongly believe that religion is a personal and private matter. No matter what you believe in, it shouldn't be used to pass judgment toward's someone.

People seem to make many assumptions about many things they know very little about these days; it's one of the challenges I am working on overcoming.

Throughout your life journey, have you heard of something, or maybe even seen something that you think we should know?

Perhaps it can help us live better lives.

I watched a video recently that made me question many things, and I think it makes for a good reminder on what is more important in life.

It says: This paradox of our times was propounded by the Dalai Lama when he said, "We have wider freeways but narrower viewpoints. We have taller buildings but shorter tempers."

Will Smith said, "We spend money we haven't earned on things we don't need to impress people we don't like."

The paradox of our time is that we have more degrees but less sense, more knowledge but less judgment, more experts but less solution.

It was Martin Luther King Jr., who said, "The irony of our times is that we have guided missiles but misguided men."

I think it was Maya Angelou who said, "People will forget what you said. People will forget what you did. But people will not forget how you made them feel."

One of the things I learned is that we are very rarely mindful of how we treat people around us, whether it's because of the misconceptions we have, or our ignorance, or because we neglect to give the respect that we expect from others.

Mindfulness seems to be very aligned with your lifestyle. What would you recommend for a happy life?

Remember you can't control everything, the past is in the past, enjoy the moment.

Be the best you can be and present the best of you to the people around you, and remember nothing lasts forever.

Most importantly, never, ever compromise who you are, and never compromise your physical, or mental state.

This book although intended for everyone, the theme of it is 30. What stage of your life were you in at 30 and where were you living?

When I turned 30-years-old, I was getting ready to become a Sargent.

I met my now husband, I got engaged, and I got married at the beginning of when I turned 31 and I moved to Dubai.

The best things in my life happened in my 30's.

What do you recommend for those of us that are turning 30 this year?

I say enjoy your 20's, travel, experience, live and learn because your 30's are where you will start to see the world in a different light.

Anything else you want to add?

Nothing, I think your questions were pretty good, they covered most of the things I would have added.

Thank you!!

ENRIQUE A. GUTIERREZ

CALIFORNIA, USA

You're so young, and yet you have accomplished a lot. You started your sportscaster career at one of the most viewed networks in this country.

The story behind how you got there is beautiful! We will get to that but before I'd love to know about you at a young age.

I know you were born in Chihuahua, Mexico. Tell me about life there. How were you as as child, were you curious about life, timid, extroverted?

It seems to me that sports is one of your biggest passions, did it start as a child?

How did it happen?

Were you influenced by anyone?

Judging by the interviews you have conducted as a journalist, I am going to guess soccer is your favorite sport. Is it?

It is a little difficult to try to describe myself as a child. Maybe those around me during that time would have a better answer.

I believe my younger self was quite calm and quiet. There is a side of me that has always been introverted, and another side that lets me be extroverted, to some degree.

That may sound contradictory, but it has more to do with the surroundings. I guess I was extroverted in certain environments and very introverted in other environments.

From an early age I felt attracted to sports. *Futbol* was my biggest passion.

"Don't know exactly why?"

It has some sort of irresistible charm that makes a great percentage of boys fall in love.

Growing up, I played other team sports including baseball, basketball, and football, but I didn't enjoy any of them as much as *futbol*. It is hard to understand how it happened, it just did.

My love for most sports included practicing them as well as following them in the newspapers and TV. By the time I was ten-years-old my favorite activities included watching every sports show possible, ranging from *lucha libre*, boxing, and *futbol* to Olympic sports, which didn't get as much exposure.

In addition to learning about the sport itself, I was also intrigued by the stories behind each athlete, learning how it was they became successful in their respective fields. In all, it could be said that sports have played a big role in my life since I can remember.

Growing up I developed a sense of respect and admiration toward athletes, as most kids do. I also had a couple of athletes to whom I looked up to. Among them, there is one that stands out as a source of inspiration due to his work ethic, discipline, fortitude, and philosophy: Ayrton Senna.

He was a Formula One driver who found success on and off the racetrack. He won three Formula One championships and built a legacy that has touched thousands of kids through his Ayrton Senna Foundation. Senna died during a race in 1994 at the age of 34.

Without ever getting the opportunity to meet him, he is one of the persons that has influenced me.

As mentioned, *futbol* is my favorite sport. But I find most sports to be fascinating. I feel sports are a form of art: they help people express themselves with creativity, discipline, and teamwork, and provide a platform to bring out the best of them.

Sometimes children have a clear image of what they want to be in life, where they want to live, even what pets they want to have.

Were you one of those kids?

As a kid I pretty much knew I wanted to be involved in sports and athletics for the long run. Watching TV and reading different newspapers, I thought it would be great to be able to cover all the important events such as World Cups, Olympics, Super Bowls or mega fights, as well as get to know the athletes.

So, there was always an attraction towards the media as well. Nonetheless, I figured I would be a professional athlete first, and then moved on to becoming a journalist. I wanted to be a journalist that covered all types of events not only sporting events, I thought I wanted to cover a war, and presidential visits and so forth.

As I got older, I started shifting my goals and focusing on sports journalism.

As a young person I thought I would need to move to Europe so that I could work and cover the most important *futbol* leagues in the world. That was a thought I had for many years, and it appealed to me to live in Spain, Italy, or England. Life took me to Los Angeles, where there is a multitude of sporting events of the highest level.

I could say there are few places in the world with the type of professional and high-level sporting activity that we see in Los Angeles.

You eventually moved to California. Did you ever think you would move to California?

How did the California move happen?

If we looked at the map to see where Chihuahua is, we would think a more convenient move would be to Texas. But instead, you moved to California.

How old were you when you moved and what were your thoughts about moving? It was such a big move in a lot of ways.

Moving to the US was not something I thought about much during my childhood years, but it was also not something I thought impossible. I had visited the US several times given its proximity from where I grew up.

Moving to California proved to be a challenge, and I encountered most of the same obstacles most immigrants face, such as leaving behind family and friends, learning a new language, trying to understand the system, and so forth.

The first few months I found it difficult to adjust to the new environment, but I eventually and slowly settled in.

I also realized that my transition was a lot smoother than that of other people. As you know, there are thousands of people who have a very difficult time by being thousands of miles away from their original home, and some people can't go back due to different circumstances. For the most part, I was able to go back home often, so in that regard, I was also blessed.

California became your home as we mentioned. After high school, you enrolled at the University of La Verne in Los Angeles.

How did you end up selecting La Verne?

What was your exact major?

What were your dreams and hopes at that age?

Did you intern anywhere?

It was thanks to my high school counselors that I found out about the University of La Verne. They took a small group of students to visit a few campuses. We went to Chapman University, Azusa Pacific University, Whittier College, and ULV, among others.

At the time I had received a few invitations and a couple of scholarship offers and the opportunity to play soccer at other small Division II and Division III colleges, including a couple out-of-state. However, I felt I wanted to stay close to Los Angeles. I applied and got accepted to a handful of private institutions. I narrowed it down to Chapman and La Verne.

They had some pretty big differences: the atmosphere, the campus, the student body, and so forth; but they both shared the small college vibe, and as far as I knew, they both had solid communication departments.

In my head, either school would have been a good fit for me. In my last high school semester, I was leaning towards Chapman mainly because it offered a better soccer program and I already knew the coach and some of the players. However, during a high school match, I suffered an injury and was advised to stop playing. That event made me choose La Verne instead.

When I entered ULV, my intention was to experience everything the Communications Department had to offer. I took every class I could that involved journalism, radio, and TV. I ended up majoring in TV broadcasting.

At that age, one is eager to get out and conquer the world. Youth gives one the certainty that everything is doable. My professional hopes were to be able to put to use the knowledge and skills acquired during my academic formation.

Back then I was hoping to work in different fields that included writing, TV production, and reporting. Also, as most journalists would say, one of my goals was to cover a war. Being a war reporter is a pinnacle to most journalists. I had that same desire in my younger years, even before I went to college. But as time went on, my perspective changed and I decided to focus on the topic I enjoy the most, which is sports.

During my college years, I completed a couple of internships. The first internship was in the production of a documentary. A European company was producing a documentary in Los Angeles, and they needed production assistants. I was able to do some camera work, and conduct interviews. My Spanish speaking ability came in handy as most of the subjects being featured only spoke Spanish, and no one else in the production did.

The other internship was for a local production company. I was entrusted with doing camera work for a season of shows showcasing a pickup truck racing series. It was a great experience; I particularly remember the times I was assigned to do the aerial camera from a helicopter. The helicopter would "hover" above the race track while the race itself took place. That was probably the highlight of my time with that production company.

In addition, there was yet another internship I was able to do post-graduation. It was on a morning TV show, where I was mainly a production assistant, making copies, answering phone calls, and welcoming guests of the show.

After completing your degree, you have previously mentioned in interviews that you started your own sports centered show, that seems amazing and such a BIG step for a recent college graduate.

How did you start it?

What did you name it?

How did you fund it?

After finishing college, I got involved in other projects and jobs, including a local TV sports show where I reported, did camera work and edited; there was also a local radio show in which I participated as a soccer analyst.

At the same time, I also worked for a news station doing a variety of jobs including being a floor manager, audio operator, editor, and camera operator. It was a great time where I had the opportunity to learn a lot about the news business.

A few months later I decided to produce my own show which was called *"Contragolpe"* I realized I had the skills needed to undertake such a challenge, so I figured I'd give it a try. It was a pretty fun and difficult experience. I learned a lot and expanded my network of contacts. It was a very fulfilling stage of my professional life.

About 6 months after having started your own show, perhaps without exactly knowing your life would be changing drastically and beautifully, it did. You were selected to compete at one of the country's leading Emmy-awarded news station for the role of a sportscaster.

How did you feel when you were applying to participate?

Were you feeling hopeful?

Did you think you would win?

What kept you motivated while being surrounded by great candidates competing against you?

Well, this whole experience was quite unique. I did not have a lot of expectations, perhaps because there was not a lot of information about it. I had only seen a couple of promos on TV, but they did not offer many details other than the date and location to audition. It was my impression that the "grand prize" was to be a guest at the station for one weekend. As the process went on, I realized it was a lot more complex than my original thoughts.

I didn't know who was going to get selected. To me, it was a good opportunity to meet new people and get a closer look at how Univision worked. I don't recall being too worried about the final outcome. The entire process took a few weeks, so I had to continue working on my own independent project/show.

My focus was on trying to enjoy and absorb the experience and let the producers decide who they wanted. At the end of the day, they were going to make the decision based on their needs, and all of the finalists offered something different.

I am not sure this is something you remember as a spectator (I am guessing you were probably 15 or 16 at the time) or something you read about. In any case, every time people bring that event up, they seem to remember it differently from how I remember it.

What was that feeling like, when it was announced you would be the next broadcaster at the most watched news station in the country?

The night of the "final," all of the finalists were excited. We all wanted to be the last man standing. As the other candidates began to be eliminated, the excitement grew. I remember one of the finalists being very upset when he was dismissed. When the time of the final announcement came, I felt very calm. I had already done everything I could, and the decision was out of my hands.

Of course, I was very happy when the verdict was announced on air.

I had been declared the winner of the competition, but even then, it was not made clear to me as to what that entailed. I was told they would call me in the next few days to give me more details.

About ten days later, I received a phone call from one of the executive producers asking me to go to the station the following day. It was then that I was told I had a couple of weeks to prove myself.

As you now know, that turned into a job I held for years, in which I was fortunate to meet very interesting people and cover several sporting events.

Over the course of your career you have covered a World Cup, how was that experience like?

Where was it?

I can imagine the whole experience was very surreal.

I have only been to one World Cup. It is an amazing and complex event. There is a lot of traveling involved, from one city on to the next. You are constantly on the move. There is a lot of energy flowing with fans from all over the world coming together for one big party.

I am looking forward to attending more World Cups, as a fan or spectator, or as a working media member.

You're clearly doing what you love. Every time I see one of your interviews, it seems as if your eyes are super lit and wide open. You seem so eager to hear everything the person you are interviewing has to say that no distraction can preoccupy you.

Can you tell me more about what you're thinking of?

This is quite interesting. When you are interviewing someone on TV there are a few factors of which you need to be aware, particularly if the interview is airing live, so it is very difficult to be able to just focus on the interviewee. Having said that, as you may know, every interview is different.

It also seems as if during that moment there is no one, in that room, or in the world that can capture your attention but the person in front of you. It's wonderful to see you that happy and to know you really are in the field of your dreams.

What would you tell someone that isn't working in their dream profession?

We need to recognize that not everyone has the blessing to work in their dream profession. Not everyone is given the same opportunities. The playing field is not leveled.

But for those who could, and are currently not doing what they love, I'd just suggest they do a lot of soul-searching.

We often hear about how short life is and that we need to do what makes us happy. I believe that's true.

In my opinion, life is more about the journey than the destination, so I'd like to convey the message of trying to follow the path that would make that journey more fulfilling.

I have seen many people give up on their dreams because they have found a comfort zone. That can be dangerous because that tends to kill the desire within. Sometimes, following one's dreams can be scary. People fear failure, rejection, and disappointment, so it becomes easier to settle for that "sure thing."

The sense of security and stability are threats to people reaching their goals.

What should we do to get there eventually?

What I try to do is to overcome those fears.

I understand life is a gift and each new day is a blessing. Having said that, I try to imagine myself at an old age reviewing my life. I ask myself, "How I would feel then with what I am doing today?"

"Will I be happy with my decisions?"

"Will I feel it was worth it to spend so much time on things that don't matter much?"

"Will I regret doing or not doing something?"

This visualization exercise has helped me in both my professional and personal life.

That's what I can share with people, hoping it helps them too.

Every day in one way or another we get reminded how hard it is getting to live in this country. How bad the unemployment has gotten over the years, how overpopulated we are getting. And how the "American Dream" is getting harder to achieve each day.

Yet your story seems to contradict this.

It looks like your story is the "American Dream," and you attained it in this day and age.

What do you have to say about the "American Dream," do you think it's still attainable?

What can you tell those of us that are still trying to attain it?

I think everyone has a different definition as to what is the American Dream, at least, I think everyone should have his or her own definition. So, I don't think there is a "one-fits-all" type of answer. I personally am not a big fan of that phrase.

I feel every person's journey is unique, and with that, every person's situation, mission, or purpose is different.

But for the purpose of answering this question in the general sense, I think nowadays the younger generations have an unbelievable set of tools to do almost anything they wish. The world has "shrunk" thanks to all the new technology that has become available in the last 10-15 years. There are amazing things happening and people from all over the world are connecting in beautiful ways.

I see a lot of young entrepreneurs building successful businesses and platforms. I think the younger generations have the upper hand on the older ones in that sense.

Despite the obstacles you have described, those of us living in the US enjoy many opportunities that don't exist in other countries. For the most part, we are given resources to turn our ideas and dreams into realities.

Reaching one's dreams is attainable.

However, I feel that in this era, people are hungry for instant gratification and that's not always the best way to go about things. I feel people are too concerned with what others think or say about them.

I feel we live in the social media era where everyone tries to make it seem like they are leading a perfect life.

Those thoughts not only distract you from what I feel should be the priority, but they also make people go in directions they don't need to go, for the sake of getting acceptance from their peers.

So, to me, the so-called "American Dream" is a personal path.

Success, triumph, happiness, peace, etc., are personal scales. What you may deem as successful, may not be valued equally by someone else, and vice versa. We should not allow others' opinions to be a determining factor of what we do, and that goes for both the positive and the negative.

I've heard a lot of ways people accomplish a dream. Some sit down and write down each step that their dreams requires. Others are spiritual about it and pray. Some do both.

What's the first step you take and how do you proceed?

I find that prayers are powerful. I lean on them often. I believe spirituality is an important part of the overall wellness of the individual.

I believe that whenever one has a goal, there needs to be a plan of action. Sometimes, one, may not know what steps to take, therefore asking around to get started may very well be the first step.

I constantly find myself involved in multiple projects at once. Some of them evolve into bigger things while others disappear in the process.

At times we are faced with triumph, and at other times we are faced with failure. The older we get the more we realize that and the more we realize failure is just as part of life as triumph is. Failure seems to be harder to deal with.

How do you deal with it?

As you mentioned, failure is just as part of life as triumph. Setbacks give you the opportunity to reassess a situation. Many times a setback allows people to readjust and prevent a bigger loss.

We all go through ups and downs in life. It all adds up to experience.

Although this book is intended for everyone, the theme of it is 30.

Do you have any advice for those of us turning 30 this year?

Life is precious, and being 30 is a beautiful stage of life. It is a time in which you are both old enough to have gained some valuable experience and young enough to do almost anything.

There is a movie I like that motivates me whenever I need to be "pushed" a little bit: *The Dead Poets Society*.

One of the mottos heard in it is: "seize the day."

I would pass on that message to all: "seize the day."

Make the most of it. Each day.

At the same time, don't take everything so seriously. There is a mysterious balance in life, finding that balance is what makes it interesting.

A book that I recommend to everyone regardless of their age is *The Alchemist*; I find it inspiring and full of wisdom.

Anything else you would like to add?

Well, this really is a broad question. I would invite people to make it a point to help others reach their goals.

That's not to say that they should forget about their own, but it is more about not being so immersed in themselves that they forget to share knowledge and experiences with others.

Being able to give to others makes life that much gratifying.

Thank you!!

CHRISTINA MCFAUL

CALIFORNIA, USA

Your latest photography project, "Water under the Bridge" is actually where your story begins, and the photos are actually from where you grew up, right?

How do you think your childhood has impacted where you are now in life and your values?

If we traveled back 30 years from today, we would find a barefoot, bronze, curious child exploring her backyard; which happened to be three magical miles of a lake in the Santa Monica Mountains of California.

At about 8-years-old I had the run of Malibou Lake. I might have been found in the creek to the west catching frogs, on Huckleberry Finn Island swinging on the rope swing, or drifting in my tin boat with about 30 ducks following as I threw out a piece of bread every few minutes.

What I loved most was the freedom I had. The ability to enjoy the quiet, or not so, quiet sounds of the lake: bullfrogs at dusk, the swallows that return early spring and build nests under the Crags Drive bridge, the red-winged black bird's beautiful song is permeated in my mind forever.

Some may call an 8-year-old running around 3 miles of lake neglectful but back then it was growing up as a free-range child. My father believed his role was to teach me and then trust me. He equipped me with the skills and knowledge to navigate the lake on my own, only after many years of exploring every inch of the lake together. I knew how to drive our boat, what to do if the motor failed, how to swim home, walk home, or call home from just about any neighbor's house.

In a nutshell, I learned to use my freedom wisely, how to be autonomous and manage myself. I learned how to handle mistakes and be more resilient. And believe me, there were many mistakes I made! But one way, or another I always found my way home.

I will always be so grateful for the childhood my father gave me at the lake. He came from a poor family and worked extremely hard to create a life where his family could thrive. Much of who I am today and what I want for my own children took root from my free-range childhood on Malibou Lake. My respect for the planet and all living things, my curiosity, desire for adventure, and love for the world all stemmed from my roots as a "Malibou Laker." I was also lucky to have an amazing artist for a mother. She planted a seed that grew into a love of the arts.

Recently my husband and I decided it was time for our family to move from Chicago to San Diego, California so that our boys could have a similar free-range childhood. Only they will be exploring tide pools, the surf, and maybe even the underwater kelp forests of La Jolla.

You have lived in a couple of different places besides California and have traveled to so many different destinations.

Do you think the exposure to different people and cultures has helped you?

Absolutely, traveling and immersion in other cultures gets you out of your comfort zone, stretches your mind, and opens your heart to endless possibilities.

Where else have you lived other than California?

When I was 18-years-old, I studied abroad in Costa Rica and lived with a host family for six months. It was a big deal because it was completely outside of my comfort zone, it was my first time out of the country, and I knew like three sentences of Spanish!

Looking back it was one of the top five events that shaped my life. I got to witness the culture from the inside and see how people in another part of the world live. The warmth in hospitality, close-knit ties to family and the healthy lifestyle are a few things that left an indelible impression on me.

I am a big believer in being an explorer, not just a tourist that scratches the surface. Think of it this way, if you bite into an orange but only a little bit, you get the bitterness of the rind. You have to get to the juicy, sweet center to really enjoy the experience.

During my time in Costa Rica, I threw caution to the wind, left fear in the rear-view mirror and fell in love with the people, the pristine rainforests, the warm hospitality, the language and of course salsa dancing!

But more importantly, after losing my father to cancer at 18-years-old, Costa Rica gave me back a life worth living and a fresh view from which to see the world again.

I know that giving back is a big part of your travel philosophy, can you tell me more about that?

Giving back is definitely an integral part of my travel philosophy. I believe if we have the means to travel the world we always have the ability to give back in some small way and therefore leave every place a little better than we found it.

When the idea of Journey 360 Degrees was born, it was all about my passion of travel and giving back. Just by starting a conversation and an online travel blog, all of these synchronistic events and people started coming into my life. One of those people turned out to be my best friend and business partner for Journey 360 Degrees. We now work as a husband and wife team bringing our two little boys along for the adventures. Together we created something much bigger by putting both of our visions together. We created a company that brought groups abroad to have transformational travel experiences. At the end of every trip, we partnered with a local school, or charity to give back.

On our first trip to Costa Rica, we aligned with Sona Fluca Primary School. We initially visited the school to see if it would be a good fit with our values. Not only were they value-driven, but we also discovered they were in desperate need of a new roof because the rainy season was coming fast and if they didn't get the leaks fixed on the roof, the children of that village could not go to school that year. It would have been too dangerous with all of the electrical elements exposed to the rain and lightning.

So, we asked the principal what he would need to keep the school open, and he said, it would take a new roof.

Thirty minutes later we found ourselves on a bumpy road to a local hardware store where we purchased about forty sheets of corrugated steel, some nuts, and bolts, and within two weeks the school had a brand new roof.

Another, memorable moment came while we were visiting a classroom of 7-year-old's and asked them what they wanted to be when they grew up. The emotional impact of that question has continued to enforce why I believe in giving back, simply put, it creates hope and dreams of endless possibilities.

That day some of the children said they wanted to be football players, some doctors, some teachers, some tourist guides. Finally, the last little girl looked at me and said, "I want to do, what you do, one day. I want to help other people."

At that moment it felt as though my whole life came full circle. Everything I had been through, all of the hardships, joys and sorrows were worth that single moment, to be able to give back to the people of Costa Rica, that had given so much to me.

We have been back several times and continued to build our relationship of service to Sona Fluca Primary School. We have assisted the community in building a library and a gathering hall. We always seem to get more than what we give with every visit. The little we invest comes back a thousand fold every time; our lives are forever changed.

A footnote to this story, is that at the time that you reached out to me, to be a part of this book, we also heard from the principal inviting us to come down and celebrate the anniversary of the school.

I love your photography, you are actually one of my favorite photographers. You capture very creative shots, and you always seem to get it right. It's obvious, it's your passion

What does photography mean to you, and why do you love it so much?

"Photography, what could be more beautiful than a medium of light?"

Much like the practice of meditation, photography is an inner practice that leads me more fully into a rich engagement with the world. Finding the light is a way of life.

To me, photography is many things: a journey of personal growth and transformation, a means of interacting more deeply with the world, and a way of expressing creativity. Photography is a mirror to oneself and a window into our world. With one eye turned inward and the other outward, you can develop self-awareness and deepen your engagement with the world.

We have a choice at every moment in our lives. We can be present to the moment and all that it has to offer, or we can stay in our habitual, distracted, often self-centered state of mind. A moment comes when we click the shutter that expresses the heart of the subject. It gives voice to our experience of the world. The resulting photograph is both a mirror and a window. This moment has magic and presence that far transcends the shallow reflection of the selfie era. We can learn about our own vision and our own voice through the camera lens. By engaging deeper with the subject, you learn to penetrate into the heart of a landscape, an event, a person, or a condition of the world. Attention brings the world to life. With a camera, we can offer our attention in the service of others and help heal the world.

The world needs our attention, now as never before. Others need our genuine care and insight. It begins with us; we can only see as deeply into others and the world as we have seen into ourselves.

Did it start at a young age, or when did it begin?

I realized the importance of an image when I was 18-years-old. There was a definitive moment as I sat in my childhood living room sorting through all of my dad's photos and dividing them up into three piles: one for my sister, one for my brother, and one for myself.

My father had just passed from cancer and although he was gone there was something comforting to me about seeing him in photos. Really, it was the most important material thing left behind, in my opinion. Going through those photos, I learned so much more about my dad's life and even my own childhood. There were many gaps where I wished that more photos had been taken, though all in all, it was a tremendous gift that I treasure and revisit often to this day. Looking back now, I can see that the loss of my father at a young age planted a seed that would eventually bloom into my "why."

As, I started college that next semester, I found myself taking photography courses for all my electives and even sitting in on lectures when the classes were full. I loved the process of creating a project and then going out into the world and finding creative ways to express it with only my camera and endless possibilities of my mind.

Seeing my visions come to life in the developing tray of the black room was like magic. My secret dream was to be a *National Geographic* photographer but I never actually thought I could attain that so, it became my hobby.

After college I got a work visa to go to Australia, and I shot 27 rolls of film and then decorated my condo with that photography. It was obviously my passion, but it wasn't until I became a mother that I decided to really go for it! Giving birth sometimes reawakens and strengthens our purpose and passion in unexpected ways.

My mom always said, "Being a mother is the most important work a woman can do." Let me add that being a mother is not only giving birth to babies but to ideas from the divine feminine heart center.

A year after Nicholas was born I started my professional photography career with a portrait studio, My Little World Photography, capturing the monumental moments of families. Knowing that one-day those children would look back at my photos and see the bond between them and their loved ones, filled my cup to overflowing measures!

I was helping families create their legacy that would be passed down for generations to come. What a gift and honor it has been to work with all my clients and what a great feeling it is to know I was living into my why.

Speaking of people and moments you have captured, what was the last photo you took and why was it important enough to capture it?

The last photo I took was of a baby seal pup in the Children's Pool Beach of La Jolla, California.

My favorite morning ritual is waking up before sunrise and walking along the coast to visit all my wildlife friends of San Diego. Spring is already here in mid-February, and there are babies being born everywhere. I counted at least thirty seal pups on this day. Brandt's cormorants are sporting their spring plumage and doing their funny mating dances while others already have a family in the nest.

I am absolutely in love with the natural world. Knowing that, one, can only protect what we love, I hope that my nature and wildlife photography will inspire others to get outside more often, fall in love with our world and join me in protecting these amazing creatures and their habitat. We only have one planet! Let's do our part to take care of it and more importantly, teach our children to protect our planet.

Are there any important lessons you have learned throughout your life? And if so, what have those taught you?

Embrace all of life and forgive often. Forgive others and forgive yourself to set yourself free. Even some of the most awful tragedies can later be seeds for our greatest adventures and transformations.

Pain is not an indication that you are failing in some way. How many spiritual masters have endured great suffering in the fulfillment of their destiny?

Growing pains are a part of the journey.

Emotions whether they are joyful, uplifting, fearful, sad, or sorrowful all come to us to teach us. The more we embrace, the more spiritual growth we have, the less we seek to blame someone else. I found that by embracing the darkness while shining a light on it, I could see the depth of my pain. All along the source of my suffering resided in me. It was not in the man who abused me as a child; it was not in my parents for what they could have done better or differently, it was not in God for making my life unfair (or whatever your religious beliefs are).

Believe me, I tried to make it all about them and, if only they would change, apologize, love me the way I deserve, etc., but the longer I stayed in that cycle of victimization, the more I prolonged the pain and suffering. It is easy to look outwards and find someone to be the source of all the pain, turmoil and darkness.

Accept right where you are, embrace all of life, have faith that we are not given anything we cannot handle. When we embrace our pain, suddenly it isn't so painful. When we forgive there is a huge weight lifted from our heart and space created in our lives for whatever we choose to create next.

The transformative life cycle of a butterfly reminds us that when things seem like they're coming to an end, we only need to look to the caterpillar. The caterpillar evolves into a chrysalis and reminds us that it's now beginning its next life. It provides a powerful reminder that there are seasons of life.

Endings are followed by new beginnings. Our lives can take flight into whole new journeys.

It is very interesting to me; I once read an article that I have never forgotten about. 80 something-year-old's were asked what they regretted most in life. The most common response was having worried too much. Worrying seems to be part of our culture. I am going to list a few common things we worry about in a lifetime.

Education

Work

Buying a home

Relationships

Weight

Did you ever worry about anything from that list? And if so, how do you control yourself from worrying too much?

Yes, I have worried about all of the above! Worry will always be there; it's just a part of being human. What I have found for myself is the practice of being present. Whether that's a photo, walk, yoga, meditation, forest bathing, or playing tag with my boys… those all snap me right back to the beauty of the present moment!

I believe, strongly, that any art form, or mindfulness practice can help awaken your soul and spark that inner flame of creativeness and expansive awareness.

There are a lot of people that really want to peruse their passion further but can't seem to, for a variety of reasons. What do you suggest they do?

Believe wholeheartedly in your dreams. Even if you have no idea how you will ever achieve those dreams. Believe! Turn your magic on, and anything is possible. If you don't believe you can bet that, you will never arrive.

Visualize your dreams like they are already here. "What does it feel like to have arrived at this dream? What can you hear, smell, taste?" Really put yourself in that feeling of already having it. There is power in where we put our attention and the intentions we set for our life.

Move the line forward every day. Make your time in this world the adventure of a lifetime!

Thank you!!

ANDREA MARADIAGA

UTRECHT, NETHERLANDS

You, and your boyfriend are living together in the Netherlands, congratulations on that milestone in your life.

How did you decide this?

Although I have always enjoyed traveling and enjoy studying different cultures, I grew up never wanting to move away from my family and friends.

Therefore, my plans were to stay in California my whole life. My boyfriend moved back to the Netherlands, and with a lot of thought, I decided to also make the move.

It was one of the most difficult decisions of my life.

My family offered me the space I needed and the support to allow me to make my own adult decision, by myself. I am incredibly thankful for their kind words and love during this big transition in my life.

Even though I saw many tears and their hearts broken, my parents told me they trusted my decision, for I am in control of my own life. My sister, brother, extended family, and family, all gave me more support and love than I ever thought to be possible.

I am now living in the Netherlands; meanwhile, I keep the doors open for moving back to California in the future.

How long did it take you to plan the move?

It took six months to decide.

I cried many nights because I never wanted to move away from California. I have always loved and appreciated California, and I still do. I moved to be able to understand my boyfriend's culture and family a bit more.

Getting to know this part of the world is a plus.

Where did you both meet?

We both met at a Halloween house party in Huntington Beach on October 31, 2015. We were each invited by our friends. There we were, both not dancing. Instead, we sat on the couch on our phones, next to each other.

That was funny.

We eventually started talking about traveling and had coffee two weeks later. We talked for 5 hours on our first date at The Camp in Costa Mesa.

We talked about almost every single topic possible: our past, current goals, and future.

We went on dates every single day, except for Wednesday, that same week. We connected instantly, and the sparks were on.

What should we know about love and relationships?

Cliché enough, respecting each other, all times is huge.

Taking the time to put oneself in the other's shoes is vital to be able to be more likely to understand each other.

The same goes for maintaining your own identity while making an effort to take care of your partner's emotional and physical needs. We each live part of our lives individually with our work environments, social circles, cultures, hobbies, and daily experiences.

We then live part of our lives together where we verbally share our individual life activities and experiences with each other. We also take the time to share new activities, adventures, aspirations, feelings, opinions, traditions and so forth with one another.

We take the time to share and listen to each other even though we don't always agree and sometimes annoy each other. It's also good to consciously avoid hurting each other, as much as possible.

Your partner should be a friend you can count on, to have the best intentions for you and vice versa.

Hollywood has created a lot of comedies based on people who fall in love that are like you, from different cultures.

Can you relate to any of them?

Do you have any anecdotes pertaining to that?

We have several differences between our cultures. A funny difference is our cultural perception of time. They, are so different. I come from a polychronic culture and my boyfriend from a monochronic culture.

I come from a culture that views time in a fluid and relaxed manner. Time is free-flowing for the most part. Distractions and interruptions are a natural part of life. Human interaction is valued over schedules, deadlines, and objectives.

Change of plans or meeting with someone a bit after time is easily dealt with.

He comes from a culture that perceives time as fixed or unchanging. Time is viewed in a rigid manner, for the most part. Interruptions are bad, for they put scheduled activities at risk. People value being prompt for schedules, and deadlines, and objectives highly.

Being late or changing plans can be viewed as being rude.

Neither is better than the other, they both have their functions. The funny thing is that there is a need to clarify whether we will meet according to my view on time or his.

It's really funny.

What's the most romantic thing you have done for one another?

My boyfriend said, one of the most romantic things I've done was bake him chocolate cookies, while he was going through a work burnout. He was having a rough time, and I wanted to cheer him up.

So, I drove to his house accompanied by my sister, at about 3 AM.

As my sister waited for me in the car, I placed several fresh homemade cookies in a brown, paper bag, and a little sock monkey on a beach chair, in front of his house door. I figured it would maybe bring a smile to his face when he woke up for work at 5 AM.

One day he showed up at my parent's house with about five dozen, extra large, roses. The roses totally stand out in my memory, they were gorgeous!

But there's also the day he drove us from Orange County to Northern California to the middle of nowhere, on an Indian reservation. By the time we arrived at the campsite, we were exhausted. Even though he was tired, he told me to stay in the car and cheerfully walked out of the car into the freezing night.

He took our cooler out of the trunk, blew up our car mattress, and started our campfire. We then ate some snacks with whiskey in front of the fire as an owl hooted over us all night. We then went camping further up north and visited other campgrounds in Big Sur. He planned the entire trip.

I will never forget it.

In the end, all the material things go out the window; the most romantic thing is that he truly cares about me. I'm truly grateful for him.

Your parents are from El Salvador; you were born and raised in California and your boyfriend is Dutch.

With such a close and direct exposure to so many different cultures, have you determined what your favorite part of each is?

Tell me your favorite part of each culture.

My favorite part of my Salvadoran culture is our spirit.

We are family-oriented, friendly, warm, and can deal with tough situations in a positive way. We are resilient and know how to stay positive even during difficult life situations. I love our jokes. I love our laughter.

We try our best to enjoy our families and our lives.

We are strong.

My favorite part of my Californian culture is how relaxed people tend to be, for the most part.

I like how exposed to so many different cultures Californians are. I love being able to be in California and easily be able to make friends of different ethnicities and nationalities. It's a beautiful thing.

Lastly, I like how progressive as a whole the state of California is.

I love California.

My favorite part of the Dutch culture is how eco-friendly their lifestyles are. I don't see a lot of plastic being used. Most people take tote bags while doing their groceries.

Cars are extremely small and fuel efficient.

A portion of the population use bicycles and trains as transportation. I think if the rest of the world would mimic this lifestyle, we would have a lot less pollution in the world.

While traveling, have you discovered your favorite place?

I've been to 11 countries and plan on experiencing more cultures.

My favorite country to visit is El Salvador. I love the laughter, the love, and all the jokes. Its people are so willing to share. I love that the people are so willing to share with one another.

Although you are so culturally exposed and have traveled a lot, you had only lived in Orange County, California.

How different is it to live in the Netherlands compared to California/ USA?

The hardest part of living in the Netherlands has been being away from my family and friends.

I can't stress that enough.

Everything else like adapting to a different climate, language, social system, and culture is something I'll be able to adapt to with time.

You've only been in the the Netherlands since the start of the year (about a month). Have you adjusted to your new neighborhood, yet?

My family, friends, boyfriend, and his family have been the most supportive people, ever. I'm very thankful for all of them. I'm trying my very best to adjust as much as possible.

Other than that, most people speak Dutch and English, sometimes three or five languages. Communicating is not a problem for the most part, and their transportation system is amazing!

Their grocery stores have delicious food, and things in cities run smoothly.

Now that you have moved, you're in a sense a foreigner..an "immigrant," even. Do you feel like the Dutch have treated you fairly thus far?

Yes, I'm a foreigner now, (laughs), I love it. Yes, Dutch people are kind and helpful. For the most part, they don't mind speaking English to you if you don't speak Dutch.

Of course, there is that occasional idiot racist who assumes the worst of you, not based on your behavior, but solely based on how you look.

Every country has their share, but for the most part, things have been good. Amsterdam people are really cultured and nice. I love that city. People there are very friendly.

Have your experiences as a recent "immigrant" allow you to view immigrants differently?

I was raised to see people all as equal people. I don't support classist systems, racism, sexism, homophobia, nor discrimination against the disabled, sick or elderly. I was also raised not to label people as immigrants or non-immigrants, but to view and treat all people with love and respect.

In 1980 a civil war started in El Salvador.

With military aid and training, and economic aid of an estimated 7 billion dollars (from the U.S.). The Salvadoran military killed its people(children included). School teachers were persecuted. Boys were stolen from their school classrooms and forced to be war soldiers. Families were purposely trapped in their houses and burned alive.

People went missing, never to be found again.

Innocent people were tortured with torture tools. Torture methods were used: electric shock, suffocation, cutting off tongues, rape, destroying eyes with chemicals, etc.

People were decapitated to be later placed on sticks in the middle of streets to create fear.

It's estimated 25 percent of the population was to flee the country during that filthy war, many of my family members included. It's estimated 75,000 people lost their lives, people did what they could to survive during those treacherous years.

My parents were war refugees and are survivors of that 12-year Salvadoran Civil War.

They experienced and saw so many horrendous things; no one should ever have to go through. Words would not be able to describe all the horrible memories. They were persecuted and were forced to save their lives by leaving their tight-knit loving families behind.

They fled their native country at a young age against their will, to survive.

Many of my Asian and Latin American friends have unpleasant war stories, they've heard from their parents. All immigrants have their own story, as to why they left many things behind. All stories are unique, but sometimes similar in the fact that war, poverty, and corrupt governments sadly force people to leave their families behind.

I have always respected immigrants and now even more that I've moved to another country myself. The only difference is that my immigration has been undeniably way more pleasant than others. I can't imagine how so many immigrants make it through, so much.

They are brave and strong. My respect goes out to them.

Are you more patriotic now that you live in a different country?

I was born in the United States, I love my country, always have.

Even though I don't support the involvement of so many dirty wars that the United States of America has been involved with throughout time, I love her people.

I love our American diners, our coastal towns, holidays, the variety of food options, our cluster of cultures, and so forth.

I also have tremendous respect for all the hard-working American activists and professionals striving hard to make the lives of future generations better.

For people of any age that are thinking of listening to their hearts, just like you did. Either by starting something, or even ending something.

What would you tell them?

I say, "Take a second to listen to what your heart tells you."

"What positive experiences are you longing for?"

When you notice a little spark coming from your heart towards things that inspire you, take a hold of it, and write your dreams down. Make a visual board.

Some dreams don't need too much thought, go for it. Just get up and do it.

If not, weigh your risks, pros, and cons and research it inside and out. Sometimes you must face and surpass your fears. Work hard and do what you must to make your dream come true.

Life is short. Make it worth your while.

Criticism, all of us are prone to it and none of us are exempt from it.

How do you handle it?

It depends who is giving me criticism and with what intentions. If someone I don't care for, tends to be a negative person, I listen and dismiss their garbage.

If the person is someone I respect, has good intentions, and I trust, I take the time to listen to that individual and consider what they have to say.

You always seem so happy, and you are always smiling. What is your perspective on life?

What should we do to be happier people?

No matter what I go through, I'm a person of great faith. I feel like God is always by my side and am thankful for my family, and my friends, and my life. Life is such a beautiful gift, and I appreciate it very much.

Some phases of life are absolutely difficult and overwhelming, but like my parents say, "All bad things pass. Good times are always on their way towards you even when you don't see it coming."

I suggest for people to appreciate every single day of life, for you don't know when your last day arrives. Also, learn to "chill-out," a bit and enjoy life. Life is beautiful. Take the time to enjoy your loved ones, nature, and your hobbies.

Be resilient when things get tough. My mom always told me to learn to be fluid, like water. Be strong and go with the flow. Take your guard down and learn to laugh at yourself.

Your laughter brings you joy. Anger brings you misery. Filter yourself out of negative thoughts and replace them with positive ones.

Anything else you want to add?

Vegetable soup is good for you. Cool people consume it (smiles).

Thank you!!

BAOYIRUOLE

ULANHOR, CHINA | NEW YORK, USA

Your passion for dance has led you to contests all over the world—you have won many awards at those contests and events.

And a BIG milestone for you was when you represented China at the 2008 Beijing Olympic Games opening ceremony.

How did your passion for dancing start?

And what does dancing mean to you?

First thing first, I'm Mongolian, the Mongolian culture is very into parties! We sing, we dance, and we know so many musical instruments. People in Mongolia like to dance…a lot.

I think that is where the passion came from, and also I am really good at dancing—since elementary I have participated in many dance performances for Mongolian folk dance. Also I joined an a cappella group at school where we sang traditional Mongolian music.

That is why people say we have that gene in our body as Mongolians.

I'm really good at dancing and singing. When music starts, I start to dance right away without choreography. I think its just about having fun, enjoying the music and moving your body.

My passion comes from naturally liking to dance.

Did you know you wanted to become a professional dancer, as a child?

Honestly, I wasn't really sure about this during my childhood. But I was really good at dancing and singing, so when I was a child, I didn't really know what type of person I would become in the future. But I really liked being on stage.

I would say, I wanted to be an actor, singer or dancer. All I knew was that I really wanted to be an artist. But if you ask me, which one is the one that I can be really good at, dancing would be my response.

What should we know about dancing?

Dancing is a human art.

We have so many types of dance styles, ballet, Latino, hip-hop, contemporary and so many different country folk dances! But my point is that dancing is just a feeling. It is just a reaction of when you feel happy. When you listen to good music, you just want to move your body.

Your body naturally reacts.

We have so many professional dancers that are really, really amazing because they have practiced a lot and perfected their movements perfectly! But dancing is not only for professionals, everybody can dance, just move your body when you feel happy, listen to music and move your body however you want!

Currently we have so many different types of dance but they come from different centuries. Hip-hop is closer to this new generation's style of dance. We are also continuously creating different types of dance styles, it is never-ending.

What I want people to know about dancing is to move their body with the music and just have fun!

Have there been any difficulties with being a male dancer?

Or have you experienced any difficulties in your industry, in general?

If you want to be a professional dancer, it wont be easy at all. You need to practice a lot, a lot and... a lot! Whatever type of dance you choose, whether its hip-hop, contemporary or folk. You still need to have a ballet foundation.

I have a big ballet foundation.

My body needs to be a flexible, so every morning I wake up at 5 AM and go to a dance classroom to stretch my body. Sometimes your body will hurt but you still have to keep stretching until you make yourself more flexible. Practicing flexibility is the most boring part for a dancer but you still need to do this.

Sometimes, I wake up so early that the sunrise isn't up yet. One time, I saw an old man cleaning the street in the cold and snowy winter season—he wakes up really early and doesn't make much money cleaning.

So many things are unfair, in this world! But I cant change it. Although maybe one day when I am become successful. I also told myself, if I don't wake up early now that I am young, when I am older like that man, I will have to.

Back to your question though, being flexible and practicing lets you control your body more easily. Sometimes when I have a show, I have to learn 5 or 10 different dances in one day and then I have to go on stage and perform those dances, shortly after having learned them!

As a professional dancer you have to learn all the movements very fast. Which means we not only need our body but also our brain. When I need to learn a choreography, I need to use my brain to create amazing art.

Since I started dancing until now, I have injured myself so many times. But I am the lucky one, my classmate broke some bones and almost lost a thigh, this happens to a lot of dancers.

"Is being a male dancer difficult?"

Honesty, male dancers have it easy because they're aren't as many male dancers as there are female. Male dancers can find a job easier than a female dancer— so many shows need male dancers.

That's the benefit, you don't have to compete with female dancers!

You are working in your dream field, was that hard to achieve?

I'm really happy with being a dancer, and doing something I like. Living in New York City brings so many opportunities for working in really big shows! You can work with so many amazing dancers. You can watch the most amazing shows in the world!

You really can feel that you are living in your dreams.

But being a dancer in New York is not easy— most of the time the salaries are low— even for some of the really famous dancers. So many amazing dancers have two or three different jobs and some of them are working in restaurants!

That is how the New York City dancers live.

In this very minute you can holding the trey of food for people in the restaurant you are servicing in the restaurant you work at and then, minutes later, you are standing on stage and everybody is clapping for you—and you are shining on the stage.

But I am lucky—I am working at a public school—I teach dance class for middle school students. I also do amazing shows. l am able to keep dancing and enjoy my dream.

You have obviously accomplished your dream, even though it hasn't been easy. What would you tell someone who also wants to become a professional dancer, or someone who wants to work in their dream profession?

If you want to accomplish your dream job, then just do it! You shouldn't care too much about anything because it is your dream job.

But never forgot, what it is about your dream job, that you want. Because sometimes when you work in your dream job, you will have many difficult moments. For example, as an artist, you're not going to be rich like *so* rich. But art is what you want not the money, so you'll be enjoying your lifestyle .

And just keep working in your dream job, money will come to you. And you will realize, one day, you are going to be rich and successful, because you have continued to work in your dream job.

How was your childhood like in China?

I grew up in Mongolia, China, I have one older brother, and one older sister. I am the youngest one. My parents never separated, so I grew up in a sweet family.

My elementary school had so many different activities because that school is the number one elementary school in Mongolia for arts—the government really cares about our culture. Every week we have an art activity, a music activity, and a dance activity.

"Maybe, that is why I'm so good in the arts?"

Other elementary school's don't have as many art activities, only my school has a lot of activities. *So*, interesting.

China is known to produce a lot of the products that are used worldwide. As someone who is ethnically Chinese, how does that make you feel?

Well, honestly, my hometown doesn't make anything.

Most of the factories are all in the south of China, so I didn't feel as if we were making *so* much. Until, I came to the US, I realized everything is made...in China! This is interesting because even though I am in a different country, I am still using Chinese stuff.

Because the Chinese prices are lower than in the US, most of the big companies like to work with Chinese factories, and they can make more of a profit—because of this China is getting rich.I feel really proud because we are making things that get sent all over the world and for a low price.

We are serving the world, its a GREAT thing.

Did it take you very long to adjust to life in New York City ?

I do miss my family.

But we live in the year 2018. So, I do FaceTime every day with my parents. And I can see what my friends post on WeChat. Also, I have many new friends in New York—everybody is so friendly. I hang out with my friends daily and living in New York allows me to never feel lonely.

What is the hardest part of life in America?

Being a dancer in New York City, you don't earn much money, even if you are one of the most famous dancers.

I used to teach a class in Shanghai and with one class, I could make $100.00. But here the dance studio's mostly just give you $20, $30 or maybe $40. And in New York City the rent is really expensive.

I feel that is the hardest part.

But like I said earlier, if you're living your dream life; you have to know what kind of life you want. Who you live with, what kind of work you do...

If the people are your favorite, in the world, then just keep doing everything you're doing.

What is your favorite part about life in America/New York City?

The culture's mixing, that is my favorite part!

New York is so inclusive, you can see so many different people from different countries, living different lifestyles. And they mix-in together. We take each other's culture. Mixing the world, is so amazing.

New York is the center city of the world!

You can see any shows you want.

And its tolerant of all cultures.

Have you always felt welcomed here in America/New York City?

I feel that American people are really, *really* kind and friendly.

It's really, *really* easy to make a friend. I like being friends with American people—they are respectful and helpful.

For me the answer is, yes.

I'm really positive and energetic. Open-minded. I am a dancer, I am an artist—I like being around stylish people. My personality is very okay living with the American lifestyle.

The most important part is you need to be confident and willing to socialize with everybody. I have some friends who are from China, they went to college in the US and they told me, they didn't fit in with the American people, because the cultures are different and you grow up, differently.

Life and our values are different.

Where you grew up, makes you who you are. That's true. But everyone's different, some adapt to new environments really fast. And some don't. I feel that they just need time. But some don't fit in because they are always telling themselves, they are from China, and they are different.

You are a very passionate person.

Why do you think it is important to follow our passion/s?

"Why did humans develop modern science and technology?" Because of interest to the unknown.

When you are interested in someone or something, you will have a passion for that. That's life.

If you want success, you need to find an interest you like, and that will help you when you're looking for a job. When you're interested in something, you will have a passion. When you have a passion, you will stay focused and step-by-step you will find success.

Do something you like and you will discover your passion, right away.

What is the meaning of you to you?

Honestly, I don't want to sound *too* dramatic about how great life is. When you're born in the world it isn't your choice, it's your parents choice. Once you're already in the world, you need to fight for your life, and try to enjoy your life!

If you feel your life is boring, you could choose to die—but doing that is not an easy thing. If you are brave enough to have those thoughts, then you are BRAVE enough to fight for your life! So, just stand up and keep fighting for your life.

One day you will be successful.

The meaning of life to me is to enjoy life! The world is so amazing, you can see so many different colors. You can hear so many different sounds. You can touch and feel so many different textures. You can smell so many different scents. You can taste so many different foods!

So, go travel all over the world, eat the food you want to eat with your lovely family!

Go, see the world!

Although this book is intended for everyone, the theme of it is 30. And I know you're not 30 yet but I feel like receiving advice is always great from everyone.

Do you have any advice for those of us that are turning 30 this year?

Everyone will get old—enjoy when you are young!

Do some crazy things.

Do not keep any regrets.

Sometimes a sudden decision can change your life.

Don't be soft and indecisive.

So, after doing some crazy decisions, it's time to be adults. When you are 30-years-old you should think about your family, and your stuff. Times goes by super fast. If you have something you really want and have been targeting but are still hesitant to it, then it's time to really implement it.

Thank you!!

ANGIE C. SEAGREN

ALASKA, USA

You're originally from Newport Beach, California but you're currently living in Talkeetna, Alaska.

Why did you decide to relocate to Alaska? Had you ever visited before moving there?

I was born and raised in Newport Beach, I had never been to Alaska before; I actually had never really thought about visiting Alaska before I moved here. I had a friend who asked if I wanted to come up with him for the summer in May of 2016, I fell in love with Alaska and wanted to stay a little longer.

How long have you been living in Alaska for?

I moved to Alaska on May 23, 2016. So, just about 2 years.

What is your favorite part of living there?

It's hard to pick one aspect of Alaska that's my favorite part. There are so many beautiful things about Alaska. I would have to say the wildlife.

When I was living on an island in Seward, I would walk to work at 6 am, (work was about half a mile down the island), and there would be whales playing about 10 feet from the shore. I saw many humpback whales, orcas, and fin whales. Fin whales are actually not very common to see. They are the second biggest mammal in the world (right under the blue whale), because of their size it's hard for them to come to the surface for long periods of time. Luckily, I was fortunate to witness 3 of them playing with each other on the surface!

Living in Talkeetna, there is different wildlife. I've seen more moose than I'd ever thought I would. Bears, too. They are beautiful and majestic animals. There is a river in Talkeetna so I wouldn't see any whales there but I've enjoyed a different kind of wildlife.

Aside from the climate, what is the biggest contrast between Newport Beach and Alaska?

The biggest contrast between Newport Beach and Alaska is the amount of people. There are 800 residents of Talkeetna, no grocery store, no mall, and the town is about a half-mile-long. It's the cutest town.

The summer is so much fun because there are a lot of tourists that come through and want to know everything about the tiny little town.

Our mayor is a cat named Denali; he just became mayor about a year ago. His brother Stubbs was the mayor for 20 years until he passed away last summer. It was actually a huge deal when Stubbs passed.

Actually, last summer Talkeetna was ranked the number 1 small town to visit in America. It's full of good food, good little shops, and even better people.

Even though Alaska is part of our country. It seems as if we know very little about it.

What should we know about it?

What everyone should know about Alaska is, it's definitely a lot bigger than you think it is. Denali National Park is 6 million acres. That's the same as fitting the state of Massachusetts 6 times just in Denali National Park.

Another thing everyone should know (and yes we get this question all of the time, especially from Americans). Yes, you can use U.S., currency in Alaska, and no you cannot see Russia from Alaska. However, if there was a bridge built from the westernmost parts of Alaska to the easternmost part of Russia, it would take half an hour to cross the bridge in your car.

What would you tell someone who also wants to move to Alaska or a place similar to it?

What I would tell someone who is thinking about moving to Alaska or a place similar to it, is really do your research on where you are going to be living.

You don't want to be stuck in the middle of nowhere like I am in Talkeetna, without the proper clothing or not knowing how to find your food. There is a grocery store about an hour and a half away, but it's hard to drive there more than once a week, especially during the winter. So, you want to make sure that you catch enough fish, or have enough, bear or moose meat to last you through the winter.

Again, really do your research on where you would be living in Alaska because it's not easy living here.

Can you tell me about the weather, when is it the coldest there and when is it the warmest?

The weather is definitely something to get used to in Alaska. In Seward during the summer, the hottest it reached was 85 degrees, let me tell you, that it may as well be 185 degrees when living in Alaska as you aren't used to that kind of heat all of the time. The coldest it reached in Seward (when I lived there) was probably 40 degrees (I only lived there for one summer), it snows a ton there, but it's absolutely gorgeous. It also rains a ton in Seward. There was a time when it rained for 17 days straight, not once did the rain stop, it just poured and poured. It can be miserable at first but you learn to adapt to it.

In Talkeetna, the warmest was also about 85 degrees and the coldest, well, the coldest I experienced was -41 degrees. Yes, -41 degrees Fahrenheit. We still had to work on that day, and at that point, I was living close enough to work that I would walk every day. Everyone went about their day when it got that cold, and I thought everyone was nuts for thinking this was normal. I had to remember that these people have lived here for 30 years or longer and have gotten used to it.

Did it take you very long to adjust to the climate change?

It's actually kind of a funny story. When I first arrived in Talkeetna it was October of 2016. So, fall had started and the trees were out of this world with color and it was one of the most beautiful places I'd ever seen.

It was 35 degrees and I wasn't used to that cold temperature. I was all bundled up in a heavy jacket, beanie, scarf, and gloves. My friend, the one who convinced me to move to Alaska, was with me and we saw someone walking around in shorts and a sweatshirt. We thought they were out of their mind! But what we later came to understand after living in Talkeetna during the winter, was that 35 degrees was still warm for them and they were still used to the warm weather.

We found ourselves wearing shorts and sweatshirts in 35-degree weather the next fall as well. So, I guess the short answer to the question is, it probably took me about a month to acclimate to the climate.

What is the biggest life lesson you have learned from living there?

The biggest life lesson I have learned by living in Alaska is honestly, learning how to fend for myself when there isn't much of an option for food.

I learned how to catch, cut and cook salmon and other fish, how to cook moose meat, (it's actually very tasty and sweet), and how to use the resources I had around me in nature to make meals. I would go camping and hiking a lot and that is a good way to figure out how to survive out in the wild.

I learned how to keep a fire going all night without having to wake up and add extra logs and just being able to be smart about surviving in Alaska.

Aside from your family and friends, is there anything else you miss from back home?

Aside from missing my friends and family, I really miss fresh fruits and vegetables. I probably would have never said that in my life had I not moved to Alaska. Fruits and vegetables have to be shipped to Alaska. By the time they get into the stores, they are already going bad. There are some veggies that grow amazingly up here, for example, kale, lettuce, tomatoes, carrots, foods like that. The soil is very rich in nutrients. But since it rains a lot some vegetables can't grow up here. I also really miss avocados and tacos!

This is your chapter, what do you want people to take away from it?

What I want people to take away from this is not being afraid to try new things. I also want people to know that you are capable of so much more than you think you are. Take it from me, I grew up in a city with lots of people, now I'm living in a town of 800 and loving my life!

Although this book is intended for everyone, the theme of it is 30. And I know you're not 30 yet but I feel like receiving advice is always great from everyone, do you have any advice for those of us that are turning 30 this year?

My advice for people turning thirty would be to not take things for granted.

You don't know what it's like to not have electricity, running water, a grocery store or mall right down the street until you have actually lived in that situation. It's definitely a tough adjustment.

Also, don't take life too seriously and go on those adventures you've been talking about forever. You have your whole life to work.

"When will you have time to travel and see the world, meet amazing people that become your family and learn a new way of life?"

I hope people enjoyed reading about life in Alaska and I would encourage everyone reading this to go and visit the sheer awe-inspiring beauty of Alaska. Seriously, you'll catch yourself in an absolute trance staring at the natural beauty of Alaska. It makes you really see how important life is and how important it is to do everything we can to keep the natural beauty of the earth for as long as we can.

Thank you for taking the time to read this! Come visit us soon, we all have welcoming and open arms!

Thank you!!

MARIO ALBERTO GUZMAN JAIME

OAXACA, MEXICO

---

*Spanish/English Translation

When I first met you, you had a pretty clear vision of what you wanted in life.

You wanted to govern the state of Oaxaca and go from there. You were very passionate, and you spoke very enthusiastically about it.

Its been about seven, maybe eight years from that conversation and now you're actually working in politics!

What's your current title and how did you get there?

Before I begin, I would like to thank you for remembering those pleasant conversations of when we were students in the city of Guadalajara, if I'm not mistaken we met in 2009, almost 10-years-ago.

I am currently the general director of the Coordination of Planning and Evaluation for Social Development of Oaxaca. In December 2016, I received the invitation of the newly appointed governor of the state of Oaxaca, Alejandro Murat Hinojosa, to be part of his team for the administration that covers 2016 to 2022.

I am very grateful, but above all, committed to being able to collaborate in the not at all easy task that it is to govern a state.

The current president of Mexico, Enrique Pena Nieto, was asked in 2011 at the Guadalajara International Book Fair what his favorite book was. He responded by saying the Bible was.

Knowing you are a future leader of Mexico I would like to ask you that same question, what is your favorite book and why is it your favorite book?

Recently, I remembered that since I was a little kid, I have been interested in politics. At that age, I found a book called *"Porque Chiapas"* by Manuel Camacho Solís, and it was very funny to me as I was only 10-years-old. I tell you this anecdote because that is the type of reading that prevails in my life—in that sense.

The political novel that I have enjoyed reading the most is *"La Fiesta del Chivo"* by Mario Vargas Llosa; it perfectly narrates the comparison of the government systems of the 60's with a great touch of sympathy and of the vicissitudes of its rulers. It is required to read that book in political science; I enjoyed knowing I had already done so at the age of 15.

There's a biblical saying that says something like,"No one can be a prophet in their hometown."

You started your political career precisely in the state where you were born and contrary to that biblical saying it seems to be working for you.

Why do you think it's been working for you and why did you choose to start your career there?

Oaxaca is a state that has many social needs, it is among the three poorest in the country, so the opportunities for academic training at a professional level are reduced compared to other states. Thanks to my parents, I had the opportunity to do my studies both in Mexico City and in the state of Jalisco, but I always had the clarity of returning to my state to collaborate in its development.

We must identify our interests and recognize our capabilities, I am passionate about public administration, and I consider myself qualified to exercise it.

"And what better than in my beautiful Oaxaca?"

Oaxaca is a very interesting state for so many reasons, one, in particular, is that there are a couple of different languages spoken there. Among Spanish, indigenous dialects are also highly spoken.

Is that an indication of a cultural separation?

Or how is the interaction between both cultures that are essentially one?

Oaxaca is a multicultural state where 16 ethnic groups coexist, and the same number of indigenous languages are spoken.

In a population of almost 4 million inhabitants, it would seem somewhat complex, but the respect for our native people, customs, and traditions of each ethnic group are what allows for that diversity. And it is translated into an incomparable cultural wealth.

Tell me more about Oaxaca, what should I know about it?

Its geological conformation allows the existence of very diverse regions, its flora and fauna are among the richest in the country. There is also a great variety of climates.

In total there are 8 regions: Cañada, Costa, Cuenca, Isthmus, Mixteca, Sierra Norte, Sierra Sur and Central Valleys.

The orography has been the main factor for the composition of human settlements; there are 570 municipalities and around 12 thousand localities.

Pre-Hispanic cultures, apart from a vast cultural heritage, is where we have inherited our great archaeological cities.

About 120 varieties of *maguey* are produced here, which makes Oaxaca the largest producer of *mezcal*.

Thanks to its beautiful colonial architecture, the Historic Center of the city of Oaxaca is listed by UNESCO as a World Heritage Site.

It has an extensive coastline that has formed beautiful beaches that have become famous worldwide.

It is the state with the highest production of wind energy in the country.

What is your favorite part of Oaxaca?

It's people.

They are people that come from hard work and from the fruits of their labor. And who day-by-day struggle to build a better place to live.

Why did you choose to study politics?

Initially, I studied economics, but my love for public administration forced me to enroll in the classes that my political science friends were taking. In the second year of college, I decided to change my career (laughs).

I've met a lot of families who regularly talk about politics, was your family one of those?

Indeed, without a doubt.

My father was a public servant for many years, from a very young age, I was already accompanying him to his work tours in the interior of the state, getting to know wonderful places but also discovering the shortcomings of the population at a young age.

Eventually, that awoken my interest in a future that consisted in working towards changing that situation.

How active were you in your community when you were growing up?

I enjoyed my childhood and my youth a lot; I made many friends.

In school, I always participated in activities that involved community work. I was also part of the political groups that encouraged our participation in our community.

Earlier you thanked your parents for the opportunity they gave you in allowing you to study outside of your birthplace.

Why did you choose Guadalajara, Jalisco as your destination for college?

There are many other destinations you could have chosen closer to home. Guadalajara is about a 4-hour flight and a 12-hour drive from Oaxaca.

Guadalajara is a beautiful city and given its development, it is fully equipped to train future professionals in the highest of capacities. It has excellent universities.

The distance was hard, I only visited my family 1 or 2 times a year, but it was worth it, I feel very satisfied with the results.

Is there anything that you admire from the politicians of the state of Jalisco?

When I lived in Guadalajara, there was a very controversial governor, but I also remember very enthusiastic mayors.

I believe that as it is with the rest of the country, it depends on the politician's vocation in order to make a notable change that can make a difference in its way of governing or administrating an institution.

While I was in Guadalajara, I attended the last meeting of the year for the House of Representatives of the state of Jalisco. It was mentioned there that the highest number of people migrating to the state of Jalisco were from Oaxaca (at that time).

They mentioned the cause of the migration was because of the high amount of violence, along with the high amount of poverty and so on.

Now that you are a public officer in Oaxaca, what can you tell us about this?

Have the numbers changed?

What about the problems that forced people to migrate to other parts of the country like Jalisco, has there been a solution for that?

I did not know that Jalisco is a migratory destination for Oaxacans, perhaps because of the variety of industries and the large amount that exist there.

Social deprivation has caused a high migratory rate in the state, forcing migration mainly to the United States, and unfortunately, it remains a constant occurrence. However, this situation generates high economic remittances for the families of the migrants, which allows them to have better living conditions in their lifetime.

The State Government has a program of support for migrants who return, so that upon returning to the state they can carry-out productive activity that allows them to reincorporate themselves to society, socially and economically.

There are two very known Mexican historical figures/former presidents that like you happen to be from Oaxaca. One was a dictator. The other one has been referred to as a "political hero."

What do Porfirio Díaz and Benito Juárez represent to you, or mean to you?

Mr. Benito Juárez García, the "*Benemérito de las Américas*" undoubtedly is a historical reference for Oaxaca and for Mexico. He is the example that the tenacity of an indigenous child can result in a great reformer and statesman. Precisely what the country needed in the 19th century.

To General Porfirio Díaz Mori, I think that history has not done him justice. He was a man who fought from a very young age and defended the country from foreign invasions; and as its ruler, his priority was to take Mexico to progression and to the vanguard. He took Mexico to an international level.

Both of them are two Oaxacans who are undoubtedly the inspiration of many; their names are written in gold letters, in Oaxaca.

I have spent a lot of my time reading about dictators and researching them. They seem to really think their way of leading their country is the right way to govern.

Their dictatorship also seems to happen in a blink of an eye.

Latin America has lived through communism, as it does currently. What can you, as an expert in politics, tell us about dictatorship?

I believe that a dictatorship is not born per se, but that different factors are those that build it. In Latin America and South America there are many cases, and in all of them, the ruler in question, came to power with the support of the majority of its voters, but it is also the majority who later removes that person from power.

We have to think about the majority of the citizens who choose their leader in order to prevent the government from becoming the government of the minority of its population instead of the government of the majority. And therefore allow the law to be the last thing that prevails.

Who is your favorite president?

What qualities do you wish to take from him/her?

And internationally, is there a leader that you admire? And if so, why?

I think that each president has his essence. I would take the rationality of Benito Juárez, the pragmatism of Porfirio Diaz, the patriotism of Lázaro

Cárdenas, the state vision of Adolfo Ruiz Cortines and the astuteness of Carlos Salinas.

I consider Winston Churchill a leader with extraordinary qualities that allowed him to not only be a great ruler, but a moral leader for different rulers around the world; his artistic ability is equivalent to his leadership.

Mexico like many countries has never had a female president.

Is there a certain female politician that you would like to see become the first one?

There have been women in different political parties with great capacities; I would like to see as president of Mexico that woman who achieves change in the social perception of its rulers, with her work and with the results of that work.

It seems to be a very hot topic, and it stirs a lot of controversy when people discover that the political party, *Partido Revolucionario Institucional* (PRI) has only been defeated twice...ever...by one other political party, *Partido Acción Nacional* (PAN).

Up until then, the party known as PRI had been in power for about 71 years.

Globally everyone asks themselves how this could happen (fairly). And why this has happened.

Do you wish to comment on this?

Society is constantly changing, so the alternation in Mexico is already a reality. The citizens freely choose their rulers, they give them their vote again if they liked their administration. They also punish them, by not giving that political party their vote, if they feel otherwise.

Out of everything that a country struggles with like, poverty, crime, illiteracy, corruption, extreme inflation, unemployment..etc.

Which one do you think is the worst?

Which one means the most to you? Why?

The fight against poverty is the great challenge of the administration of Governor Alejandro Murat, and in the Coordination of Planning and Evaluation for Social Development of Oaxaca we are responsible for designing and implementing a social policy that responds to the needs of the population, and that aligned with the Sustainable Development Goals of the 2030 World Agenda can generate an economic development that allows us as a society to have a better quality of life.

There are many relevant issues of a country or a state, but it is Social Development, the area where, as a public servant, I put my best effort, so that good things happen.

What is the hardest part about being a politician?

More than a politician, I consider myself a public servant of vocation and conviction; the most difficult thing is to try to understand that not all of us who work for the public function necessarily have the same interest in doing things in favor of the development of the state.

Last year (2017) it seemed as if Oaxaca was struck with numerous natural disasters (more than the usual). The last one we heard of on an international basis was the 6.1 magnitude earthquake that also severely damaged Mexico City.

How badly did it hurt your population and how fast are you recovering from it?

It has been the natural phenomenon that has caused the most damage to the state.

It left around 70 thousand damaged houses, 30 thousand of those were entirely damaged and therefore a total loss. 3 thousand schools were left with partial damages; roads and drinking water systems were also affected.

It will be an activity that will occupy us for the following three years.

At a time like that, when a natural disaster hits, a politician is both there professionally to aide its people, but at that moment they themselves are also just civilians who don't have a response as to why things are happening.

How do you continue your job in a situation like that?

When you hear the devastating stories of families who lost their loved ones and their patrimony, your position as a public servant detonates the possibilities of helping those in need, and you stand in solidarity with those affected.

It seems that politicians are constantly receiving heavy criticism. They are made fun of at times. They are also constantly being judged.

How do you handle criticism?

How tough do you have to be emotionally?

I don't know if this is going to always be like this (laughs), but I recognize that the line between public and private is very thin and as you say, sometimes people without knowing the personality of a public servant generalizes our behavior by the behavior they have seen in others.

When its happened to me, I try to do the best that I can to demonstrate that is a false stereotype.

We all have bad days, how do you handle them?

Arriving home in the evening and having dinner with my family, telling my daughter a story, talking to my wife. Those are all things that make my profession easier and remind me of the motivating factors of my efforts in public service.

A career in politics comes with both victory and loss. How do you overcome loss and failure?

I think that when you compete for an objective, whatever it is, you should always think about winning. Otherwise, your destiny will be failure, but if you put your best effort and do not succeed, you have to take into account that life is made up of failure as well, so you have to better prepare yourself and try again, only then will new opportunities arise.

You've stayed very focus on your desire to govern Oaxaca, and you're getting there. I have no doubt that you will get there.

How are you so disciplined?

Do you have any advice for achieving a goal?

On the contrary, I would like to receive a lot of advice. I believe that success is based on that, observing, asking, consulting, listening, understanding, learning and improving. But the most important thing in your career is to enjoy what you do, in my case, every day is a victory conquered towards my final goal.

You have been exposed you to a lot—including natural disasters.

You see contrasts daily (victory, loss, poverty, wealth).

You meet with world leaders, and you also meet with people who come to you with the most unusual and desperate circumstances.

What do you think life really is?

Whats your perspective?

Life is what one decides to build of it. One also is the one who decides what path to take.

I am very aware of the stages of my life that made me grow as a human being, at 8-years-old I experienced the separation of my parents. I also lived through the rebellion that comes with the adolescent years, and the death of my brother in 2014. All of those circumstances can provoke any person to have an emotional imbalance, but the values and the upbringing that a family can equip you with are what help you overcome those and allow you to move forward.

Therefore, if you build a solid foundation and direct yourself towards the right paths, you will enjoy your life to the fullest.

Do you really think a person can overcome his or her obstacles and become the person they want to be?

If so, why do you think so?

Of course. As I mentioned, it is one who decides the way and the direction we want to give our life. For that reason, obstacles become secondary when you have clear objectives.

Is there a particular story that stands out to you, of someone who overcame their obstacles?

The one of my parents, both come from humble origins and from rural localities. Waldo from Chilapa de Díaz, Oaxaca and Marina from Amacuzac, Morelos. Despite their shortcomings and the adversities they faced, they studied, they became professionals, they worked hard, and despite not getting married until recently, they managed to have four children who admire them for their dedication towards our family.

And for working hard towards our well-being.

Although this book is intended for everyone, the theme of it is 30. Where were you at 30-years-old, what stage of your life were you in? And what would you recommend those of us turning 30 this year?

I am 31-years-old, at 30 I was just starting my current job with great preparation, with a lot of energy, enthusiasm and with the clarity of doing things well. Age gives you that, which is why we should never waste any moment of life.

Thank you!!

MICHELE AND KEITH GREEN

NEW YORK, USA

Do you remember the day when you first met?

When was it and where was it?

Michele: Yes, it was September 9, 2000. For a long time, that day was our anniversary.

In my car, in front of his music studio in New York City.

How did it happen?

Michele: My childhood friend Christina introduced us. She holds a very special place in my heart. Our dads were best friends, and we grew up together.

She lived with me for about a year. We both don't have sisters, but we consider ourselves to be sisters.

She met Keith's friend and business partner Jay, and when Christina met Keith, she knew we would get along really well.

How old were you when you and Keith first met?

Michele: I was 19-years-old, and Keith was 28.

A lot of people say that when they met the person they eventually married, they instantly felt something different, and they immediately knew they were the ones they'd marry.

Did that happen to you, or what was the first reaction you had of one another?

Michele: My girlfriends and I went to the music studio where he was working. My friend (Christina) went inside to get Keith and his friend Jay. They came in my car, and at the time I had a mini-van. I was in the driver's seat, and he was sitting in the 3rd-row, and every time I turned around to talk to him, I was blinded by a bright light surrounding him. It was almost blinding. I later learned that he had a very bright aura. I had never seen that on a person before.

That night I thought he was nice and funny, but we really didn't connect.

The second time we were around each other, I was able to have a one-on-one conversation with him.

We talked all night.

We were so engaged in our conversation.

Keith: Our friend Christina had been telling us about each other for a month. Finally, the day came when Michele and friends made it to the recording studio where I worked (at the time).

I am the kind of guy who appreciates a woman's smile. I was blown away by hers. It was warm and authentic.

I tend to be a class clown among friends. We all joked and laughed.

I was pretty guarded at the time, so I wasn't quick to picture marriage when we met, but I definitely knew there was something there that felt real, and natural.

I knew I wanted to get to know her.

I think all of us at one point in our lives has agreed to attend something we're told about, but we are dreading it and feel like nothing is going to come out of it.

This happens a lot when it comes to dates and especially when our friends are the ones who are acting as matchmakers.

Was that the case for you, or were you actually excited to meet each other?

Michele: When Christina met Keith, I was studying Fashion Illustration in the Dominican Republic at The Altos de Chavon School of Art and Design. Oscar de la Renta attended that school many years earlier.

I was there for about a month.

I would call Christina after-school "sometimes" and she kept telling me that I needed to meet Keith. She kept saying that, "He was a funny guy," and she thought we would really hit it off.

I kind of got sick of her mentioning him all of the time. I had friends in the past that would try to set me up with their friends.

So, in my mind, I'm like, "Oh boy not another guy."

But I was curious.

Keith: Like Michele, I had been told so many times that I HAD to meet her, that I was a little bit indifferent.

I was however interested in meeting this person that was so perfect for me.

Can't say I completely believed the hype but I did want to see for myself.

When did you officially become boyfriend and girlfriend?

Michele: We took our relationship very slowly. Keith was busy and working a lot. I was going to school, so we saw each other maybe like once a week in the beginning. We didn't make it official until Valentine's Day.

I believe that's when we really fell in love.

How was your love life before meeting one another?

Were you actively dating?

Michele: I never had a serious boyfriend because I was only 19. I would have "small" relationships, but it was never serious.

Keith: It was one year after I had been in a 3-year relationship that ended badly. I was not seriously dating.

How was the proposal like, did you have any idea it was coming?

Had you talked about it?

Where did you get proposed to?

Michele: Keith proposed to me while on vacation in the D.R. in front of my whole family.

We were at a resort and during one of the night time live shows he had the host announce that we had won a free 2-night stay at the hotel. When our room number was called, we both had to get up on stage to " claim our prize."

My husband knows that I am shy and knew that was the only way that I would get up on stage. He knows I love free things (laughs).

My best friend Mala who also came on the trip told me Keith was going to propose twice. Once before the vacation and again in the D.R.

We had talked about marriage, and we had been together for nine years.

How long did it take you to plan your wedding?

Michele: About four months.

Where did you get married?

Michele: We got married at the Hilton Hotel in Hasbrouck Heights in New Jersey.

The ceremony took place in the garden of the hotel. The cocktail hour and reception took place indoors. It was convenient for us and our guests to have it all in one place.

After the wedding some of our guests stayed the night.

You have very diverse backgrounds, and your family is very multicultural.

Michele, you have Chinese ancestry through your paternal side of the family, and Dominican Republican ancestry through your maternal side.

And you, Keith, you are African-America.

That's my favorite part of your family, I feel like looking at your family is like visualizing what our country will resemble more of in the years to come.

Tell me how life is with one another when there are so many different cultures involved. Cooking, for example, I can imagine you always have great food.

How does it work?

Do you take a little bit from each culture and make it your own?

Michele: Cooking is very big in both of my cultures.

My dad was born in China and moved to Cuba when he was a young boy. It was during World War II. China and Japan were at war, and two of his brothers were killed.

My grandparents escaped with all their remaining children and moved to Cuba.

My dad went to regular Spanish-school, and at night my grandparents taught him to read and write in Cantonese.

He also helped my grandfather with his tailoring business.

Then Fidel Castro came into power, and my dad found out that Fidel was having his people take over businesses all over Cuba.

They were going to my grandfather's business, so my dad and grandfather packed up their shop and fled Cuba.

They found out later, one of Fidel's people went looking for my dad and grandpa, the very next day.

My dad and his family came to the U.S. and moved to Chinatown in New York City. He opened up a restaurant right next to The Copacabana.

My mom came to the U.S. when she was 8-years-old with her two brothers and mother. My grandmother worked all of the time, and my mother cared for her two younger brothers. She cooked and took care of them.

Growing up, I watched my parents cook together. My dad taught my mom to cook Chinese food, and that was mostly what we ate.

My parents never showed my younger brother and I how to cook, but we watched them cook all of the time.

We always ate amazing food.

My parents divorced when I was about 12-years-old, and my younger brother and I lived with my dad. He passed away a month after I turned 18. My brother was 17.

I have been cooking for myself since I was 18. There were a lot of trials and errors. I cook a lot, and right now I cook mostly Dominican food. I mix it up with Italian, Soul Food, Mexican and Chinese dishes.

We are both foodies and enjoy pretty much all cuisines.

Hollywood has created a lot of comedies based on people who fall in love that are like you, from different cultures.

Can you relate to any of them?

And was the introduction between families as funny as we have seen in movies?

Michele: Not really.

When we go out, people do stare at us. I'm not sure if it's because we are a bi-racial couple or because of our size. Keith is 6' 3, and I am 5'1 (maybe 5'4 with heels). I am used to the stares. I have been stared at my entire life.

People look at me and know that I am of a mixed race and have always tried to figure out what my background is. That was and still is the first question people usually ask me when they first meet me.

When I met Keith's family, they accepted me immediately, and the same goes for my family.

Do you have any anecdotes that pertain to that?

One year, for Valentine's Day we went to a Korean restaurant on the Lower East Side. We noticed that every couple that came in were an Asian and Black couple.

We were very surprised to see that.

What are the benefits and challenges that come with having a biracial family?

Michele: We have been lucky enough to not have any challenges.

The benefits would be having handsome boys, people are always commenting on how handsome they are.

My husband always says that at some point in the future there will not be such racial difference. We feel proud that our family simply represents the human race.

Is there any advice you have on dating and marriage?

Michele: We have been together for 17 years and married for 8 years.

I would say, "Do not rush into marriage."

Have fun dating.

Travel to as many places as you can.

Go out together but also make sure you spend time with your friends without your significant other around. It's not healthy to be inseparable. You need to have a social life with your friends too.

Always love and support each other in everything you do.

What is the most romantic thing you have done for one another?

Michele: I would say the wedding proposal was the most romantic thing. Keith put lots of thought and effort into pulling it off.

Keith: As far as the most romantic thing, I would have to say our Valentine's Day tradition is the most romantic.

Every year Michele makes white-chocolate-covered strawberries. We put the kids to bed, exchange cards and feed each other the strawberries.

Physically as we discussed, you are pretty different from one another. What about in personalities?

Michele: We do have different personalities.

Keith is funny, very intelligent and very social.

I am more of a quiet person when you first meet me.

What we do have in common is that we are very down to earth, real and caring people.

Both you and Keith, have seen the different types of love there are. Love between the two of you, love for your children, love for your extended families and so on.

What can you tell me about love, and what is love to you?

Michele: We have a deep love for each other. We've been together for so long. We are each other's best friend. We are always there to support each other.

Keith is an amazing person and an amazing dad to his four boys.

He treats me with love and respect.

He's an easy person to love.

Early on in our relationship he told me that he didn't want to play games. He wanted to be in a real and honest relationship.

And that's how it has always been.

Keith: True love is a privilege that we are not automatically entitled to, but it is something that we earn.

Once you are in a relationship, you have a responsibility to the person to continuously work to deserve it from one another.

Having experienced everything you have lived thus far, what is your perception of life?

Michele: When Keith and I met, I was very depressed.

My dad had passed away from cancer a year before, and my mom had been living in New Jersey with then-boyfriend. They have since married.

I lived alone in my dad's house with my younger brother.

He came into my life when I needed him. I wasn't looking for anyone at the time. I believe that's how you find your true love.

When I became a mother and wife, I decided to dedicate my life to them. I am a stay-at-home mom right now, and I enjoy every moment I spend with them.

To me, family is everything. They will always support you and be there for you.

Keith: Life is just existing with people to share it with, and be loved by.

When we have kids, we are responsible for what kind of people we add to this society. When we are old and gray, I can't imagine anything more gratifying than being surrounded by generations of loved ones that will carry on your legacy.

Is there anything you think we should know about life that you wish you knew?

Or that you think we can benefit from?

Michele: Life can be hard at times, but everything always works out.

Keith: Always do everything with genuinely good intentions.

Although this book is intended for everyone, the theme of it is 30. Where were you at 30-years-old, what stage of your life were you in? And what would you recommend those of us turning 30 this year?

Michele: I was living in New Jersey and Keith, and I decided it was time to start a family. I became pregnant shortly after turning 30 with my first son, Kairo.

I was also working at Purdy Girl.

My advice to all of you turning 30 this year is to focus on your career and who you want to be. When you're in your 20's, it's all about working and having fun. When you're in your 30's, it's time to get serious and focus on your career and family.

Keith: When I was 30, Michele and I had just recently moved in together in New Jersey. I had broken off from my business partners and started my own music production company.

At that point in my life there were a lot of new chapters beginning in my life.

My advice to the new 30-year-old is to reflect on the experiences you've had through your 20's. Take the good, and the bad and figure out the lesson hidden behind every one of those experiences. Then make sure you apply those lessons to your life moving forward.

Thank you!!

YASMIN SIQUEIRA DAHÁS
SÃO PAULO, BRAZIL

It seems as if every little girl wants to be a princess, when they realize they cant be that, they switch to wanting to be a model. You actually happen to be a model, and you have been so for sometime now.

When did you start and how did it start?

Well, unlike some girls, I didn't imagine that one day, I would work as a model. I started in 2009, I was very young, I was 14-years-old. But even before that I already loved art, photography, and fashion.

One day, there was a casting call that took place in my hometown (Belém). My father was my biggest motivator to participate because he believed, I had the potential.

And then I was selected in that casting, I was surprised, and after that, a lot of work began to appear, and I just started to fall in love with my profession and lifestyle.

Do you remember the day when you signed your modeling contract? Can you tell me about that day and the emotions it brought?

Yes, I remember! I was very nervous during that new phase, and, very anxious to start working. I had a feeling of responsibility, as if, at that moment I was becoming more mature.

I know you briefly mentioned that when you were growing up, you weren't like one of those little girls that I described. If you weren't the little girl who dreamed of princesses and models, what type of little girl were you?

I became very independent, disciplined and responsible from the start ... so I was not dazzled by things. I thought everything was serious and I was very committed. I just thought of working and earning my own money by doing what I liked.

Do you have a favorite model?

I know it sounds a bit cliché but I've been inspired by Gisele Bündchen. Not only for her beauty but for her determination, and of course for being Brazilian. And for being recognized worldwide.

However, even though I have a favorite model, I have always tried to create my own style because each person has a personality and a type of beauty.

What about a style icon, do you have one?

As incredible as it might seem my style icon is a man, Jared Leto is my favorite. He undoubtedly has his own style.

Do you have any fashion tips?

The most important fashion tip is to always be comfortable and feel good.

For me in particular, I seek to always have neutral colored clothing in my closet.

So, that when I want to wear clothes with more color, I can use the clothing I have to combine it.

And I let the hem to bend, its a "rule" that I always follow.

It seems to me that models are always traveling for their jobs, where has modeling taken you?

The opportunity to travel to various places and meet new people from different cultures has always been one of my favorite things in this profession. I have worked hard in many cities, in my Brazil, in Italy, in France, in Africa, in the United Arab Emirates, and in the U.S.

Do you have a favorite out of those?

Even after getting to know those places and several parts of the world, I fell in love with New York City, that city, is simply just the way I am.

Do you have an anecdote you want to share of your modeling career?

Once I was in a fashion show, and the high heel I wore was too big for me. I taped duct tape under my foot to prevent it from coming off. But in the middle of the catwalk, one side of the high heel came off. Even though, I had put the tape on it. I had to return to the beginning from where I had started, I was limping to get the high heels and to put them back on.

All of the people who were watching began to laugh, I could not take it, and I started laughing too.

Every job has their benefits and disadvantages. What are the benefits you believe your job has and what are the disadvantages?

One of the benefits is for sure the knowledge you are always getting, traveling, making connections with people from all over the world, creating trends, among other things.

And the disadvantages, I think, is the uncertainty of getting a job. Sometimes we have work, and sometimes we don't. As models, we are always looking for something, preparing physically and psychologically to get the job we want and when we aren't selected for that job, it is a bit frustrating.

Just this past year (2017) there was an entire movement on women coming forward and speaking about being harassed by men at the workplace. Most of those women happen to work in jobs similar to yours.

Have you ever encountered any type of harassment, or anything that has made you feel uncomfortable?

Unfortunately, in the past, women who chose to be models were highly disregarded, they were considered prostitutes and dumb. In addition to suffering from the disrespect of the people, they were also being targeted by profiteers.

I believe that nowadays, thanks to the freedom of expression, communication, the media, and the attitudes of women, and also of some men, the industry is more enlightened and a part of the world has evolved through that.

I had some difficulties in positioning myself in this market, to impose myself and try to prove that even though I was very young, I was mature and capable of making my own choices.

What should we know about being a professional model?

First, a professional model has to have conviction, make sure you want to work in this area, and you have to want it as a job, not for the glamour of it.

Then you have to dedicate to the maximum, in all the jobs you do, and always keep the focus with a lot of energy and pleasure, being punctual and organized, always.

It is very important to have your own personality, your formed opinion, willpower, information.. attitude.

I always wonder how models know how to pose when they are being photographed; I guess that's the secret behind the success of each and every model.

Is there something you are thinking about when you're posing in front of a photographer, or do you have a technique for knowing how to pose?

I think the only thing that comes to mind when I'm posing is the next posture I'm going to do, the next cannot be repeated. It's always good to be attentive when the photographer is clicking on the camera, a click, indicates it is time to change the position.

I don't think too much ...I just do it. My technique is always to allow the lips to be a bit open, and allow my eyes to be very expressive.

Your career is very competitive, especially in your country, and yet you're making a living from it. What would you tell someone who is seeking a career in a competitive industry like yours?

Always make connections, always try to be sincere, and be humble. Have an interest in learning everything because the more knowledge you have, the more chances you have of growing within your profession.

What is the best advice you have ever received, that you would like to share?

That it is better to ask questions, than to believe that we know all the answers.

Your country has made itself famous for winning the most number of World Cups from any other country—5 to be exact. It's also famous for having the biggest Carnival in the world. And of course, it's also famous for all of the top models it produces.

What else should I know about your country?

It's a country of beautiful beaches, rich in ore, with extremely welcoming people. And of course, we have our wonderful Amazon.

Throughout your life and your career, I assume you have seen a lot and have encountered a lot. After having experienced what you have, what is the meaning of life to you?

For me, life is trusting in our feelings, knowing how to face challenges, finding happiness in the simplest moments.

Valuing the presence of all the people we love. Valuing our memories and learning from the past.

And never forgetting to be grateful.

You have followed your dreams, and you are continuing to you, what would you tell someone who is also trying to accomplish their dreams?

Run back and fight for what you want.

Never give up on your dreams, or your goals.

Let your heart decide without fear of making a mistake.

This is your chapter, what do you want people to take away from it?

Dream big, fly high. Be grateful and love yourself.

Although this book is intended for everyone, the theme of it is 30. Do you have any advice for those of us that are turning 30 this year?

Love every phase of your life and don't be afraid to go through any of them. Let yourself be inspired; you are unique.

Anything else you want to add?

No.

Thank you!!

SONIA MASTERS
CALIFORNIA, USA

I was in high school the first time that I heard about the bar exam; I remember hearing how unbelievably hard it is. In fact, it is known to be one of the hardest exams to pass. And it happens to be required to practice law in this country.

How hard was it and how long did you prepare for it?

Taking and passing the California Bar Exam was one of the hardest things I have ever done in my life! Especially with the pressure of passing on the first time since California has a pass rate that is so low. Typically, a student graduates in May then has about two months to study. That's exactly what I did.

I graduated and began bar preparation on May 30th, so I had just under two months. I stuck to a rigorous schedule. I took a commercial program (Barbri) and I also took advantage of my law school's bar prep program taught by Professor Mainero (I graduated from Chapman). In all honesty, the amount of work and material that needed to be studied and memorized was overwhelming.

My girlfriends and I studied together, supported each other and had many meltdowns together.

But, what worked best for me was to realize right away, I could not do everything that I wanted, needed, or was told I had to do. I focused on general concepts and understanding the material. I studied and, thank goodness, passed the first time!

I was more than thrilled…on November 17, 2017, when we got the results, I must have checked the website 20 times to make sure it wasn't a mistake!

I have to mention that I got help from my family with my daughter, Yasmina. My mom came to visit me for my graduation and when bar prep began, I asked her to stay in June to help me with Yasmina so I could stay at school and study late.

She did, and it was such a help. My mom has always been supportive and amazing when it comes to helping me with Yasmina. Then, when July came, and Yasmina was out of school, she went with my mom to visit my sister in Hawaii. So, for that month I was able to just focus on studying.

I don't know what I would've done without the help of my sister and mom. I am very lucky.

Was taking the bar exam, the hardest part of your road to becoming a lawyer, or what was the hardest part?

Going through law school the first year is very tough. It's been described, a lot, as feeling like you've been hit by a freight train, without notice of it coming. I definitely felt like this.

I started school while being so excited, and I was a good student, I had great grades at UCLA—I love to learn. I had a career in special education before this, I thought that law school would be difficult but not as much as it was. You have to learn a different way of reading, listening, learning, writing, competing, and you have to fit in a certain amount of studying a day that doesn't even fit in 24-hours.

It was insane.

On top of that, I had a full scholarship going into law school and in order to maintain it, I had to maintain a certain GPA. So, the stress of my first year was incredibly high at the time and along with being a single mom, it was one of the most difficult years.

Thank goodness, I kept my scholarship throughout school, but it took hard work and I had to give up friends, family, etc., most things. I didn't even have time for sleep!

The bar was a different kind of hard. I thought to myself, "This is it. My entire career depends on this. If I don't pass, I cannot practice law. The one thing I worked so hard for." It was as if my first year of law school was condensed into two months, all of which my life and my daughter's life depended upon.

I know it sounds silly, "Right?"

You can always re-take it—many people do and are amazing attorneys. But for me, that was not an option. I was 33-years-old, a single parent, my path had taken *too* long as it was, I couldn't have it take longer.

So, the stress and mental exhaustion the bar exam had on me definitely made it difficult.

If I was more prepared my first year, I could have been less stressed. But there was nothing I could have done to prepare better, or be less stressed for the bar exam, so I would say for that reason it was definitely harder!

What type of law do you practice and why did you choose that type?

At the moment, I practice personal injury (PI) law. It was my first job coming out of law school, and I am still employed with my firm, Bergener Mirejovsky. I never, ever thought of doing PI law! It never dawned on me, once in law school!

But I was talking to one of the most amazing professors I had at Chapman, Professor Dowling and he asked me, what I was looking for?

And spoke to me about the firm. I was interested, so I applied.

After hearing about PI law, I realized this is exactly what I have always wanted to do, be a voice for people who don't have one. Here, I am able to be their voice and fight insurance companies for the compensation they deserve after being injured.

"Will I be in this type of law forever?" That's another question…

You were a mother when you entered law school, as you just mentioned. Its pretty amazing to know you were able to do both.

How did you manage and how old was your daughter when you entered law school?

My daughter was 10 when I started. Luckily, I have been in school since she was 4-months-old so I had many years of experience of juggling work, school, and my daughter's schedule.

I have to say, my daughter is amazing. She would wake up, make her breakfast and make her own lunch for school.

I would go to school, get off at 5:30, run to pick her up at her after-school program, run home and make dinner, shower, put her to bed, then study! I would then usually wake up at 5 AM to get study time in the morning too, because at night, wasn't enough.

Of course, there were times when she didn't have school, and I did, and I had no one to watch her—a special thanks to Professor Rosenthal, Professor Howe, Professor Litwiller and Professor Gibbs! Those professors allowed me to bring Yasmina to class with me when I didn't have anyone to watch her.

I am forever grateful for that.

Anyone who has been to law school knows that missing one day of class, your first year, feels like you've missed an entire week!

So basically, a strict schedule, no social life, help from family, professors and friends…and lots of coffee is what got me through it!

As a side story I'll mention, there was this one time during my first year where I missed something important of my daughter's.

In the first year of law school, at the end of the year, all students have to argue a brief they wrote in a competition against each other. At Chapman, its how you get onto Moot Court (if you do well).

I made it to the top 16 (out of maybe 180 students, I can't remember the number). I really wanted to be on Moot Court, so of course, I had to compete in the top 16.

It was an hour before my daughter's geography bee. But the judges who were judging my rounds were extremely late. After 30 minutes had gone by and I hadn't performed yet, I realized I would miss it. I competed, ran out of the run with my heels in my hands, and drove to my daughter's school.

She was crushed. She said she, "Didn't do good because she looked at the audience and didn't see me."

My heart broke!!

I tried to explain to her this was the first time in over ten years I had ever missed anything like this and I thought *that* was a pretty good record…she wasn't having it though! After some pizza and ice cream, she forgave me. But she's 13 now, and I'm sure she still remembers this!

In our country in order to become an attorney you have to have a bachelors degree, a law degree and of course pass the bar exam. In total, it takes about eight years, or maybe even longer to actually become an attorney.

Out of all the other careers that perhaps only require a bachelors degree, why did you choose to become an attorney?

I have always wanted to be an attorney for as far back as I can remember. Even before I knew what it would take—I always found it amazing that someone can use the law to get people what they deserve.

I was always fascinated with injustice. I asked myself, "How could this be? This is the law, why is this person suffering?"

So, when I realized there was a profession that helped those people, even in preschool, I said, "That's what I want to do."

How did you stay so focused all of those years?

Determination. I knew I wanted to be an attorney and there were certain things that you mentioned above that I needed to do to get there.

So, I kept thinking of the end goal. It's what kept me going.

That and teaching my daughter how important it is to work hard for what you want and to keep trying until you get there.

Over the years there have been many shows centered on law, even movies, do you have a favorite?

I have to admit…I don't watch TV! I used to though, so the last series that was law-related that I watched was *Ally McBeal* and *The Practice*.

I loved both of them. I am sure things have changed drastically in TV series now though!

Wait…I have watched *Scandal*, and I do love it and love Olivia Pope (before she turned into her father)!

I am always supportive of any show that shows a strong, successful woman doing amazing things and, let's be honest, in a man-dominated career.

Did any of those inspire you to peruse law, or what inspired you to pursue it?

The TV series were really just for entertainment, I didn't think any were really reflective of what it was like to be an attorney.

There wasn't ever really a person who inspired me…it was just the idea that I could help people.

I could use the law of this country to get people what they deserved. No gimmicks, tricks, or anything else like that, the black letter law to argue to get something, someone deserves!

What should we know about law and lawyers?

The law is an amazing thing. I could read a statute, or court ruling and interpret it to mean something. Someone else comes in, reads the same thing, and interprets it in the completely opposite way.

The law is never, ever, black and white. It depends on who's reading and interpreting it. Sometimes, it's easier to first understand why the other side believes what it does before being able to make your argument strong.

It's extremely interesting and it's what keeps this country going. There is always something up for debate when it comes to making and interpreting the law!

Lawyers are not all the same. The profession is filled with so many different kinds of people. Introverts, type A personalities, liberals, conservatives. Hard- working, intelligent and dedicated attorneys.

Lazy, corrupt and selfish attorneys. Ones that hold the profession as high as it should be held, and ones that take advantage of people by abusing their position.

We are all different, but it's important to understand that.

Some people call PI attorneys "ambulance chasers" but then they watch the *Erin Brockovich* movie and think, "Wow, what they did was amazing!"

But they were a personal injury law firm! So, its really important to separate the bad, from the good, just like in any profession.

Do you have a favorite part, maybe saying, "objection" when you actually do have to go to court?

I have never actually had to object anyone because I have never tried a case. Maybe one day I will have that experience!

But thus far, my favorite part is the exchange between myself and the judge. If, the judge asks me a question, and I can answer with caselaw to support what I am saying, that's a pretty good feeling.

There are many successful female attorneys in our country, one of them is, Gloria Allfred.

But there are also a lot of successful male attorneys. This seems to be a male-dominated profession.

Through the course of your career, have you felt like you have been treated fairly as a female attorney?

Yes and no. I think in any male-dominated profession, there are going to be some people who still continue to treat women in that industry as less than, or less capable of.

It's a shame, and absolutely ridiculous, but it's nice to see the movements that are happening right now to change that.

I find it especially interesting when I am on the phone with a law firm, or even a new client, and they say something like, "Pass that on to the attorney."

When I say, "I *am* the attorney."

There is a response of, "Oh…"

As if, a woman couldn't have possibly been the attorney.

Pretty sad.

There is a certain image I have of attorneys, I always picture them very sleek, clean and tailored, and they usually always are.

What do you wear to work, and how much fun do you have when selecting what you're going to wear?

Every firm is different. Some more casual than others. The firm I am at actually has a pretty strict dress code. Business attire, blazer, the whole works.

So, the firm I'm at, I'm guessing is pretty close to that of which you picture attorneys looking like!

You have obviously followed your passion even though it hasn't been easy.

What would you tell someone who also wants to become a lawyer, or someone who wants to follow their passion in an area that also requires a lot of dedication and study?

Never give up! I know that sounds cliché, but it really is my best advice. When you think you don't have the time, money, strength, opportunities that others may have, just don't give up.

Make opportunities for yourself. It's so incredibly difficult, but so worth it. And after, you'll have a sense of appreciation that is beyond what you could even imagine.

Just keep going. And don't be afraid to ask for help along the way.

As a lawyer, I am sure you have seen a lot, maybe even the most unusual of circumstances. Knowing what you know now about life, what is your perception of it?

This is a tough question…I think the hardest part is, if there is an unusual circumstance that we experience, or witness as an attorney, the difference between us and others in their profession is the attorney/client privilege.

We are bound by it and there is almost nothing that can break it.

What makes the justice system in America unique from any other?

Our tort law system is amazingly different from any other countries' in the world. We allow people who are injured to get compensated for their monetary losses, as well as pain and suffering. It's an amazing system in my opinion.

It not only compensates victims but also penalizes those who do *really* bad things.

For example, when Ford (years ago) built a car, that it knew would blow up into flames if it were to be in an accident because of where the gas tank was placed. Ford actually calculated the numbers and determined that they would make more money placing the car into the stream of commerce and paying out any personal injury, or wrongful death claims, than they would if they didn't place the car into commerce.

That to me is sickening and overly absurd.

I am happy to live and work in a legal system that punishes behavior like this with punitive damages.

If someone is in need of legal help but can't afford a lawyer, where should they go, or what should they do?

Always go to the local courthouse—there should be information on pro bono services and firms.

What is the biggest life lesson you've had?

Becoming a mom has been my biggest life lesson.

Understanding that even when I do my best, I don't always know everything, and that is something I have to admit to my daughter at times.

It's a humbling and amazing experience, knowing that in order to raise her to be the best she can be means being completely honest with her about life.

This is your chapter, what do you want people to take away from it?

I am a pretty normal person! I get asked all of the time, "How did you do it? How did you go through school, work two jobs, and raise this amazing little girl?"

And my answer is, "It's all I knew."

I only knew how to be a single mom. I did what I could, and when I needed help my mom and dad were amazing and always there.

I had great friends help along the way who were always supportive.

Just like anyone else, I don't think there is anything extraordinary about myself…I just knew I wanted two things out of life: "1. Raise my daughter the best I possibly can, and 2. Become an attorney."

Although this book is intended for everyone, the theme of it is 30. What stage of your life were you in at 30, and where were you living? Do you have any advice for those of us turning 30 this year?

I was not afraid to turn 30 at all. I welcomed it!

I just kept thinking, "Wow the twenties were a mess and so hard!" In my twenties, I thought I knew what I wanted. I thought I was strong and confident.

But everything was so difficult! Dating, communicating with the world, making a name for yourself in whatever field you worked in…everything just seemed so difficult.

I realized later; it was a false sense of confidence I felt. I was scared and unsure of myself. I think this was because instead of understanding that I was still learning and growing, I thought I knew everything, and so, I was the one who knew what was best for myself.

At 30, when I finally understood what "confidence" really meant, it was a game changer. Being confident doesn't mean you know everything. It doesn't mean you always know what you want.

It means knowing that when you don't know, or understand something, you can ask for help. It means knowing the difference between what you do know, and what you don't, and doing something about it. It also means knowing that you control your surroundings and what you allow in your life.

So, it's a great time to take out all the toxicity in your life that you may have allowed during your 20's.

Anything you else you want to add?

Just a big thank you for thinking of me for this book! I really appreciated these questions; it made me look back on my own path and what it took to get me where I'm at today. It makes me want to call everyone in my life and tell them that I love them and that they are amazing people. Because, I am who I am, and I am where I'm at, because of the support and love I had through the years.

One of my good friends always says, "It takes a village to raise a child."

There is so much to that saying! It's not just for the raising of a child; it's also for the parent as well! I couldn't have gotten through college without my dad watching Mina on Monday nights while I had to sit through 4 hours of my physiological biology class. I couldn't have gotten through that same year without my mom watching Mina, Saturday and Sunday mornings as I took my English classes.

I am forever grateful for the love and support Mina, and I always received.

Thank you!!

CHATO

CABO SAN LUCAS, MEXICO

*Name has been changed.

It is very interesting to me; before I sat down to write the questions for our conversation together, I randomly read that the human body is built to thrive in any situation.

I thought it was very special that I read that just before this.

That's exactly what you have done during the most difficult, and unusual circumstances of your life. Thrive.

You were born in Mexico and moved to California as a little boy, from then on, you pretty much lived in California your entire life.

Do you remember the move?

How old were you when you moved?

My move to California was an experience for sure. I was 11-years-old when I moved to California. I had to wait to finish the 5th grade in Michoacán, Mexico before I could move.

I remember that I didn't want to move to the U.S.

My mom was already living there, and we (my brother Rod and I) were living with my aunt (my mom's sister). But my mom promised to have a Nintendo for us if we agreed to move there.

So, she basically bribed us (laughs).

I'll fast forward to the experience of crossing.

Since we were little, obviously, we could not cross over to the U.S. on our own. So, we had to figure out how.

Luckily, we had a friend in my dad's family that was planning on going to the U.S., so she became our helper.

Remedios is her name.

We started our trek in Mexico City, from there we said, "bye" to our dad, who lived in Mexico City, with his family. He was always absent from our lives, but that is another story.

We took a *camion* from Terminal Central del Norte to Tijuana. It took about 40 hours to reach Tijuana, that was the longest bus ride we had experienced, up until then.

Maybe, it was that bus ride, that has made me love the road.

I remember staying up at night just to see the white lines on the road while I heard the humming of the *camion*.

I also remember, experiencing the heat in Mexicali; it must have been about 110 degrees when we crossed the border.

Once we arrived to Tijuana, that was when the strategy to cross to the U.S. began. I remember we met with the *coyote* (the person that crosses people into the U.S. illegally) and he gave us the scoop on how it was going to happen.

We were clueless of what was about to happen.

So, first, we stayed in a cheap hotel until the *coyote* had gathered all of the people that he had to cross. Once, he got the group ready, then we could start our entry into the U.S.

Back in 1990, crossing the border was like, a piece of cake.

We started the cross in late August of 1990 at about 11 PM. All I remember was that Remedios had my brother Rod by her side at all times, and I just followed along. Rod was 8-years-old at the time, and I was 11-years-old.

For me the trek was easy, but for Rod, it was a bit challenging.

I remember seeing all of the different groups of people trying to cross. There was helicopter action every now, and then. They called the helicopter *Mosco*. Every time we saw *Mosco* we knew it was time to look for a hiding spot under the bushes.

Our *coyote* was very experienced (I have to say). He knew exactly when to run and where to run when we had to.

We actually saw groups getting caught by the *migra* while we hid. We ran for about 7 hours.

I was concerned for Rod, but he was a stud. It was funny how when we ran; he just looked like a doll being dragged by his arm, there was no other way, other than that way, though.

Once we had reached the strategic point of pick up, a truck came, and we all jumped in. It was an old, beat-up truck, and we were squished like sardines.

We were finally in America. The land of the free.

We, stayed in a *guarida* until the *coyote* was paid, and until there was a truck that could drive us to Orange County. But before then, there was one more obstacle to beat, the San Clemente checkpoint. We stayed in the *guarida* for about three, long-days.

We could not go out, at all, so that we would not be seen.

I remember we were in a residential area; I know this because I broke the rules and I peeked out the window. I remember that I saw the first Black person ever in my life walking by, on the sidewalk.

It was *so* cool.

So, the day came when we were going to be driven to Orange County. We all somehow fit in an old Econoline van. There must have been about 20 of us in it. We were all sitting strategically one behind the other.

It was like a human puzzle.

The van had no seats, so, we all sat in the back portion of the van, with our legs open, so, the other person could sit in front of that person, and fit in-between our legs and so, on. I remember that my legs got numb from not being able to move.

After about 5 hours of dropping people off in different places, we reached our destination. We (Rod and I) arrived at our uncle's house at 123 El Camino Street, apartment D, in Costa Mesa, California (laughs).

I still remember the zip code, 92626.

A few hours later our uncle took us to *La Conasupo*. A little grocery store in Santa Ana, where our mom used to work. It was a happy day to see our mom after not having seen her for three years.

You are a great storyteller, by the way. Thank you for those details.

Just like the two of you, there are millions of other people who were brought into this country illegally as children. And because of that, the Obama administration of our then-president Barack Obama established the Deferred Action for Childhood Arrivals policy in 2012 (often referred to as DACA, or the DREAM Act bill).

The purpose was to facilitate a way of residency/citizenship to those that qualify.

It was however revoked by the new administration of our current president (Trump) and in fact, during the last couple of weeks, there was a government shut down because both political parties (Republicans and Democrats) could not come to an agreement.

How do you feel about this, do you want to comment?

"How, do I feel about this matter?"

First, let me tell you, that I am the last person you want to talk politics with, but I will tell you how I feel.

The U.S. has all the right to protect their citizens and do whatever is best for them. I am sure there are lots of good-hearted people on both sides of the political parties.

I believe that most of the DACA beneficiaries are outstanding citizens. Unfortunately, though there is a small percentage that might not be, and for this reason all of them have to pay the consequences.

Like in all cultures there are good people, and there are bad people.

I do believe that we, Latinos, are hard-working *vatos* (laughs). I happen to have worked with immigrants from Guatemala, and those guys taught me a different level of toughness. They always did the hard work and never complained, they were appreciative of their work and very respectful of it.

Those are the people that have done so much for the country. The people that go to America and work extremely hard and make something of themselves and allow their families to have a better life. This has been the story of America and the reason why America is so great. Every new group in America has been discriminated against. The Irish, Chinese, and Japanese. Those people came to work and work hard.

Now the people South of the border are going through the same thing.

I am not sure if, I answered your question, but my point is that America has to be grateful for the hard work that most illegal immigrants do for America. And in the same way, there are laws that the immigrants have to follow in order to be good, admirable, citizens.

America is in all its right to protect its citizens, and it isn't easy for America to legalize all its immigrants, especially when there are all different kinds of opinions about the subject.

Let's not forget that America is a democracy.

When we are little, we are so innocent to a lot of things. Part of our innocence triggers us to believe everyone else lives like we live and likes what we like.

For example, if we attend church on Sundays, we assume everyone else does too..and so on.

Did you think everyone else that surrounded you at school, was also like you?

Born in a different country from the one they were living in.

Or did you know your situation was unique?

"You mean when I was a kid?"

I happened to be very perceptive as a kid. For some reason, I knew that we had very little and had to live the way we did.

We had lived with four different families by the time I was 11-years-old. We lived with our grandma, our aunt, and at our dad's (I lived with our dad for a year when I was eight). Our parents wanted to split Rod and I, between our family and obviously with our mom.

In every situation, I had to adjust to the circumstances, and I knew that not everybody lived the same way that I did. I knew there were income levels and different social situations.

It seems as if we never really talked about our immigration status as openly as we currently do. At least in past years I feel as if speaking about this was never relevant to our conversations, but suddenly it has turned into "the thing" that keeps coming up.

Through the regularity of this topic, a lot has been said, and there have been a lot of opinions shared.

You're a perfect person to ask, what's your opinion on everything pertaining to our immigration issues in the U.S.?

And whats your opinion on the entire topic that surrounds it?

"What can I say...?"

I have a different view than most of the people that have gone through what I have gone through. I really have no issue with the system.

I think America tries to be as fair as possible with its policies when it comes to immigration. We, as Mexicans do get the short end of the stick, but that is because we are the majority when it comes to illegal bodies in the U.S.

I will tell you this; I was treated fairly when it came to me trying to become a legal resident in the U.S.

When I was 20-years-old, I was arrested on Wilson Street, in Costa Mesa in 1999. Two friends and I were walking late at night with some alcohol (from beer) in our system. The police stopped us and asked some questions.

My friends thought that it was racial profiling and got all excited about the situation. Of course, they arrested us, because we were walking intoxicated on the street. Drunk in public.

I thought, "Okay, one night in jail in Costa Mesa won't hurt."

To my luck, there were immigration officers that night at the station. They asked me if I was a legal resident and I said the truth, "NO!"

So, that is when I became legal in the U.S. or semi-legal. I was taken to a detention center in Lancaster, California. I was there for a week, and I hired a lawyer that helped me get out.

The state gives you all of the tools you need to fight your case in the U.S.

I was given a work permit, so I was able to work while I fought my case. I think that was fair. Since I had my work permit, I could also get my driver's license. I no longer had to drive scared of driving without a license.

I fought my case for 11 years, and I appealed my case 3 times, and I finally lost. I had no ties to the U.S. that would help me stay there legally. I could have married and stayed, but that was not an option for me. I was waiting for the Dream Act to go through, but it never did.

What I'm trying to say is, that I was given the tools to become legal and also the opportunity to live a normal life, while I fought my case. I think that is a very humane thing to do. Unfortunately, I did not become a legal resident, so now I have to live in Cabo San Lucas…so sad (laughs).

I don't believe that I did not benefit from living in America. Living in America opened my mind to many different views on life. I lived in a little town in Michoacán; I knew exactly how I was going to end up if I had stayed in that little town.

Living in America, especially in Orange County, was very cool. You get to experience different cultures and see people from a lot of different social statuses.

Where I lived I think was cool, because you get to live next to the kids that had the nice shoes, and that had brand new bikes. Then a year later, you and your parents, could go to their garage sales and then you can have that cool bike with just a few scratches on it.

In my little town, I would never been able to buy that bike. And believe me, I love bikes.

"I don't know if, I answered your question?"

What I'm trying to say is, "I have no bad feelings."

My brother went through the same [thing] that I went through, and now he has a beautiful family in Cottonwood, Arizona and is working as a firefighter. If anything, I'm grateful for the opportunities that my brother has had.

I think God wanted it this way.

What was your favorite part of life in America?

Working as a mover for 13 years. I got to travel all over America. I got to hear all of the different accents, and I got to know the different types of people in America. There is a whole other side to California in America (laughs).

Being that I love the road and I love physical work, moving was the perfect job for me. There is nothing like seeing a sunrise in the middle of the I-40, surrounded by the immense desert, listening to country music (laughs).

I still transport myself to some of those driving memories; the desert has something majestic to it.

"Do you remember the movie, *Forrest Gump*?"

"Remember the running scenes, when he is running in the desert, and then he finally stops?"

Well, it's that kind of desert, but much nicer because you're all alone.

See, I told you this would be therapeutic (laughs).

I am happy it is, but I am sorry to take you away from that desert scene and take you into another deep question.

Although you were born in Mexico, you were raised in the U.S. (as explained earlier). And every Monday through Friday, you attended an American school. Therefore, essentially you were an American, an American, little boy who recited the Pledge of Allegiance every morning at school.

How did you feel when you were asked to leave the country where you felt was your home and that *really* was your home for 21 years?

Did you ever get flashbacks of the days when you placed your right hand over your heart and recited the Pledge of Allegiance?

I remember doing the Pledge of Allegiance at school. I thought it was cool. I kind of felt patriotic (laughs).

I remember when that immigration officer came to my door. I peeked through the window and saw some men who were standing straight, outside the door. I asked Ray (my friend) to open the door while I hid in the house.

They didn't find me.

But I had to go to work, and after waiting for about half-an-hour I exited the house and jumped a couple of fences to lose my tracks. Once I came out and stopped my car alarm, they came out of nowhere.

I guess, I didn't do a good job of losing my tracks (laughs).

So, I was put in custody and taken to a Santa Ana facility to process my deportation. I remember talking to the officer, driving me to the station. It was like talking to a buddy. It was weird (laughs). We talked about sports, and I remember that I told him that I was not mad for him arresting me, but I did ask if, I could stop and get some money because I had very little on me and he said, "No."

So, to answer your question. I was not mad for what happened. I lived 21 years in the U.S., most of my life and for sure, all of my adult life up until that point. I was a little scared. I'm not going to lie, *pero me los tuve que amarrar.*

Sorry, it's just a Mexican saying.

After you left California and the U.S., entirely, how did you determine where you would relocate to and where did you relocate to?

First, I thought, "How God knew I needed a vacation," (laughs).

That is what I did. I traveled a little all-around Mexico; I even went to Guadalajara to visit Betty, you might know her (laughs).

I really didn't know where to relocate to.

I knew that my dad lived in Mexico, so, I tried to contact him to see if I could stay with him for a little bit. I told my cousin to reach him. I took a flight to Mexico City the next day after being kicked out of the U.S.; my dad was there at the terminal, my cousin did a good job. I went to my hometown to visit and then I did some traveling to see where I would fit in.

Then, I started my job-hunt.

I had no proper job training other than having my two hands and lots of will to work. Since I loved my job as a mover, I got a job as a mover in Mexico City. I did that for a couple of months then moved to Cancun and tried work there.

After that, I moved back to Mexico City and got a more stable job as an English teacher during the day and at a call center during the night. I did that for about a year-and-a-half.

After that, I moved to Cabo, and this is where I am now. It took some time, but I found the right place for me.

It would be normal to feel out of place, in a place where you didn't grow up in, even if it happens to be your ancestral country.

Did you ever feel like that, out of place?

Absolutely, I did feel out of place. I happen to be Mexican, but I had no clue how to live like one. I was Americanized. My accent was a bad thing, and I got a little discriminated.

I am not going to lie.

I was very surprised to see how people live here in Mexico. There is a different level when it comes to income. I lived in a place in the Estado de Mexico where I saw a lot of poverty. I saw how people just bought the essentials for the day, nothing more. I was not used to that. I even saw ladies coming to the little *tienda* just to buy one diaper for their babies; they could only afford one at a time.

That was a little shocking.

I adjusted quickly though. I got used to taking the public transportation, and I even learned how to walk on the street.

Yes, there is a way you walk in the streets of the Estado de Mexico.

This I learned because I was robbed, after living in Mexico for a month. I guess I was not walking properly and the thieves could smell a newbie from miles away (laughs). It taught me a big lesson.

That was my welcoming to Mexico.

What was the hardest part of living in your new neighborhood and adjusting to it?

The hardest part was trying not to look like I didn't belong there (laughs).

I did miss my family and friends, but to be honest, I had been used to being kind of alone. I adapt quickly, so, I really didn't have a real hard time adjusting.

Aside from missing your family and friends, what else did you miss?

Aside from family and friends, I missed driving; I did not have a car for a while. I did miss having the freedom to drive anywhere I wanted.

I did miss the financial freedom I had in the U.S. I'm not saying that I had a lot of money, but I could do more things with what I earned in the U.S. than here in Mexico.

I remember one day, I went to work at my moving job. At the end of the day, I was paid $300 *pesos* (less than $30.00 USD) for my duties that day. I decided to buy an *agua fresca* on my walk to the metro.

Then, I bought some tacos because I was starving.

Then, I bought candy and paid for the metro.

When I got home, I had spent close to my $250 *pesos*. So, I came home with $50 *pesos*(less than $5.00 USD) only (laughs).

That was something I was not used to. People have it hard here in Mexico.

People that have gone through a hardship of any kind seem to believe that burdens turn into blessings.

And that what seems to be a burden is actually a blessing.

Ever since your departure, you have traveled a lot, met a lot of people and it seems as if you actually belong right there, right where you are at.

What do you think?

Do you think that at the end of the day, we end up where we were intended to be, in this case, Cabo San Lucas for you?

I do think that things happen for a reason.

I for sure was meant to live in Mexico.

Remember when I said, "God wanted for this to happen to me, instead of my brother Rod?"

Maybe I didn't say that right away, but I was meant to come back.

"You know how your brain is so strong that if you plant a seed in it, it will flourish?"

Well, I was always in love with Mexican art, Mexican food, and Mexican history and I was always thinking about those things. I always cared about

Mexico; I never forgot where I came from. I think that secretly I wanted to return to Mexico. I don't know if Cabo is the place, but it is the place for now, for sure.

Speaking of Cabo San Lucas, how did you end up there?

I know previous to that; you lived in Cancun.

Someone suggested it. It was a great suggestion, for sure. Cabo is a small town, and the only industry here is tourism.

Being that I speak English, it has been a great help. There is a lot of work here in Cabo. So, I'm happy that my friend suggested it.

Out of everything you have lived, while living the U.S. and after leaving the country, what has been your biggest life lesson?

The biggest lesson life has taught me, "Hmm?"

That not everything is for sure, life can change any second. You have to live life in the moment because you never know what tomorrow will bring.

And it is true what my stepdad once said, "If you study, that is the only thing that no one can take away from you."

I wish I would have studied a little more.

What about the meaning of life, what do you consider the meaning of life is?

This is a hard question for me.

I think that life has to be lived the way you really want, but you have to do this without harming anyone.

It is really important that you leave something behind. Whether you give-back or create something to help the future, then you are doing something.

I think that teaching is the most humble of careers. Teachers have a very important job and that is to mold the minds of children.

It doesn't matter your social, or economic status, you can always give something to help someone.

Even if all you do is sweep your front yard, you are creating something nice for people to look at. I am a very simple person and don't have a lot of things, but what I try to do is at least give a smile when I can.

Even if that person has said something bad to you, just smile, and the outcome will always be positive.

Over and over again, we hear about family and friends not being supportive through the hardest of our hardships, and the number of those that are oftentimes is very low.

Was that the case for you?

I was always getting support from friends and family, but I am very stubborn and like handling things on my own.

If anything, maybe I'm the one rejecting support, but I've had no problem with that.

Just like you, many people have had to pick up the pieces of their lives. And whether we find out about it or not, there are people doing this every day. Maybe they were laid off from a job, lost a home, a loved one. Or, maybe even experienced something similar to what you have.

What would you tell someone experiencing something like that?

I think that when bad things happen, this is the time to show what you are really made of. It's the time to find yourself. This is the opportunity to learn.

My advice is just to stay positive, no matter what, even if it's really hard.

Crying is okay.

In fact, I suggest that you cry and then smile. And attack the situation piece by piece.

When I used to move furniture, now and then, we would have to move really heavy furniture up a flight of stairs. Things like refrigerators, grand pianos, etc.

They would always be intimidated and asked, "How are you going to move those up those stairs?"

And then I would tell them, "Don't worry about putting this on the third floor, worry about putting it on the first step, and then the second and so on."

You wouldn't believe the look of relief on their face. I think that is how we have to handle every situation.

Step by step.

There are people that support the DREAMers as we referenced earlier in our conversation, and there are those that don't support their initiatives.

If you could tell both sides, anything you wanted, what would it be?

To those that oppose it, I would tell them that these are good people, that DACA is good for the country.

DACA is only helping immigrants that came at an early age and have no criminal record. Most of these kids have college degrees and are in all terms Americans. Some of them have to do jobs under the table, and this does not benefit the state.

DACA would just be bringing out all these people out of the shadows.

For those that support it, "Hmm, good job," (laughs).

Currently, a person who enters our country with a work visa, can eventually become a resident in X amount of years, depending on their specific case, of course. From then on, after X amount of years, they are eligible for citizenship.

It's a pretty straightforward path for them in becoming a citizen of our country.

The difference is the fact that those people entered the country legally as opposed to illegally.

In short, a native from a completely different country, who on the contrary to you, did not grow up with an American education, nor pledging an allegiance to our country. Has an easier route to their residency and eventually citizenship, than a child who arrived to our country illegally, as a minor, without a choice.

Do you wish to comment?

If so, what is your opinion?

This is a great question. I had never thought of this.

I think that is great that someone coming with a visa can get a chance to be a citizen within a certain amount of years. Most of those people are doctors or have a high level of education, I am guessing. This is obviously very good for the country.

On the other hand, it is kind of unfair that someone that has been brought up American can't have that same chance.

Is there anything you feel that you have learned about life that you want to share?

I have learned that life is like a box of chocolates, you never know what you are going to get (laughs).

I really don't know what I have learned in life that could make a difference in someone else's.

You have never complained about anything you have lived.

But ultimately you are human and therefore have feelings and emotions, it is normal and rational for them to make you feel a certain way.

What was the hardest part for you to comprehend out of the entire situation, and how did you get past it?

I'll be honest; I was a little terrified that I would have to make my life in Mexico. But not once did I think of going back. The moment that I stepped on Mexican soil, I knew that I would have to make it, in Mexico.

I knew that I did not want to be illegal in the U.S.

Every, now and then, I would get anxiety attacks. The way I fought anxiety was to go for a run. I was running for a good three months.

I got in really good shape (laughs).

Once I stopped my vacation mode in Mexico, that was when the anxiety attacks started. But I knew that by working and exercising those attacks would go away.

I once had an English professor at Orange Coast College who said: "The best way to attack anxiety is with action."

He couldn't be more right.

Little by little, with every run and hard work, I became more Mexican.

I'll share a quote from one of my favorite movies, "How much can you know about yourself, if you've never been in a fight?"

It was said by Tyler Durden in *Fight Club*.

I thought about that quote on my runs.

This was a fight for sure. Running has always helped me when I am down.

Maybe that is why *Forrest Gump*, is my favorite movie; he did the same thing when he was down.

It seems that when we are going through something unexpected, we turn to our faith and to God.

Did you?

I sure did a little prayer in the morning, and one at night. Along with my runs that was the recipe.

This book although intended for everyone, the theme of it is 30. Where were you at 30-years-old, where were you living and what stage of your life were you in?

I was living in Huntington Beach with my friend Ray. I was working at a moving company and enjoying life. I remember that 30 was a big step. I remember thinking that my thirties were going to be great and was very enthusiastic.

What advice do you have for those of us turning 30 this year?

"What advice would I give, hmm?"

Your 30's definitely go faster than your 20's, that is for sure.

I would advise you, to- do a bucket list of things that you really want to do.

Anything from traveling to doing something that you are scared of doing. If there is something you have not done that you think, you can't do when you are 40, make sure you do it now that you can.

Age does come at you quickly. I'm not as agile as when I was even 30-years-old.

If you care about your friends, make sure you stay on top of them because friendships need to be attended to just like a plant does.

And for sure take care of the family. But I know for sure, you guys don't have a problem there. You have such a beautiful family.

That is really all I have, I am sure you will do great in your thirties.

Write lots of books, *pon el nombre en alto*.

By the way, *feliz cumpleanos*!

Thank you for this opportunity.

Anything else you want to add?

I hope that I have answered things well.

Thinking about my life and me crossing into the U.S. was hard, I hadn't thought about that in a long time.

What I maybe want to add is that I had a great time in America and I wouldn't change it for anything. It made me who I am, and I met lots of great people there.

I really don't have any hard feelings towards the U.S.

Thank you!!

POLEN PULLUOĞLU
ADANA, TURKEY

Its hard to believe you're now 19-years-old. You were a teenager when you and I first met in New York City; I remember you were on a summer trip with a group from your high school and it was your first time in New York City. You seemed to be very happy.

How meaningful was that trip, and how hard was it to be away from your family? After-all you flew from Turkey..it was a long flight I bet.

It's hard to believe for me too, time really does fly by.

That summer in New York was epic and an unforgettable experience. It was the end of my freshman year in high school, so I didn't really know the people I traveled with. And to fly from Turkey to New York, first, we had to fly from Adana (where our group lived) to Istanbul. Which was 12-hours of flight in total, not including the time we spent waiting at the airport, or the delays.

Now imagine being a 14-year-old, really, really, shy teenager, away from her parents in a country she has never been to, with people who are her friends but not the type she can trust with everything.

Even though I was with a close friend, we weren't that close. So it was a pretty hard trip but every second of being in New York City was worth it.

I remember missing my family so much that it made me cry but at the same time I was mind-blown by the fact that I was in New York City (as a real *Gossip Girl* fan). It wasn't my first trip away from my family, but on that trip to New York City, I was in a bigger city. I felt strong, happy and free but sad at the same time.

I can't even explain how meaningful that trip was for me. Actually, my parents were the ones who wanted me to go to New York City that summer and I didn't, but now thinking about that summer and the memories I have; I'm glad that my parents didn't listen to me and made me go.

Do you have an anecdote you want to share of that trip?

I have so many good memories from that trip but what I want to talk about is a feeling, actually. When we went to the Empire State Building, I could see the whole city, like it was right under my feet. I felt so tiny, and big at the same time. Seeing all the buildings that I had walked by, all the streets, and all the places was unbelievable.

It felt so peaceful that I could've stayed in that moment, on the 86th floor of the Empire State Building. The altitude was so high-up that it made me nervous and scared at the same time.

I still want to go back to that exact moment sometimes.

You were very brave in choosing to spend a summer away from your family; I know you're parents as you just said, were the ones who sort of insisted on that trip.

But did anything else motivate you to choose to spend a summer in New York City?

When I first heard about the trip, I didn't even consider going. My parents were the ones who made me change my mind actually. I didn't even think about the opportunities because I was so afraid of the idea of being alone in New York City. But then somehow, I started feeling a little less scared.

Since, it was my freshman year, I didn't have many friends. Another girl from my class was also considering the trip, and while talking about it, we became friends. And then we started feeling confident and not afraid of the trip because we had each other.

There were teenagers from all over the world who also participated in that same summer program that you did.

What did you learn from their cultures?

Since, we were all teens back then, we didn't care about cultures. All we cared about was having fun, and making new friends. But I can say that even though we were from different cultures, we had so much in common.

Having said that, do you think we as humans, have more in common than we think we do?

Yes, I totally do think that way. Everybody, I mean every country, thinks and pretends that they are so much different than other people from a different culture than theirs. But it is a huge mistake.

There were girls from some countries that I can't really remember now; they didn't try to communicate with us. But the people from the French group were so friendly that they wanted to learn a Turkish dance called *Damat Halayı* and then they danced with us.

Aside from those girls and the groups that came from France, Spain, Italy, Romania and the ones I can't remember, they were really friendly. I can almost say that the only difference we had was our language.

Do you remember who you bunked with?

I shared my room with the girl I mentioned earlier, the one who encouraged me to go to New York City that summer.

Upon arriving to America, was it how you envisioned it?

First of all, I must say that I didn't have huge expectations. As a 14-year-old teen, I only cared about candy, malls and the places which were showed in *Gossip Girl*. But America was something different. I have only been to New York City that one time but I immediately fell in love with the city and with America. It was more than I could have envisioned as a teen.

Being a teenager can be very hard for many reasons, it is the stage of our lives when we are learning a lot about life, while also experiencing a lot of changes within ourselves. Even though you're an adult now, you kind of just experienced your teenage years.

What did those years teach you, and what was the hardest part to overcome during those years?

Those years taught me so many things. They are the reason, I am who, who I am, now. But the most important thing those years taught me is that I don't always have to be with someone; that being alone is something normal, acceptable and even peaceful.

I used to be afraid of being alone in crowded places, where others were with their friends and family. For example, I couldn't even go grab a coffee, if I was alone. But after having so many close friends over the years, I can't call even one of them a friend now. They either argued with me for foolish reasons, or just broke my heart.

I used to think that having a lot of friends was something super cool. But my teenage years have taught me that the coolest thing is being happy when you are left with yourself, when you can do whatever you want by yourself.

In your opinion from what you have experienced, what has been easier for you, your teenage years, or being an adult?

Being an adult is a challenge for me that I'm still trying to get used to. During my teenage years, I didn't have very many responsibilities as I do now and my parents were the ones who did everything for me. So, I think my teenage years were easier.

You were born and raised in Turkey and you currently still live there, what do you think we should know about your country?

I think, what you should know about Turkey is that it isn't what it looks like from the news and other things.

I used to hate living in Turkey, but as I grew older, I realized that I live in a very unique country with a very unique culture. I think people should visit Turkey to have an idea of what Turkey is like; but not only the big cities, they should visit the small ones that have less of a population too. Because that is how they can get to know Turkey and our culture.

What is your absolute favorite part of your culture?

The urban language is my absolute favorite part, I guess. I wish I knew a way to explain this to you, but you have to be Turkish to understand what I mean. But I can say that the urban language we use in Turkey bonds people together, and by people I mean strangers. There is a kindness and sincereness in that language.

Your country is predominantly Muslim. I don't know, if you happen to practice it, but if you do, what should we know about being Muslim?

I am a Muslim, but I'm not a huge believer.

What you should know about Islam is that it's not about war, bullying, a hijab, or women wearing pieces of all-black clothing; it is about being kind and being affectionate.

There are some parts that are confusing to me, but I don't want to talk about those parts and give you wrong information.

This is a time in your life when you are welcoming adulthood and facing the new challenges that come with adulthood, what is your current perspective on life?

Uncertainty. I had so many expectations about university life and living in a different city. But they all failed. Every single one of my classes are a challenge on their own. And I'm just a 19-year-old woman, trying to make things work.

I hope I can have a better perspective and don't let everything fall apart.

This is your chapter, what do you want people to take away from it?

It's a hard question, to be honest. But I think I want people to think about their lives and the way they do things after reading my chapter.

I used to be so cautious when I wanted to do something, I'd think about a million things. But after I started university, I realized that when you don't think about every-single-detail, and don't plan everything, life is so much more fun. I started doing things without overthinking about the results and without making excuses. And I can say that I'm enjoying my life now.

So, to everyone who is reading these sentences right now; don't make excuses just because you're afraid of the uncertainty of the results. If you want to do something, you can. All you have to do is stop making excuses and start trying a little harder for what you want.

I love that you love reading, is there a book you think we should read?

The Divergent Trilogy. They may seem like just some young-adult novels, but those books affected my personality a lot.

The main characters, Tris and Four, affected me a lot. I don't want to give too much information about the books, to avoid giving any spoilers, but I think everyone should read them (even if they have watched the movies).

Speaking of books, this book although it is intended for everyone, the theme of it is 30. There is still plenty of time left before you turn 30. But have you thought about it?

Of course, I have thought about it. I still do sometimes.

Do you have any advice for those of us turning 30 this year?

I can't really advise anything since I'm only 19 but I hope they have lived their teenage years to their fullest and I hope they have good memories.

And if they don't, then I advise them to live their upcoming years to their fullest.

Make good memories and have enough fun that when you get older, you can think about the good old days with a smile on your wrinkled faces.

Live a life that you'd be happy of. Don't have any regrets and don't leave something you want to do for another day. Do it, the moment you have the opportunity; you may never have that opportunity again.

You don't have to live a life that makes you or others proud. You just have one chance, make the most of it.

Thank you!!

RODRIGO NAVARRO-RAMIREZ, M.D., M.S.

NEW YORK, USA

There is a saying in this country that goes something like, "It doesn't take a brain surgeon to do it," or "This isn't like brain surgery." Both quotes are usually said when explaining a simple task.

Given that you actually happen to perform brain surgery, what do you think of those quotes?

I find those phrases funny and I think it should be changed to, "It's not like putting IKEA furniture together," those are really difficult things to do.

Brain surgery is as difficult as any other professional task.

You're the first neurosurgeon that I have ever met. I would love to know what it actually takes to become one, especially since according to the American Association of Neurological Surgeons there are only about 0.5% of medical doctors that are neurosurgeons in our country.

Being a neurosurgeon does not require anything other than a love for neuroscience.

Love and passion for what you do.

If you want to become a chef, or a rocket scientist, or a neurosurgeon just to beat the challenge, I guess your career and professional life will be miserable.

So, the answer is, you need to focus, be patient and feel passion and love for what you do.

The easiest way to identify this is, work on what does not feel like working.

You became a medical doctor, specialized in Neurosurgery and later obtained a master's degree in Molecular Neurobiology.

How old were you when you realized you wanted to become a doctor?

I think I always wanted to become a "fixer." That is what I used to tell my mom. I was like 8-years-old when I told my mom that.

Back then, I didn't know that a "fixer" career did not exist. But with time, based on my background, I wanted to become either a chemist, a lawyer or a physician.

I chose on becoming a physician mainly because it's a career that becomes better and better as you get older since you get experience and people trust you more and more.

On the other hand, with all the other jobs, your best years are the initial ones and then you start going down as you grow older.

When you realized that was what you wanted to be, a doctor, did you know the long road that was ahead of you?

At first, you are willing to take the challenge, but I don't think anyone understands the commitment.

Medicine took me 4-6 years, master's 2 years, specialty 6 years, sub-specialty 2-3 years. It takes 16-17 years just to become a "beginner."

How were you as a child? Society seems to think that people that grow up to be doctors were once timid, studious and soft-spoken kids.

Does that describe you as a child?

Not at all. I was active, I questioned things in a nice way, not in an annoying way but the common factor I would say was that I was always curious.

I asked questions like, "How things worked? What made them fail?" And I asked how to disassemble them and fix them. That was what I thought about when it came to furniture, TV, my parent's car, people…

I know you were born in Mexico City and then later moved to Cuernavaca, Morelos, the city that is referred to as "Eternal Spring," about an hour and half drive away from Mexico City.

How was life at that age with your parents and your brother?

Life was great. I moved at the right age to the right place.

My parents were struggling because of a national economic crisis but we managed to be together.

I was transferred from a private school to a public one and had to physically fight for respect, but I made the best of friends that I possibly could have made.

At the same time, my brother was struggling because he was older than me and I think he had the hardest time, but we managed to survive and enjoy the ride.

As soon as he got into college, he found a way to be transferred to a university in the US.

Were you ever influenced to become a doctor through your family?

Somehow, yes. I think looking at my dad struggling to find a better job made me think about finding a career in a field where I could be more productive as I got older.

My options were to be a chemist, lawyer or physician.

Eventually, with none of them other than with medicine I felt like as if I wasn't working although I was actually working, sometimes for more than 36 hours straight.

I feel as if all of us as children at one point in our lives is given a toy doctor kit. Maybe to motivate us to become one, or maybe really because parents genuinely think it's a fun toy.

Did you ever have one?

I think that as kids, we may identify with doctors just as a role but the love towards the career will not build until your first encounter with the actual field.

Medicine is about finding beauty among disaster, chaos, smells, sadness, crisis, stress, pressure, and sleep deprivation altogether.

As a little boy, did you ever choose to play "doctor?"

I think I never chose to play as a doctor, but I remember writing a letter to Santa for a chemistry kit. I asked for that because I wanted to be innovative and discover something new by mixing substances.

By the way, that Christmas I got an electric music keyboard, and I still remember asking for my chemistry kit.

Most children are terrified to go to the doctors and even some adults.

How were your doctor visits as a child, were you one of those kids that hated going?

I didn't hate going to the doctor, but I think the doctor was not my biggest fan. My mom used to tell me stories about my behavior and how active and curious I was.

For example; she said that once at the pediatrician's, he got distracted, by listening to my belly with his stethoscope and I grabbed it and said, "Hi" as loud as possible and my mom said that the face of the Dr., just changed and then the physical examination was over.

Now, I don't wonder why.

What about now as a doctor yourself? Do you ever go to a clinic as a patient, or do you treat yourself?

I think I am just like all doctors: paranoid..I never go to the doctor's unless it is strictly necessary. Doctors tend to minimize their symptoms maybe because we have seen critical patients and we understand the concept of "emergencies."

I try to be up-to-date with my preventive medicine appointments, but I do it more because it will be a shame not to do it rather than because I feel like doing it voluntarily.

I mentioned earlier that according to the American Association of Neurological Surgeons there are only about 0.5% of medical doctors that are neurosurgeons in our country. Most are males about 45-47 years old.

What was it, or what is it, that interests you about this specific area of study?

There are a lot of other specialties to choose from like Family Medicine, that seems to be very popular.

Why did you choose Neurosurgery as your field of expertise?

I think it made me feel intrigued, motivated, and happy. I like the challenge of understanding something that we know very little about even today with all the cutting-edge technology available.

We have to understand the following: The brain and nerves are something that is anatomically mixed, impossible to differentiate even with magnification. And that it is a structure that uses chemical elements and electricity to work.

"How complex could that be?"

There are no circuits, no defined paths, no parts. We know what "region" does what. But I think that in comparison with any other specialty even when it seems that we understand a lot, I think we cannot explain more than 2% of how the central and peripheral nervous system works.

Why do you think there are very few neurosurgeons in this country?

The average time it takes to become a neurosurgeon in this country is 12 years.

Could it possibly be because of the length of time it takes to become one?

I think the proportion will remain constant and grow as the population grows.

Also, I think neurosurgeons are not driven by money nor prestige.

Neurosurgeons enjoy the specialty and it allows them to feel satisfied. I will say this rationale is based on several factors.

Neurosurgery is not the best-paid specialty.

It is a relatively long and a stressful specialty.

In recent times medicine, in general, has been conceived by the general population as a "service" and those that look just for the challenge or prestige immediately get discouraged.

With the increase in specific demands on positive clinical outcomes, the physicians are prone to lawsuits and increased insurance quotes. Making the field less and less attractive and making the specialty so hard to practice that after analyzing the cost-benefit they may decide to pursue another career.

It's very interesting to me that the two neurosurgeons I know of, Dr. Quinones, the internationally known neurosurgeon, and you, are both Mexican.

Do you think there are more neurosurgeons in Mexico than in the US?

No, I don't think so. I think the proportion of population to neurosurgeons may be around the same in Mexico than in the US.

I am sure it was a milestone for you to have been mentored by Dr.Q. He was named 1 of the 100 most influential Hispanics of the U.S., by a Hispanic publication.

How did you meet him?

What did you learn from him?

I met him after a scientific lecture. It was right after I graduated from my master's in Molecular Biology and at that time I was interested in brain tumors and brain cancer.

He was already famous but not as he is today. I think that helped me to have a more personal connection with him.

After that, I just kept in touch and one day I found myself at Johns Hopkins as his mentee.

Do you think there will be a growth in neurosurgeons in our country?

Yes, but the proportion neurosurgeons/population will remain constant or will decrease because of the reasons I mentioned before.

The cost-benefit proportion is close to 1 and for some people that is too much.

Molecular Neurobiology is what you received your masters in.

What exactly is it?

How does it relate to your neurological studies?

Molecular Neurobiology focuses on the molecular aspect of the structure and function of the neurological systems.

A simpler way to explain it is that Molecular Neurobiology is the part of neuroscience that focuses on all of those microscopic parts that have a structural or functional role in the brain and nerves: proteins, chemical elements, molecules, neurotransmitters, etc.

Looking back at your journey that brings you to today, a Neurosurgeon Fellow at one of the hardest educational institutions to be admitted into.

About 106 applicants are admitted out of the 6,000 that apply each year.

There must have been sacrifices you had to make along the way. Which sacrifice was the hardest one?

I don't know. I cannot recall one in particular.

The most dramatic response will be, Christmas, family time, friendships, girlfriend… but to be honest I think all of those have not been sacrifices. They have just been enjoyed in a different way.

On the other hand, one thing that as a doctor in training you sacrifice is comfort and personal time.

Sleeping on a chair, on the floor, eating low-quality food, rushing because you have "things" to-do are very common.

It seems as if we are mostly motivated towards the beginning and then as we progress it gets harder and harder.

How did you motivate yourself year after year, while you were in school to keep going?

It's interesting, at first during your life in medical school and residency, there is a linear progression. You join a program and you have milestones decided by others; classes, tests, courses, meetings, board exams and the competitive environment keeps you motivated.

But after training, it's a random progression. You are the owner of your priorities, and what keeps you motivated is family, friends, your girlfriend, kids, academic career, achievements, etc.

In my case, I tend to do my best in an "only for today" basis and I try to split my day into work, personal life, and social life.

Every day has to have some of everything.

Doctors are very logical thinkers.

What do you recommend we do when attempting to achieve a goal?

Well, it's very difficult. Depends on the goal.

"Are your goals achievable or platonic?"

Achievable goals are short-term goals, and you should do whatever it takes to accomplish them. However, the advice here would be.

"Don't stop living and don't stop doing what makes you happy to achieve it."

Otherwise, you will feel miserable, and there is a high-risk of getting disappointed and tired if things do not happen as expected.

Platonic goals should be far on your sight and will help to give you direction, but you won't die if anything changes in the process, or if you never make it. Anyway, you will be trying, and that should keep you satisfied.

I've asked many people what they do on a bad day, but I have never asked a doctor.

Can you tell me what you do, or is there something we can do that would help shift our brain from feeling bad or being negative on a bad day?

A few tips:

Work issues should stay in the office or hospital (if you work there).

Life could always be worse, and people are still smiling, having fun and living. If you have a place to sleep, something to eat and you are healthy, then all the rest is extra, and you should not stress about it. It will come and go.

Use your common sense, the less common of all the senses (sometimes).

What is something you and your doctor friends laugh about that we repeatedly do as patients?

I think a funny situation is to think that doctors are better if they have a lot of grey hair.

What about something annoying that we do, what is it?

Nothing is annoying.

Most of the actions of patients even in a subconscious mental state are valid and authentic.

We need to be considerate of the kind of situation our patients are going through and remember that no one comes to the hospital just for fun.

You were recruited to come work in New York City; how did that happen?

Was it hard to leave Mexico, your family, and friends to come live in New York City?

I first came to New York City to observe and do research with my current mentor, Roger Härtl.

During that period, my performance was well-accepted by him and the group. One year after the instructor of the team was leaving to pursue better opportunities, he contacted me to fill that position.

It was at a time in my life when I thought I was still young and could receive more training and improve my skills and CV. So, I decided to accept.

Leaving Mexico was not hard. New York City is the number one city in the world, and I was invited to work here.

Also, thanks to the current technology, I am in close communication with my family. And my brother lives in New York as well, and I have two beautiful nephews, so that helps to calm the family love cravings.

When did you learn English?

I was too hyper to attend a full course. I did not take anything other than the basic courses given in elementary school. All the rest has come from, TV, the media, books, etc.

What's your favorite part about life in this country?

The fact that regardless of if there is crime or not, you feel safe.

That the institutions are respected.

That this country has been developed by first, second and third generations of immigrants who wanted to become a better version of themselves and help their loved ones.

Aside from our heart, the brain is the most important organ a human has. Ironically it seems as if we don't know much about it.

What should we know about it?

Your brain is not a solid organ; it isn't an interchangeable structure.

It's a "jelly" with cells and invisible paths that uses molecules, proteins and electrolytes to create thoughts, language, and concepts that we barely understand.

If you are reading this, you should understand and never take seeing and reading for granted. Understanding this paragraph is so unique that if every single human could read it, maybe every single one would have a different interpretation.

That is how amazing the brain/mind interaction is.

By now in life we know alcohol alters the brain significantly.

Can you as a "brain expert" explain in what ways it does?

And, I've always wondered, does it look any different when its altered?

For example, perhaps it expands in size, shrinks in size, or the shade of it changes for the time being?

In a very brief way. Alcohol modifies the dopamine, GABA and glutamate interaction with your brain (neurotransmitters) trigger it. Reward, pleasure, and relaxing feelings.

The brain macroscopically (to the naked eye) does not change.

Currently, there are imaging studies that can track chemical substances and effects on the brain by transforming these changes into a colorful or distinctive image, but that does not mean that the shape or size of the brain is changing.

What about when someone consumes drugs they shouldn't be taking?

What is happening to the brain and how does it affect it in the long run?

Legal and illegal drugs both interact with the brain, and they do it by changing or modulating the effects of molecules and neurotransmitters.

Same as in alcohol, but the cognitive and secondary responses are what makes them different. But none of them change the macroscopic structure or shape of the brain.

People complain about headaches daily. The first time I experienced a headache, or the first time that I actually remember of one, I was in elementary school. It was painful and horrible. But I was also very intrigued by it. I couldn't understand what it was.

Usually, when something at that age hurts, there is a visible sign, like a bruise or blood coming out. However, with a headache there is nothing visibly painful.

Taking painkillers alleviates the pain, but before then it seems as if the pain worsened.

What is a headache?

Well, any kind of painful experience is driven by pain receptor activation. The origin is different.

Headache origin can be classified as tension, migraine, organic, etc. Long story short: a headache is the stimulation of pain receptors in the head or surrounding structures most commonly secondary to muscle tension, stress, or migraine.

What happens to the body when the painkillers are consumed?

It depends on the mechanism of action of a specific painkiller, but most commonly, they block the pain receptor response either at the "pain functional brain areas" or at the pain receptors level.

Everyone has a different opinion on intelligence. Some people say it's genetic, especially since certain countries are known for specific traits within their population. And of course, there are others who say the human brain can be trained to be intelligent.

As an expert, what do you think?

Intelligence is the capacity to interpret knowledge, experiences, and thoughts and create new information to solve problems.

I think this capacity can be spontaneous and is used to solve new situations. This type of intelligence is not trainable, and I would call it. "Real intelligence."

The capacity to solve the same problem over and over in a more repetitive way is what I will consider trainable and I will define it as, "pseudo-intelligence" because this does not necessarily mean that you are more capable of solving problems, only that you know how to do a task faster or more effectively based on repetition.

What would you suggest parents do when raising their children?

Is there something they should be doing to nourish the development of their baby's brain?

There is no way to boost your intelligence in a significant way, but there are ways not to affect it.

In this regard, I will just say that a balanced nutrition and social interaction is enough.

There is a misinterpreted correlation between intelligence and success.

IQ is determined by "nature" but there is a point in life where the IQ and experiences combined with personality and luck become the real factors that will determine success or not.

The first time I met you, I asked you if the size of our brain determined our intelligence.

Does it?

No. There is no correlation.

What happens to our brain as we age?

Anatomically, the brain "shrinks" in a non-symmetrical nor consistent way.

Which means that the amount of "shrinkage" among individuals varies.

Some neurons die. Some connections get lost. Chemical circuits disappear. The ability to create "new connections" (acquiring new knowledge and memories) decreases and only the very old memories and strong connections will remain.

Psychologists study the brain differently, but they are also experts on that subject.

What do you have in common with them, aside from both knowing the same organ very well?

Not too much. They study the mind.

We mostly study the structure rather than the function.

Some occupations are closer to seeing life and death situations, yours is one of them.

What is your concept of what life is?

What about death?

Life is a human concept to define a temporary state or stage; sometimes lasting, a few minutes, hours, months, or years.

Death is a human concept as well, that defines an end to that state or stage. As a scientist, I am a strong believer that energy just transforms.

Knowing and actually seeing that life can end in seconds, do you think we waste a lot of our life worrying about insignificant things?

YES.

What about as Americans, what should we worry less about, or what should we do to enjoy our life?

Focus on being happy and understand that happiness is found in the "road" and not at the "destination."

Happiness won't come with tomorrow, with a new car, new job, new house, new relationship.

Happiness is here today and now.

We see this scene in so many movies; it seems like almost all of them have it, actually: the scene where the doctor delivers news that is not only sad but also life-changing. I assume it is tough to do.

Do you remember the first time that you had to deliver it?

Where were you and how old were you?

I was 29, and fortunately for me, my patient was chronically ill, and I think the news for the family faded with time and it was easier for them and me to explain and to accept respectively.

Earlier we spoke about how much time you spend in school, is there a course devoted to that, or are you trained on that (delivering sad news)?

Not that I know of.

How does your body adapt to the long hours you spend working?

Often times you are standing.

You get used to it. Adaptation.

No secrets. It's not easy for anyone.

I've read that a brain surgery can take about 4-6 hours, although it's a case by case issue.

It's obvious you are thinking of your patient but what else are you thinking of?

Are you nervous?

Are you full of adrenaline knowing you are doing what you LOVE most?

Yes, surgeries last long and I will describe it as a dissociated state, it's very difficult to describe.

Never nervous, just weird.

When performing a type of surgery like that, who else is in the operating room aside from the patient?

A group of around 6-10 people: nurses (2), anesthesiologists (2), assistants, (1) or technicians (2) at least.

The more that I learn about neurosurgeons the more I've learned that there is a lot of research involved. It's very aligned with your job description. In fact, the introduction written for you for the institution you work for mentions you have written more than 20 articles, contributed to book chapters and have various patents.

When do you conduct research?

Is it while working your shift, before, or after?

What have you discovered during your research?

Altogether, organizing the day and making small progress every day.

Are we progressing in neurology?

Yes, every day, but we are still in a very early stage of understanding it all.

What do you have patents on?

A couple of research products for intervertebral disc regeneration.

If we were to pause for a moment and look at all of the questions from this interview, we would realize you have had to make a lot of decisions your entire life. The irony of it all is that you also have to do this while you're at work as Dr. Navarro-Ramirez.

Does decision making get easier the more you do it?

Is there something you can suggest we do that works for you?

Not really, just start multitasking. This for me means doing several things the same day, but never at the same time.

That does not work, and it's inefficient and has been proven before.

What about life? Is there anything you think we should know?

Yes, stop taking life for granted.

Stop thinking 1,2,10 years ahead of you, be responsible and live today, love today, enjoy breathing, walking, and eating and think about those that cannot do those basic things and are still smiling.

Although this book is intended for everyone, the theme of it is 30. What stage of your life were you in at 30?

I was in my final years of general Neurosurgery training.

Do you have any advice for those of us turning 30 this year?

Invest on yourself.

Work hard but don't sacrifice your time or the time with your most significant ones; no one is going to thank you for that.

Have fun.

Stay healthy.

Start and finish your day with a smile, and don't bring work issues home.

Anything else you want to add?

Welcome to the 30's CLUB!

Now, you are the perfect combination between experience and life.

Thank you!!

RUTH AND MARCO ARGUETA

CALIFORNIA, USA

A lot of people say that when they met the person they eventually married, they instantly felt something different, and they immediately knew they were the ones they'd marry.

Did that happen to you, or what was the first reaction you had of one another?

And where did you meet?

I had returned to Guatemala after having lived in the US for 10 years attending school and working in a couple of states. My mom's friend from work could perceive that because I had been away for so long I might be in need of meeting people and making friends, so she invited me to outings and activities.

One of those was a big birthday party (Marco's sister's) where I met her friend Marco who used to work with her. At the party, I noticed that Marco was attentive and polite to everyone, and I also sensed that he came from a very tight, close family. We danced all night, and I had a feeling that something big could happen after that evening, as I was attracted to qualities I had not seen in a guy in a long time.

The confirmation to my feelings came a couple of days after when I was riding the bus to my new job, and he got on the same bus a few minutes later; we talked about the night of the dance, and when we got off the bus, he walked me to work.

The rest is history!

How old were you?

I was 30-years-old, and Marco was 26; because of my religious upbringing, I was ready for marriage. He said he, hadn't thought of marriage before, as he viewed it as a huge responsibility.

However, it didn't take long after we started dating for him to propose.

I knew what I wanted and what I was looking for at that time and he did too, although I realized that I was already set in my ways and it wasn't going to be easy to take me in any other path than the one I had set for myself.

My only concern in saying, "YES," to him was the difference in religious beliefs. However, I soon realized that he was not practicing the faith of his family and felt that he wasn't going to oppose raising our children in my religion.

How was your love life before meeting Marco?

I had not dated for quite some time before meeting Marco; after a few dating disappointments, I had decided to do the things I enjoyed as opposed to wasting time trying to pursue love and romance; so I always had plenty of rewarding activities that I was involved in.

I had unfortunately as a foreigner acquired a negative perception of the dating pattern, I did not accept nor understand the way things (related to dating) were handled in America. Therefore, I was going to wait until I could feel that being in a relationship was something a little more natural.

Where did you get married?

Because of the religious differences between Marco and I, we only had a civil marriage at our reception venue, a nice hotel, which still exists today, with about 50 guests.

The feeling of real happiness I remember of that day and of the ones that followed when I started getting to know the man I loved and had married, is a feeling I would want any person on the pursuit of marriage to experience.

When did you decide to move to California?

Since I had lived in America for ten years, I was missing somewhat of the lifestyle here, like work and the transportation, so coming back to California was an easy and inviting possibility for me. However, Marco wanted to start his career in Guatemala; he was a production manager, and his job was being rewarding to him at that moment.

The funny thing was that he said, "I will go to America for a year, and then we'll come back," that happened 30-years-ago.

30 years of marriage, how has that been?

When I see couples who've been together for a long-time, I always wonder who of the two had to give up a little more than the other on the things he or she wanted to accomplish or pursue in his or her married life.

For us, our business is what has been a unifying source in our marriage; even though the challenges and struggles have been many over the years when tending our business together, we've also experienced many rewarding moments and growth which has brought us closer together.

Our three daughters have been our primary source of joy and fulfillment as a couple, and the sacrifices of raising children together have given our home and our daughters a sense of stability and of purpose in life.

Although this book is intended for everyone, the theme of it is 30.

What stage of your life were you in at 30? Do you have any advice for those of us turning 30 this year?

I believe "30" is the most wonderful age to be in for many things in life.

When it comes to love, I'd say that for both men and women this is the time when permanent love and friendship can be offered to someone unconditionally.

I have always been glad and grateful to have waited to be 30 to get married; things in my life especially the decision to get married happened the way they did when I was that age, but I would advise young people to wait to be 30 to make such an important decision, as his or her offer of love, and companionship will have the level of maturity and commitment that LOVE requires.

I was able to audition for a musical group in college, which I greatly enjoyed when I was 24, and from that experience came a trip to China, and other places in the world, which turned into an educational experience and perhaps a once-in-a-lifetime experience.

The personal growth I attained in pursuing different interests and working on different projects as a single woman before turning 30 helped me tremendously in preparing for motherhood. And for future obligations in life that would eventually require my commitment, dedication, and expertise.

Thank you!!

STEFHANIA MEJIA

WASHINGTON, USA

You obtained your degree in business administration from a university in Bogota, Colombia. Soon after earning your degree, you were offered a job in your field of studies.

From then on, you continued living in Bogota while working in the corporate environment. It seems as if you were living the life you wanted to be living.

Tell me about that stage in your life.

I got my degree in business administration from my hometown Pasto, Colombia. My city is located in the southern Ecuadorian border. It is a nice place but a small town.

In the beginning, I decided to move to Bogota because it is the capital of Colombia and also it was a big opportunity for my career. On the other hand, my sister was there too. I was really excited to live with her, in a huge city, far away from home and maybe try "adult life," I thought.

I got my first job in my field of studies at a company called SKYONE, a telecommunications company in Bogota, Colombia. I was a human relations assistant. Everything was good for my sister and I, but then my sister was notified she needed to do her specialization in Mexico City and it was necessary that she move to Mexico.

So, the hardest part began when my sister left me alone.

First of all, my salary was not enough to cover rent, transportation, or food; it was really hard. It was like starting all over again and worse, alone, so I decided to look for a fast solution and something that could allow me to live with my budget. I decided to leave my first job and look for another one because I wanted to know if I could do it by myself.

I got a job at ARAMSE SAS, a construction company in Bogota, Colombia. My role was to manage the organization's administrative department. Technically it was a really good job.

I worked one year, and I felt really comfortable and confident.

Also, I learned a lot of things, and my salary was pretty good, but one day everything started to change when the company could not cover the financial problems it had, anymore. In the past, the company had been able to solve those kinds of problems, but this time, unfortunately, the company wasn't able to pay the salaries for any of its workers, including me.

I was in a huge problem again; I decided to retire from that job. I was very disappointed because I had really huge projects and also I learned so many things there but that was probably part of my destiny.

Finally, after that experience I returned to my home and lived with my parents for a while, I thought, "Things happened for a reason and probably for the best of things."

Perhaps that destiny involves you becoming an au pair, or how did the au pair idea come to be?

The idea to be an au pair came from me wanting to challenge myself to learn and improve another language and speak really fluently. So, I decided to look for some programs that work with student exchanges.

In the past, I traveled to the US and I worked at a camp, as support staff for three months, it was not one of my favorite experiences, but I felt really good to get over the fear of going out by myself. So, I thought about doing it again but made a better choice instead.

Finally, I discovered an agency to work as an au pair, and I decided to try it and started the process and maybe take another risk again for new adventures.

What is the job description of an au pair?

The au pair job is to assume responsibility, take care, educate, and be of support to an American family during a certain amount of time.

The au pair also has to represent the country that it comes from, share customs, traditions, and of course be apart of the host family.

I know there are a lot of requirements for being an au pair. You told me about the driving test you had to take that was really hard for you, especially since you were coming from Latin America.

Can you tell me more about the requirements for being an au pair?

When I started my process, I had to accomplish some requirements to be eligible for the program and to live with an American family; these are some of the requirements:

Be 18-26-years-old, be single, don't have any children, have a drivers license of the country where you work in, know intermediate English, have a university degree, and have experience in childcare.

The process has two important phases; the first one starts at the respective country of the person who applies. That person needs to interview with the company, create a profile on its web page of the au pair company, wait for the selection of the American family, this takes between one to two weeks, even a month.

When the au pair is selected, they need to interview with the American family, when the family matches with the au pair then they can start to pay for the different payments that are required. The fees for the national license and international.

A student visa, if its necessary, travel insurance, and flights.

The second phase is when the au pair arrives to the US. Some host families work in different ways. Some give the au pair some benefits, out of the contract, like a family phone with cellular data, a bank account, a driver's license for the country.

In my case, one of the requirements of my family was to get my driver's license from Washington, and this is one of the processes that for me I was most scared of, but it was a good experience.

First of all, I had never driven in a big city like Seattle. I had never even driven on a freeway before. It was kind of hard for me because even in the big cities of Colombia we don't have large roads and the traffic laws, I could say, "They are not so strict."

My next steps were to take a written test and then a sign test. I passed these with the support of my host parents. They were really patient and taught me everything that I had to know. So, now I'm really proud of myself and feel like a great driver.

Its always good to learn new things and to be able to overcome fears.

How supportive was your family when you spoke to them about wanting to become an au pair?

I had a lot of support from my parents. They are always involved in my important decisions.

They agreed that I take the au pair job because they know that my future and living in the globalized world imply many reasons to explore new paths and grow as a person and professionally.

Also, for them, it wasn't easy to let me go, but they knew that I'm an independent woman and brave enough to discover my own destiny and the opportunities that I can get by myself.

Had you ever met anyone who had been an au pair, or anyone who cared for children outside of their native country?

Yes, actually before I started this program, I met a girl who did some traveling with the same au pair agency that I am with. She was a good support for me.

When I met her she was back in Colombia, and she told me about her experience, so I felt more motivated and more confident to accept this program and do it.

Once you were admitted into the company you're currently employed with, you moved to the United States. And once you were here, you attended a training session that was held in New York City.

How important has that training session been for your career?

And what were you trained on?

I think the training in New York was a good start to being in the United States. We developed more knowledge and felt comfortable with the program.

In addition, the company that offers it, sends the best representatives from around the world and prepares us for everything, especially for being with the kids. In that training session, we learned how to perform first aid, the traffic laws and ways to entertain the children.

For us there, the company offered a tour of New York City. They showed us important avenues, they also took us to different museums.

At the end of that training session, you were told what city you were going to be living in and more importantly what family you would be carrying for. I can imagine you were anxious and excited.

How was that feeling like, and how did you feel when you heard you would be moving to Seattle, Washington?

At the training session, we are placed into groups with the city where we are going to be living at. So we knew since we started the process when the family chose us what city we were going to be living in.

In my case, I was selected for Seattle, Washington, and I felt really excited. Actually, I was really excited to meet my family.

As I mentioned earlier, we need to fill out a profile online and when the family chooses us, we are notified and can see their family profile. We get to learn how we are going to work with them and some general tips from the family.

My family and I did a real match when we did my first interview. I felt really nervous and happy in the beginning, and I read a lot about Seattle. My family and I prepared myself for the best version of myself for me to get this challenge.

Had you ever been to Seattle?

No, this was my first time in Seattle, Washington.

Do you remember the very first day when you met your host family?

I'd love to know about that day, can you describe it?

Yes, I remember that day. I arrived to Seattle with a group of the au pairs that were in the same area as me. I remember there were six girls that would be going to Seattle. We were all from different countries but had the same goal.

Our host families knew what time we were arriving, so they would have to be at the airport and pick us up. All of my friends left the airport, and I was the last person waiting for my family, then my host mom arrived, and she gave me a big welcome hug.

Afterwards, she drove to her house, and when I arrived, the kids were waiting for me with a big poster in my room. They also made me a special dinner. It was a nice surprise for me since I had just arrived that day.

What does a typical workday consist of?

My day starts at 7:30 in the morning. My host parents make the breakfast for the kids. We like having breakfast together. Then they leave the kids with me, and I just start with my routine, like prepare the kids for school.

I have three girls who are 8, 5 and 3-years-old, all of them go to school. I take the first one to the school bus at 9:00 AM, then I drop-off my other two girls at school.

From 9 AM until 12 PM, it's my own time.

Afterwards, I need to pick up the younger girl and spend time with her and sometimes she needs to take a nap. The other girls don't return back from school until 4 PM, but on some days the girls have extra activities after school, so I need to drive to different places for their activities like piano, gymnastics, music.

Then I make dinner for the kids and my day finishes when my host parents arrive home usually at 6 PM or 7 PM.

I work 45-hours during the week; I have weekends off.

I feel really good with my schedule and my work. My host parents are really good people, and we work together so that everything works for the best.

Every job has its benefits and disadvantages. What are the benefits you believe your job has and what are the disadvantages?

The benefits are getting to improve the language and perfect it.

Travel as an au pair and have the possibility to see different places. Meet new people from around the world.

Get studies or certificates in the United States in English or focus on my professional profile.

Learn a new culture. Share the culture with other people.

It helps to be brave, independent and mature.

It adds additional points for the resume.

The disadvantages are that sometimes it is difficult to adapt to the style of the family.

Working with kids can be difficult sometimes.

Sometimes it is kind of difficult to separate "work" from family life and to identify free time.

Bogota is the capital of your country, and like most capitals it's a big metropolitan city where there is a lot of constant movement in all sorts of ways.

Seattle, however, is quite the opposite in a lot of ways, including its climate. In fact, when its winter in Seattle, it's summer in Bogota.

Out of all the differences between both places, which one has been the hardest for you to get accustomed to?

Colombia is a country that doesn't have the four seasons because it is located in the equatorial region of the Earth; therefore, there are no seasons. So, Colombia has the Andes mountains, that means a lot of different climates depending on the altitude over the sea level.

When I arrived to the United States, to Seattle, Washington, it was fall and then winter. Two of the most difficult things to adapt to was that it was really cold and rainy, but also it was the first time that I saw snow. It's kind of difficult to say, but it was pretty cool because during winter it was one of the most difficult and scary things to drive in.

Otherwise summer and spring, they were good seasons and the most beautiful to see and to do fun things in the pretty cool weather.

You now have been living there for more than a year. What's your favorite part of what Seattle offers, or of life in Seattle?

I have been living in Seattle for a long time, and I can say that I like to live here so much because Seattle has a lot to offer. So much outdoor activities and I can discover life at a maximum level.

Seattle is one of my favorites cities now.

It's a walkable city and not too crowded, and the best it offers me is good coffee.

Also, the life here is nice because you can discover activities like hiking and camping. It's so full of greenery, wonderful mountains, awesome landscapes and also you can find many important companies like Microsoft, Expedia, Amazon and other kinds of icons for Seattle like museums and markets.

I think I feel really comfortable and happy to spend my time here and enjoy every moment that I live in this city.

Did you ever think "America" would be your home when you were growing up?

What are your thoughts of life here?

I always thought I would come to America since I was a child and for this reason I learned English. I think it's every Latin American's dream to come to the United States because it is the maximum power in the world.

Now that I am finally here, I can see many possibilities for getting something bigger and better for me.

No matter what, dreams do come true here.

This opportunity has been one of the biggest challenges for my personal and professional life. I'm really grateful for my destiny, and also with the education that I received from my parents, thanks to that, I could overcome my fears, discover and adapt to other cultures and be able to accomplish my dreams.

My thoughts now of life in the United States are good.

Also, it depends on me because I need to be prepared to handle any opportunity or change that life brings me. On the other hand, in this moment I need to continue the same way that I started and turn this experience into something enriching for my life.

Like many professions, your job requires you to live at the place where you work. How hard, or how beneficial is that?

I think it depends on the personality.

In my case and in my experience, I always desired that my work be at the same place as my home. Its good in a lot of ways, for example, if you work from home, you can skip traffic, sleep a little more, even take your time to have good meals.

But, also on the other side, it can be the same routine, the same space, and it can be boring and hard. But it depends too, on the style of the life that the person can handle. For this kind of work, it requires creating your own space. I mean so that you don't fall into the same routine. Also, always seeing it on a positive side is important.

It's like a parallel world, while some want to go back home, in the au pair world, we want to leave home.

But now with my experience, I think it's not too much different from when you get a job at a company, you must go to the same place, see the same people, and probably do the same things over and over. The only thing that changes is the space. I think for me it is something beneficial because I also have the opportunity to change my space and during my free time I can get out of the routine, and that doesn't make it difficult.

You left your family, your lifelong friends, your favorite restaurants and everything else to come live your dream here in this country.

What would you tell someone that is trying to accomplish their dreams?

I recommend taking the risk to accomplish your dreams no matter what because there is only one life and we must live it to the fullest.

If you are full of dreams, you need to be prepared for new challenges, opportunities, fears, and difficulties that you can find in your path.

Sometimes it is difficult to leave everything and start again, but when you insist on accomplishing a dream, it takes time to accomplish it. You win with experience and when this experience grows it could be the key to your dreams and really come true.

You were very brave to leave the known, to enter the unknown. What helped you, or what pushed you to be brave?

I think what made me brave was the challenge within myself to prove to me that there were opportunities to take advantage of and difficulties to overcome, that life is not easy and that we live in a world who gives us many ways to get, but the only obstacle is oneself.

You have met a lot of people throughout your journey and are living outside of your hometown. What is the meaning of life?

For me, life is something that transforms us and helps us discover our potential. We evolve and transcend, in order to know who we are.

Life presents us with experiences and people who allow us to develop ourselves and we learn that we should work hard on our ideals.

Life will give us a good push to work and build our destiny and to also recognize where we are and where we want to go, no matter what the circumstances are.

Although this book is intended for everyone, the theme of it is 30. And I know you're not 30 yet but I feel like receiving advice is always great from everyone, do you have any advice for those of us that are turning 30 this year?

I recommend to live life and take risks no matter what age you are, or another type of excuse is a refuge for not fulfilling your dreams.

It's worth dreaming and getting over the challenges that can be put in our way.

We only need attitude, constancy and the perseverance to get wherever we want at the time that we want them.

Also, I think life can bring good opportunities to the people who know how to be visionaries and who see the future with prosperity and joy. It's hard sometimes to change, but sometimes the circumstances or moments of crisis allow us to use our strengths and put them into action to achieve our goals and enjoy the road.

Thank you!!

GLORIA BARRERA

CALIFORNIA, USA

To see you now, pregnant, expecting your second baby. Totally healthy and happy. One, would never know all of the time you spent in the hospital and all of the agony you went through when you were waiting for your kidney transplant.

It's an amazing story and a great testimony of life.

Having experienced that and experiencing all of the joy you are experiencing now, what is the meaning of life to you?

"Oh gosh, where do I even start?"

After experiencing that at such a young age, it made me look at life a whole lot different.

I was put on this earth for a purpose. To live life one day at a time, to fulfill God's plan.

Do you remember when you were told you needed a kidney transplant, how old were you?

I didn't have any symptoms leading up to my kidney's failing.

One day I woke up and my legs and feet were swollen. I went in to the doctor to get labs done because my mom knew in her heart that I was not doing well, even though I felt completely normal.

When my lab results came back, I went in to see the doctor. He advised us that there was something wrong with my kidney's, but he wasn't sure how severe.

He said, "Drive over to CHOC Hospital there is a room waiting for you."

I was admitted to the hospital at 16-years-old.

What were your instant thoughts?

"Uhm, What? What do you mean my kidneys don't work?"

"There must be an error."

I questioned the doctor, if he was sure those lab results were mine. It was really hard to wrap my head around the results.

How familiar were you with knowing about what you were going through?

I was completely clueless.

"Who knew your kidneys played such an important part in sustaining your life?"

I had never met anyone with end-stage renal disease.

Did you have any specific symptoms before your diagnosis?

I didn't have any symptoms leading to the failure of my kidneys. No pain over my kidneys, nothing. But some swelling in my legs.

What was the process that you followed after you were told you would need a kidney transplant?

Can you explain the steps you had to take, is there a waiting list you have to be added to, or how does that work?

I was placed on dialysis two days after I found out my kidneys weren't working.

Dialysis works similar to your kidneys. They remove the excess water from your body.

I was added to the transplant list immediately.

I once read an article that was very interesting to me, 80- something-year-olds were asked what they regretted most in life. The most common response was having worried too much. Worrying seems to be part of our culture. I am going to list a few common things we worry about in a lifetime.

Education

Work

Buying a home

Relationships

Weight

Although those might not have pertained precisely to you since you were a teenager when you were dealing with your kidney situation. However, the teenage age does come with its own set of worries.

What did those from that list, and those that aren't listed, mean to you when you were going through dialysis and everything you were going through?

Were they as significant as we make them seem?

Did they mean anything to you?

I was in high school when I went through all of this. I was finishing up my junior year.

"How was I suppose to finish school?"

I was very worried about being able to finish high school with my peers. Working, buying a home, relationships, nor weight worried me.

I was worried that there wouldn't be a kidney available for me.

"How long would I have to stay on dialysis until a kidney was ready for me?"

And if I did get one off the waiting list, "Whose was it?"

"How did they pass?"

"How was their family grieving?"

What about now that you have lived through something so hard, do you ever worry about anything other than your health?

After receiving my kidney, nothing worried me except my kidney.

Now that I am a mother, I worry about my daughter.

"Do I need to buy my first home at the age of 30?"

"No."

"Do I need to have a top-of-the-line car?"

"No."

Those things don't worry me. Having good health is the most important thing.

After what I can imagine felt like, forever, you finally received a kidney transplant and the story is even more beautiful than that.

The kidney you received was your dad's!

How long did you have to wait for the new kidney to be implanted and how did you learn your dad was eligible to give you his kidney?

Both my dad and older brother were tested to see if they were compatible with me. The evaluation is performed to make sure that no adverse physical, psychological, or emotional outcome will occur—before, during, or following the donation.

They got tested as soon as I started dialysis. I was on dialysis for one year and three months. I found out my dad was compatible over the phone in July of 2006.

They scheduled the transplant for August 2006.

I know you and your family are very close and you have always been close to your dad—you're the only girl.

But just how special is it to live knowing you have your father's kidney?

Parents always say they would give anything for their child's happiness and well-being and your dad did just that.

You actually have one of your father's organs in your body, what's that like?

I am forever grateful to my dad.

I have always been a "daddy's girl." His selfless act of wanting to give a piece of himself so that I can live a normal life is astonishing.

He gave me a second chance at life. I feel like we are even closer now. When people ask me, "Who gave you your kidney?"

I proudly say, "My dad!"

How were you told your dad would be your donor?

I received a phone call from the transplant team at UCLA. I literally got off the phone with tears streaming down my eyes.

I was jumping for joy. I was ecstatic!

Last year, 2017 proved to be a great year full of births and innovative products that help us with our daily lives. But it was also a year that

was full of natural disasters. People here in our country and all over the world lost their homes, family members, their businesses. All of that was unexpected to everyone who went through it.

A lot of the people that were affected are still recuperating from everything they were faced with. You went through something very hard and very unique but now are past that.

What would you tell the people that might be experiencing a tough time right now?

Keep your head up. This will pass. God doesn't give you any more than you can handle.

There *is* light at the end of this dark tunnel.

Over and over again we hear about family and friends not being supportive through the hardest of our hardships and the number of those that are, can be very low.

Did you ever experience that?

I received a lot of love and support from my family, friends, and my school. The school accommodated me in order for me to leave two days out of the week to get treatment. They arranged my schedule in a way that I wouldn't miss too much school work.

In your opinion what's a respectful, non-intrusive way that we can be supportive of someone going through a medical hardship?

Be present.

I don't mean be there every day, but sending them a nice text saying, "Thinking of you!"

Not treating them any different. And really just being their friend.

I've heard many people refer to their hardships as blessings. They claim it was through those hardships that they really discovered their potential and life mission.

Do you find this to be true after your experience?

As cliché as that sounds, yes.

This was a blessing for me and my family. I am still not sure what my life mission is, but I am educating everyone I know about what I went through.

Is there anything you want us to know about kidney failure or of something pertaining to it?

Your kidneys are so important to be able to live a healthy life. Take care of them because they play an important role.

What was the most difficult part of your battle, the dialysis, the diet you had to keep, having to miss school?

Perhaps something else?

The diet!

It was so hard to only be able to drink a liter of water a day (that included soup, ice cubes, ice cream, etc). To know you cannot drink more, and the thirst was horrible.

I was on a low-sodium diet, more like NO sodium.

I loved bananas, and I wasn't able to eat them because they are high in potassium.

I couldn't have chocolate or coffee.

I had to take so many medications.

Love, faith, hope. We hear those words constantly especially when trying to be positive in life.

What do you those words mean to you?

Love, love with all your heart.

Faith is the last thing that dies.

Never lose hope.

I know you are a devoted Catholic, did your faith increase after having experienced everything that you did?

Oftentimes we hear that is the case.

I believe it did increase. Before any of my surgeries, I would go in with my Virgin of Guadalupe in one hand and St. Judas Thaddeus in my other hand.

I've noticed a lot of characters in our culture that are portrayed as sweet and approachable are the characters that have experienced a struggle in their life. Discrimination of some sort, poverty, etc.

Ever since discovering that, I have a theory, I feel like the nicest people are those who have gone through difficult times. You are very approachable and very sweet.

What do you think of my theory?

Do you think it takes us, humans, the need to experience a hardship in order to be more prone to empathy?

I've always thought that the nicest people have gone through the hardest of hardships. I think because you go through a difficult situation you put yourself in other people's shoes.

Death is a strong word, and it might produce chills in our body. But when we are sick, sick enough to have to need dialysis, it might pop in our heads.

Did you ever fear death, or even think about it when you were battling through your kidney failure?

At first no, I didn't know how serious it was. But after talking to so many doctors, I realized this was a much bigger deal.

I did see my life flash before me. And the fear of dying was very real.

While going through your treatments and all of that, did you ever think of the day you would be living what you're living right now, motherhood and everything else that life has brought you since then?

I never thought I'd be able to conceive and become a mother.

And look at me doing it all over again.

Luckily this kidney has been very good to me. The life-span of the kidney reflects how well you take care of it.

Are you happy with the way you were treated during your hospital stay and when going through your treatment?

Yes, both CHOC Hospital and UCLA Hospital were amazing. I had an amazing transplant team.

After having been a patient for so long, do you feel like everything that can be done to save the life of a patient, is being done?

Yes, I do believe that the doctors are working very hard in order to save a patient's life.

Kidney. What does that word mean to you now?

It means life to me.

Recovery is also part of the journey.

How is the recovery process like and how did you keep going after everything?

The recovery after surgery isn't long.

I was in the hospital for a week after the transplant making sure the kidney was working. I then visited the hospital for follow-up care.

I still see my nephrologist 3-4 times a year. Now that I am pregnant I see him more closely.

There might be someone right now that is going through something similar but feels like they're never going to get to the happily-ever-after part of their story like you have.

What would you tell them?

It's there; it is waiting for you.

There is a light at the end of this dark tunnel. We may not see it yet, but don't lose faith because it is there.

You are a living testimony of so many things. What can you tell us about your life lessons that can encourage us to live life to the fullest?

Be the best you that you can be. Never stop bettering yourself.

Always love. And never stop dreaming.

You're about six months from turning 30, but even then we all have advice we can offer one another, what advice would you offer those of us that are turning 30 this year?

Always follow your dreams, no matter how far and difficult they may seem. Never stop dreaming.

And we are never too old to reach our goals. They may have been put on pause, but it's never too late to resume.

Thank you!!

GINAMARIE AND ANNAMARIE RUSSO

NEW YORK, USA

Even though being a twin is more and more common now the fascination is still very strong. There is just something so cool about the whole thing and so intriguing.

You both happen to be twins!

I am sure you have talked about it your entire life but can you say it once more...how is it like to be a twin?

Ginamarie: Well, we actually don't know the difference! We weren't born single; we were born together so naturally when we are separated it feels like half of us is somewhere else.

Annamarie: You kind of always have this feeling like something is missing when you're physically separated, and when together, there's this complete ease. I love it more than anything, actually. It's my most favorite part of life.

Who is older?

Ginamarie: I am one minute older (smiles).

How do you celebrate your birthday, do you spend it together?

Ginamarie: Always and forever, we celebrate together. Double the cake, double the wishes.

Annamarie: Of course, we do and wouldn't want it any other way.

You're identical twins, which means you are...IDENTICAL. But what about your personality traits, are they similar?

Ginamarie: We have the same moral and spiritual compass. I can be referred to as more patient than assertive! Nonetheless, we are both kind-hearted, honest and warm. Annamarie says that I am more "sugary" and I say that Annamarie is more forthright. We balance each other. Definitely each other's right arms.

Annamarie: We share the same dreams and similar goals, but as far as personalities, we totally compliment each other. I am more vocal, and I tend to be a bit bolder when it comes to addressing things and matters of the heart. And Ginamarie is the BEST listener EVER. She responds with the utmost sincerity.

"See?" Totally ying and yang.

Are there any other twins in your family?

Ginamarie: Not identical, no.

What should we know about being a twin?

Ginamarie: It feels like Annamarie is more than my sister— she is part of me. I care and love her the way I imagine the unconditional love of a mother and child is.

Annamarie: We affectionately refer to non-twins as "singletons" and have our own language we call "twin talk."

When you're together, how many times do you get asked if you're twins?

Ginamarie: A billion and one. Never gets old.

Annamarie: Over a gazillion.

Do you have an anecdote that pertains to that?

Ginamarie: When someone is staring, we will just respond, "Yes we're twins," (laughs).

Is there something that one of you struggles with that the other one strives in?

Ginamarie: The only struggle is if I didn't have Annamarie to be there for me and motivate me. We complement each other and inspire each other, despite our adversity of rheumatoid arthritis. Anna has been my magic right hand since growing up.

What is the best part about being a twin?

Ginamarie: Having a built-in best friend. There's no one in the world I would rather share the adventures of life and just life in general with.

Who's the funnier twin?

Ginamarie: Equal. We love to laugh. We have our own twin language, and the slightest word or visual can get us into endless bursting of laughter at the most random times ever.

Did you share a room when you were kids?

Ginamarie: Absolutely, and throughout university, while studying abroad and throughout most of our adulthood.

Annamarie: Yes, we shared a room as babies and while dorming in college and while studying abroad.

Do you have a favorite memory of your childhood together?

Ginamarie: Just the simplicity of adventure— having someone to share a dream and struggles, and life itself has created countless favorite memories.

When we think of identical twins, we tend to think of the perks that can come with it.

Have you ever taken advantage of the fact that you're identical?

Ginamarie: We naturally confuse people, and we always grew up with double attention. We never need to take advantage. We are just grateful.

Do you tend to agree on most things?

Ginamarie: Yes, 99.9% if not— than 100%. I don't like fresh tomatoes, Anna does.

You've worked together in a couple of different TV shows and movies.

How was that experience like?

Ginamarie: Like no other, sharing our dream together is a dream come true itself. It is beyond fun and super exciting, acting is one of the ingredients that keeps our spirits alive when we work together on our dream.

Annamarie: It's incredible to live your dream with your life's dream partner. No words, just love, and graciousness.

What is the biggest life lesson you have learned while working on a TV and movie setting?

Annamarie: That, "As long as there's the two of us, we've got the world and all its charms and when the world is through with us, we've got each other's arms."

To work hard and go on a journey together living our dream, getting the job is the icing on the cake...the actual cake is being able to do it with my twin, side by side.

You both are open about of having been diagnosed with arthritis and just recently you became the first adult honorees of the Walk to Cure Arthritis.

What should we know about arthritis?

Ginamarie: Rheumatoid arthritis is incurable, which is why we advocate to create awareness. I have been in pain every day since 11-years-old but

I grew with my condition and I have my twin and mom who have motivated me and taken care of me to feel my best although it isn't always easy. It affects my joints and can affect the eyes and the heart. My joints get inflamed and stiff.

Dealing with RA has also made me realize how narrow-minded people can be, they judge me based on the outside without knowing my inner and painful struggle. This is one of the reasons I do not tolerate negative and stressful people. I have far too much understanding and empathy for others and there's no time for mean-spirited naysayers.

After experiencing everything you have, what is your perspective on what life is to you?

Ginamarie: Life is fragile and unpredictable. With joy, there is suffering too.

This is life.

It isn't perfect but I count my blessings and am very appreciative. I try to conscientiously be happy and at peace. God is in charge.

Annamarie: The meaning of life, or rather what gives meaning in life is being able to stay positive when faced with adversity. It's being able to see the silver lining in everything you do. To turn lemons into the sweetest lemon pound cake, or on some days, limoncello.

In my personal experience, to have empathy for others through compassion and self-love for yourself. To make each moment count and realize how precious life truly is.

This is your chapter, what do you want us to take away from it?

Ginamarie: Don't judge a book by its cover.

Be courageous and kind.

The simple things are the big things.

Talk to God.

I am grateful for my loved ones.

Although this book is intended for everyone, the theme of if is 30. What stage of your life were you in at 30 and do you have advice for those of us turning 30 this year?

Ginamarie: Make healthy and smart decisions, but get out there, grow your wings, and believe in yourself. Life is far too unpredictable to not have an open-mind. Show the good of the world, don't just talk the talk. And turn your experiences into lessons— it is priceless.

Live and let live.

Annamarie: Don't ever save anything for a special occasion. Life is short; every second you are breathing is a special occasion. Make the moments count.

Love the ones who love you. Never take the special people in your life for granted.

Go for your dreams.

Be grateful for all your working parts.

Have a kind heart.

Anything else you want to add?

Ginamarie: A smile is the prettiest thing you can wear.

Annamarie: I am so lucky to spend my life with my best friend.

There's magic for people who choose to see it.

Thank you!!

ANGIE AND JORGE GARCIA

TEXAS, USA

How does your love story begin?

Angie: Our love story is not like typical love stories, where two people meet, look at each other, and right away they know they are meant to be together.

No. Our love story is different but very special to us. It took time to develop and to flourish to what we have now. I guess one can say that's what has made it, strong and long-lasting in a society where divorce is more and more common, our love has lasted more than 19 years.

Now, every story is unique and special but every time Jorge and I retell it, we always end up telling each other. "It was meant to be."

It's amazing how God placed us both in the right place, at the right time!

The irony is, it all started because I was disappointed and heartbroken. My boyfriend of that time and I had just broken up, so my younger sister Dulce, and some friends decided that I needed to go out.

I wasn't really up for it, but I knew that a good and sound distraction wouldn't hurt. But before I can go on, you must know I love dancing, I love to dance to any type of music, but being that I am Hispanic, Latin is my favorite type of music! I grew up going to family gatherings where dancing was part of everyone's interest. Having said that, my sister knew that if I was going to feel any better, I had to go do what I enjoyed the most...dance!

That evening my sister and two other friends, and I went to a popular nightclub in Anaheim, California called JC Fandango's. And it was there when my life changed.

Jorge and I, met on that evening of December of 1999, on the dance floor of JC Fandango's.

How old were you?

Angie: I had just turned 20-years-old, and Jorge was 22-years-old.

You were both on the dance floor when you met and then..?

Angie: I clearly remember looking at him while I danced with another guy. He stood near the dance floor, and I remember thinking… "He seems familiar."

Jorge: When I saw her, at her table, I decided to approach her. But I did feel nervous because I thought there was a possibility of being rejected. But she said, "Yes!!"

I was excited, but I tried so hard, not to come out too giddy. I didn't want her to notice my excitement.

Angie: The music ended, and as I was sitting, the DJ began to play another song, one of my favorite *cumbia* songs. Every time I hear the music I like in places like that, I hope that someone will ask me to dance! I just want to dance!

It was then that Jorge approached me. He seemed too serious but the nice type.

Of course, I accepted right away! While dancing, I remember loving the way he danced (now for someone like me that loves music and dancing, dancing is a must). I always told myself that, "The person I married had to like dancing as well."

I also remember looking at his face and thinking, "Hmmm, he's not smiling, he must not be enjoying it."

After a few minutes, the song ended, and he walked me back to my table and asked me, "If I cared for a drink?"

I hesitated for a few seconds, but I said, "Yes!"

He bought me a Coke, and while I drank it, we had a short conversation which ended with a question.

"Can I have your number?"

I froze. I didn't know what to say or do.

Other times I had given a fake number, a number I made-up, but this time, I didn't know what to do. You must know, that I did own a cell phone and a pager at that time. But, I knew if I gave him one of those numbers I would be more accessible and I wasn't sure I wanted that, but I also felt he was a nice guy and I liked him enough to give him a way to contact me.

So, I took the safe road and decided to give him the house number.

I believe, we danced the rest of the night, and at the end, he and his friends walked us to my car. It was a cold December night, so he offered his jacket when we walked out which I replied, "I had my own in the trunk."

I knew that if I took his jacket, he would use it as a hook to see me again. Which I didn't mind, but I had to play a little hard to get. He and my sister insisted so much, but I didn't budge.

The following morning was a Monday. I was a student at Orange Coast College; I was walking to class while talking on my cell phone. As I was walking, I saw Jorge approaching me. I didn't know what to do, whether to pretend I didn't see him and walk by him, or just wave a quick hello. I just waved.

That same evening he called my house, and right before we hung up, he said, "So, I see that you have a cell phone."

Which I replied, "Yes, I only use it, in case of emergencies."

We continued to talk on the phone from time to time and got to see each other at school. But didn't go out.

Valentine's Day came. I still remember getting a call from him a few nights earlier, asking me out to dinner that night. I remember telling him over the phone that I had gotten back with my ex.

All I remember him saying in a sweet but monotone voice was, "Oh okay, well good luck."

We didn't speak for months after that.

Okay, maybe two months after that. I had broken up with my ex one more time, but this time my heart was shattered, I was disappointed on a different level and didn't know how I would get out of that dark, and deep hole.

I cried day and night for a whole week. I wanted answers as to, "Why it had happened to me? What had I done wrong?" But after a week of tears, pain and unanswered questions I get a phone call!

A phone call that changed my life forever!

That afternoon Jorge called, and we spent a good solid hour on the phone catching up. He asked me on a date, and although I wasn't feeling 100% yet, I knew that it would do me good. So, I accepted.

He invited me for lunch at the Rainforest Cafe in South Coast Plaza. I remember being very nervous. As I drove into the parking lot I saw him leaning against the wall waiting for me; he looked handsome. That made me even more nervous. We got to talk and got to know each other a little bit more.

When did you become boyfriend and girlfriend?

Angie: There were many dates after that, but it wasn't until my 21st birthday when he officially asked me to be his girlfriend. He stopped by, to wish me a happy birthday, he hugged me and slid a kiss.

He was sneaky. But I sure didn't complain. It felt right! It actually, felt perfect!! After seven months of just being friends, we were officially boyfriend and girlfriend!

What about the proposal. When did Jorge propose and where was it?

Angie: Fast forward one year from that night, he proposed on a hilltop in a restaurant in the city of Orange with the song *"De Rodillas ante Ti"* from Grupo Yndio, playing in the background.

Where did you get married?

Angie: A year after that we got married on November 16, 2002 and have been happily married ever since.

We have two lovely daughters Aileen, 12 and Vanessa 9.

What is your favorite characteristic of one another?

Angie: How committed he is. He works hard and is such a wonderful husband and a perfect dad!

Jorge: How reliable she is. I know I can count on her to do anything and do it right. The best part of it is that she does it without having to ask her. She just knows what needs to be taken care of; she knows what each of us needs and when we need it.

You met in 1999. That was before social media. How was dating during that time? And how did you communicate with one another during the day?

Angie: I had a cell phone, Jorge a pager. We used the Internet to write love notes to each other. We looked forward to reading our emails, it was nice to get those notifications of, "You got mail."

We feel it was more beneficial because there was no social media to distract us from spending quality time when we were together.

The first date is a BIG deal for us females. We think about all of the details, and of course, we take what we are going to wear for it, VERY seriously.

Do you remember getting ready for your first date, Angie? What did you wear?

Angie: I have always loved dressing up. I love wearing dresses and heels!! But on that particular occasion, I didn't wear a dress. I wore jeans with a beige top, black blazer, and black heels.

I do remember clearly what Jorge wore, loose jeans and a black and gray plaid shirt

How was the actual date?

Angie: We both had pasta that day. It was the first time for both of us at the Rainforest Cafe; we really enjoyed the ambiance.

Jorge: The right ambiance with the perfect person.

You mentioned a past boyfriend you had before Jorge, Angie, how was your dating life before meeting each other?

Angie: I dated a boyfriend on-off for seven years, but didn't get to date other people while we were off. I had a few admirers and lots of friends.

What about you Jorge?

Jorge: I really never dated. Angeles was my first and only date/ girlfriend.

Thank you!!

MARISOL UGUES
GUADALAJARA, MEXICO

*Spanish/English Translation

I know you have participated in the Global Big Latch On, for several years now. And you have become a key component for that cause.

Tell me more about the Global Big Latch On.

What is it and when did you get involved with it?

The United Nations has declared the first week of August, the week of breastfeeding. And it is celebrated on that week, every year.

During that week different activities are carried out that involve this movement (at an international level). In different places of the world, mothers breastfeed simultaneously for 1 minute to join the cause. There are so many different countries and cities that participate. In Guadalajara this activity has been carried out for 5 consecutive years, and every year it seems to gather more and more mothers.

The first year of the Global Big Latch On Guadalajara 2013, I participated in the event, as a participant. The following years, I have participated as an activist giving information to, those mothers, that are looking to breastfeed and want to learn more about how to perform this act of love—and this health choice.

This is all done in a respectful way, always respecting the mother who has chosen to breastfeed.

The day of the event, when the time comes, we are given a signal, and all moms will start to prepare themselves. And when the time comes we simultaneously start breastfeeding our babies, for a lapse of one minute. The babies who manage to be breastfed for a minute, are counted as part of the record for the Global Big Latch On breastfeeding record.

Why is participating so important to you?

What should we know about breastfeeding?

These events are created in an effort to show, breastfeeding is a natural act, and so that the mother may know that there are many mothers in the world who are also, "normalizing," breastfeeding.

We give brief talks about the benefits that come from breastfeeding—for the mother and for the baby.

We invite the mothers to attend as a family, the fathers have taken a very important role, in supporting the mother and baby. We teach everyone what they can benefit from and what they should know about breastfeeding. The concerns are also discussed and we are able to see the similarities in what concerns most people, when it comes to this topic.

Breastfeeding is an act of love, of life—it is a connection between a mother and her child and something that benefits everyone. There are innumerable benefits in health, affection, economy and many other aspects that not only favor the baby and the mother but also their family and society in general.

Now that you have become an activist for this cause and also now that you are a radio host for *"Nishanti Prenatal,"* a show devoted to giving parents advice on everything that pertains to children—I'll ask you, what are the techniques that have helped you while parenting?

We are very aware that we are not born with a tutorial on how to raise us—parents have made this very clear. And by now…we get it.

But perhaps there are tips and suggestions for parenting that you can offer, that can help?

Above all inform yourself, create healthy habits for your baby that is about to be born and is in its process of birth.

Not all techniques work in the same way, one must evaluate the personality of each member of the family and realize that not all are composed in the same way, so I would recommend reading and reaching a communal agreement between that of yourself and that of your husband/wife.

Create a healthy environment for the child.

Read, ask questions.

Re-invent yourself.

Make mistakes.

And create the best "manual" of how you can carry-out being the best family, you envision.

Can you tell me more about *"Prenatal Nishanti,"* your radio show?

Ever since becoming a mother, I have taken courses on different topics related to pregnancy, birth, breastfeeding and parenting. I have supported to spread and create more networks of support for the mother who decides to breastfeed and raise their children in that way.

"Prenatal Nishanti," is a space where moms and expecting mothers, can find support, and reliable information for their pregnancy, childbirth and upbringing of their children.

In *"Nishanti,"* we have the professionalism and the experience of maternity and we use it for the service of the newly turned mom.

Being an activist, allows you to change an aspect of our society. You are able to teach us about something of which you are, an expert of. And of something that you strongly believe in.

What is your favorite part about being an activist?

I tell every baby, I encounter and my colleagues (who are actually the ones who do the work) to use my voice and my knowledge.

As an activist, I am able to inform people a little bit of what we have in this world. I am able to inform families of their options so that they can choose their best option. I provide truthful information, tips that are clear and real.

Above all, I believe the motherhood we live day-by-day can be experienced in plenitude and overall in successful breastfeeding.

As the mother of a precious little boy, what is the greatest lesson, you have learned in your trajectory of being *his* mother?

My main role is to be a mom who is day-to-day and 365 days, a year, with my son.

My son and I have grown so much and without a doubt, its the main reason why I share what I know and why I give the information that I give on pregnancy, breastfeeding and parenting. I think its very important for all of us to be well-informed.

Nahum has been my engine in the days that one wants to "turn into a monkey." In days when the sun rises, I am able to share it with him, and I am able to share everything with him. I learn from his simplicity, analysis and constant improvements. I learn through that innocence that he has not allowed me to lose and I hope, I never do.

Do you have an anecdote you would like to share, of your mother-son relationship?

He's so ingenious and inventive.

When he conscientiously saw a baby being breastfed (he was about 3-years-old). He walked-up to the baby's mom and said, "I also ate from my mom and my mom's milk was the best milk."

I keep that memory and that scene in my soul.

Anything else you want to add?

In 2017, we were expecting a total of 150 mothers but 240 mothers attended our event. Those mothers managed to breastfeed at a minute of 2:20. At the same time (at an international level), 17,790 mothers were also breastfeeding simultaneously. This activity and many others that are done every day, especially in the week of breastfeeding, are aimed at improving the rates of breastfeeding in the world, in addition to making breastfeeding a normal event in our lives.

This year, thanks to the government, who helped this cause—we were able to create designated breastfeeding areas—in public places for mothers. Certain places of the city are marked in pink and in those areas mothers are able to sit and breastfeed—in public. This allows for all of those, "warrior mothers," who have to go out there and continue their busy schedules, to stop and breastfeed when they need to—before resuming back to their schedules.

We managed to do this after 4 years of fighting criticisms of people who argue against this and refer to breastfeeding as "exhibitionism," without ever thinking of the baby that needs to be fed. And without thinking of the possibility that perhaps the mother doesn't have a bottle of milk to feed her hungry baby with.

Thank you!!

ALEXANDER YU

CALIFORNIA, USA

As a realtor, I am assuming you see people at very happy stages of their lives. Perhaps even the happiest stage of their lives, considering they are about to purchase a home.

Some of them will become first-time homeowners, and some of them are purchasing their dream home through you.

Do you think their happiness is contagious?

Yes, because the more that they are grateful for…including a new home, it has the ability to transform their quality of life and those around them.

After experiencing the contrasts you see while working, what is your perspective on life?

I feel that every person is looking for something unique in a home. Often times, they grow up in very modest means, and they are searching for all of the things that they wished that they had in their home when they grew up.

An example would be a room for every child without having to share. Or if they lived in an apartment and played in the streets, they wish they had a backyard.

Most of us are seeking to improve the lives of our children, siblings or the world around us. And where we came from provides the contrast to what we should and will give.

What is the biggest life lesson you have learned while working?

I have found that regardless of the size, price, or location of the home, every home becomes a place where people can retreat and use their time to plan for how they plan to connect with the outside world.

Every home starts with a house, and it becomes a home over time.

Is there an anecdote of something you have experienced while working as a realtor that you would like to share?

I have seen families in great distress when they are losing their home. It always starts with blaming others…even sometimes in the family, but eventually, it brings them together, and they realize that you can take a family out of a home, but you can't take a home out of the family.

A home is not only the four walls that surround them, but a place in mind and heart.

What should we know about being a real estate agent?

The job is centered around making other people's goals happen.

Only when I am successful in helping others reach their goals, do I create an income, which helps me reach my goals.

My top goals are to donate back to the causes I believe in and build a business that encourages others to be successful.

What's your favorite part of your job?

People often don't understand a realtor's job. They think that it is just to drive them around and help them find a house or put a sign in the ground and sell their home.

But my goal is to be their trusted adviser and layout the game plan, educate them about the current market environment and make them an empowered buyer or seller and help them make smart decisions and informed buyers and sellers.

Even when they have purchased or sold a home before, and they tell me that, "This was a much better experience than last time," I know that I have done my job.

Previously to selling homes, you worked for a bank.

Why did you decide to change careers?

I enjoyed my time at a Fortune 100 Bank, but I realized that I could make a bigger impact in fewer people's lives working for myself.

In addition, I negotiated for the bank, but everyone deserves the same quality of representation. And when I had greater control of my schedule, I could focus more on the causes that are important to me, including youth services, family support, and animal welfare.

There are a lot of people that would love to accomplish their dreams. Maybe their dream is to have a career like yours.

What would you tell them?

I would tell them that anyone can accomplish their goals. But the most important place to start is understanding why they want their goal.

What about advice for first-time home buyers.

What would you tell them?

I would tell them that when you buy a home, make sure that you understand your budget.

Once you buy a home, you will have to be more careful of your expenses.

And you should generally know where you want to be in 3 or 5 years so that you pick the place that will serve you for at least that amount of time.

You work in a very competitive industry and in a very competitive market (Southern California).

How do you manage to not only keep up with it but succeed amongst that competition?

I have been told that it is the most competitive real estate market in the country, but I know that if I take care of my clients and serve them to the best of my ability that I will always be successful.

I may be the highest producing agent, but I know that I am always proud of the work that I do.

And the majority of my clientele are from referrals.

The competition is good because it requires agents to improve and deliver the highest quality experiences to their clients.

This is your chapter, what do you want people to take away from it?

I want people to know that regardless of what your goals are for a career, or in life, that if you commit yourself to a vision and surround yourself with people that support you that your results will not only meet but exceed your vision for yourself.

Although this book is intended for everyone, the theme of it is 30. What stage of your life were you in at 30 and where were you living?

At the age of 30, I was living in Cypress and working on trying to figure out what I wanted for my future.

It was time to get serious and focus on doing things that I wanted to be proud of.

I spent more time volunteering than ever before in my life. And the people and lessons I came across were really surprising.

Do you have any advice for those of us turning 30 this year?

A new decade can be daunting, but it is more important than ever to count your successes and the failures that you have learned from…that I would count as successes.

Anything else you want to add?

At my age, I have known incredibly successful people (financially) that were broke emotionally and other people that didn't have anything in the realm of material things that were so fulfilled and rich in every other area.

We can always make more money, but we can never make more time.

Create an impact in the world around you, and then anything is possible.

Thank you!!

ARACELI TORRES PADILLA
A CORUÑA, SPAIN

---

*Spanish/English Translation

The start of the Millennium brought us a lot of new things. Among them was high-speed Internet something that I can imagine was very beneficial to you, as you began a relationship with someone you met online.

Nowadays it is very common to start a romance with someone through the many online dating platforms that are available at a cost or at no cost. But at the start of the Millennium—when you met your now husband that was not common at all.

I would love to know more about your story.

When I met you (2009), you and Roberto were the first couple I had ever met, who had met online. You both were very ahead of your time.

Can you tell me your love story?

My thoughts on relationships were like those of my parents and ancestors, of going to the movies and to the park...like the olden day romances. At 15-years-old that's what I thought of relationships and of marriage. I thought I would marry very young at 23-years-old and that one day, I would have children of my own and in a way, we would grow up together. My idea was to have 4 children.

My parents are from a town close to Guadalajara, my father is from Poncitlán, Jalisco and my mother from Jamay, Jalisco.

My mother moved to the town of Poncitlán (my father's town) when she was young. And my dad remembers always seeing her walking passed him by where my father worked at as a bus driver. He tells me he always used to look at her when she walked by him wearing her high heels. And my father said that from those moments of seeing her from afar, he developed his love for her, and he told himself she was going to be the person he'd marry.

They did marry eventually.

And my childhood was very beautiful—I was surrounded by my 10 brothers and sisters. I enjoyed it a lot. I remember that every eight days we would go to the Poncitlán, we loved going swimming in the river there. I grew up closets to my brother Genaro, the youngest of the family.

That's what I envisioned for my own life.

My first boyfriend was at the age of 14, I met him in my karate class, he was my teacher's brother. One day, he asked me if he could be my *chambelan* at my *quinceanera*— and that ended up happening. When the day of my party finally came he asked me, why it hadn't been a wedding instead of my birthday party? I told him my dad was very protective of his daughters.

Years passed and I had many boyfriends but they resulted in very bad experiences, they didn't want serious, committed relationships. And I did.

Eventually, 3 years passed and one day I told myself that, "I was not born to get married." I thought perhaps it was meant to be like that. I figured I would work and look after my mother. It was during that stage of my life that I decided to enroll in a computer science class. And there in class on a dating website was how I met Roberto, my now husband. It was during the start of the Internet—when it was just starting to become more popular.

I had been registered on the dating website for 6 months before meeting him, none of that was common back then. I met him on September 6, 2000—I will never forget that day.

I worked and also studied at that time. I worked as an administrator at a transportation company and in the afternoons, I studied computer science. That was a very happy stage for me in my life, I loved spending time with my friends and I enjoyed listening to them share their love stories from online. But to me, even though I enjoyed listening to those stories, they sounded like a joke, like something silly.

You "met" and then...?

He would send me jokes so that I would smile.

His online screen name was Vamy and mine was my actual name, Araceli. When I asked him what his name was, he told me, it was Roberto. He asked me where I was from and I told him I was from Guadalajara. Roberto wondered if I was referring to Guadalajara, Spain, or Guadalajara, Mexico. But when he realized I was referring to Guadalajara, Mexico, Roberto mentioned he knew a lot of things about Mexico—including it's history—that was the start of how we met.

The time difference was not a problem for us to speak, I would connect at midnight (7 AM his time).

When I met Roberto online, it was interesting to me, how he was dressed in the pictures I saw of him. How he spoke was also interesting to me. We slowly started to know more about each other through our online conversations. No one suggested him to me and he actually didn't interest me in the beginning. When 5 months went by, he asked to meet me in person. But he lived in Spain and I lived in Mexico. And I thought, "He doesn't even interest me."

But a friend of mine suggested I go forward with the plan and spend time with Roberto in person.

When I told my mom she was very happy but my brother told me to be very careful because maybe Roberto would just play with my emotions and not be interested in anything serious. At first, I thought of that possibility but I also thought that whatever was meant to happen, would happen. I wanted to take the risk.

Roberto wanted me to go to Spain first but my mom didn't like that idea. She told me that Roberto should come first to visit me and then I could go visit him. And because of that Roberto was the first to visit me in Mexico. Later, I went to Spain but I had to be accompanied by my sister Estela—mom's orders.

How was your first date like?

What did you feel when you first met "Vamy" (Roberto) in person?

Finally, the day arrived and we met in person! Our first date was in Guadalajara, Mexico and we talked a lot about his country (Spain).

When I first met him in person my heart was accelerated, his was too, I know this because I could hear it (laughs). We were finally able to look at each other face to face. When we spent time together in person it was different— it's different to know each other in person—than to see each other through a camera. It was an incredible thing…the emotions, the heartbeats, and the enormous happiness of finally meeting each other.

In Guadalajara is where I think we really fell in love.

The next step was your turn to visit Roberto in Spain.

What did you pack for your trip?

What emotions did the trip bring you?

Next, it was my turn to visit him in Spain. Estela, my sister and I went to Spain but waiting for the date of the trip felt eternal. I packed Mexican things for his parents like tequila, spicy food, CD's of mariachi music and other things.

When I arrived to A Coruña—for me it was a thing of another world. The buildings, the people were blond, tall, thin, everything was so clean. And it was different from Mexico. It was another world, something so incredible. I also felt weird—the people spoke differently.

When did Roberto propose to you?

When did you get married?

And how was moving to A Coruña?

We were online chatting when he asked me for marriage and I was *so* in love that I didn't believe it was happening (laughs). By this time, it had been four years from when Roberto and I first met in person in Guadalajara.

We got married in Guadalajara, Mexico—my hometown on September 14, 2004. It was very special to me that we got married in September because Roberto and I met in September and years later, our son Juan Ramon was born in September—without planning it.

For me, in the beginning, it was very hard to get accustomed to living in Spain because of the weather and the people aren't very trusting—and the food is different but little by little I got used to it and I liked it.

Since 2000 people have sought online romance more than before and in fact more than ever. Why do think you online dating works for some people, like it did for you and your husband?

What works for online dating is how everything starts unfolding itself by itself, on its own— that's the secret.

Getting to know each other through a dating website, I think is very normal and it's nice to know you are able to get to know each other little by little and it is something…"How can I describe it?" Something very exciting.

For everything to work out, it is necessary to be sincere, understanding and affectionate.

Although this book is intended for everyone, the theme of it is 30. What stage of your life were you in at 30? Do you have any advice for those of us turning 30 this year?

Thirty I think is the happiest age you can be in. You've enjoyed half of your life already. The advice I give is that— it is the perfect age to get married.

Thank you!!

TINA CARSTENSEN
GUADALAJARA, MEXICO

My sister has mentioned all about your advocacy in Early Childhood Education for the American School Foundation Guadalajara, A.C.

Shes's marveled about you.

Through that persistent advocacy that she describes, is how you managed to bring the Reggio Emilia approach to ASFG.

That's a significant milestone considering very few schools in the world practice that approach.

And, to think, that would have never happened had you never moved from New York to Mexico .

When did the idea of moving to Mexico arise?

In 1985, one of my best friends from grade school was studying a semester abroad in San Miguel de Allende and invited me to visit her for the winter holidays.

At the time, I was teaching at a public daycare center in New York City and reading an early biography of Frida Kahlo—that book was the first contact I'd had with Mexico.

I flew to Mexico City where my friend met me, and we stayed near *el centro* and walked around old buildings and the markets.

Then we took a bus to San Miguel.

Buses were different back then, wood floors, no air conditioning, I think there were even chickens on the bus, but maybe I am imagining that part!

I fell in love with the quality of life in Mexico, the handmade paper doves and tiny *piñata* ornaments sold during Christmas, getting fresh squeezed orange juice at the market, the beautiful tiles, bougainvilleas climbing up the walls, children in the streets, and the stories my friend told me about the Virgin of Guadalupe and Juan Diego.

Do you remember the day you decided you'd be moving to Mexico?

Why did you choose Mexico?

I taught at the Lilian Wald Day Care Center in New York for three years while studying my first master's degree in Education and I was hoping to eventually become a bilingual teacher in the public-school system.

My plan was to move to a Spanish-speaking country for a year to master Spanish (little did I know that would take a lifetime) and then return to the US. I was 25-years-old.

First, I traveled to Spain, but I didn't feel the same way about that country as I did with Mexico, so I returned home.

This was before there was the internet, so I visited the public library in my hometown one evening, found a book that listed all the American schools in Mexico, and sent out my resume to several.

A few schools got in touch with me, but the first contact I received was a phone call one Friday from Dr. Argenziano, the director general of The American School Foundation of Guadalajara, A.C., offering me a job as a pre-kinder teacher for the following school year.

He told me to think about it over the weekend and call him (collect) the following Monday with my answer.

I said, "Yes" without having seen the school! And began planning an adventurous five-month solo trip to get to know more about Mexico and Guatemala before starting work in August 1989.

Although hired by Dr. Argenziano, I never worked for him as he had left the school before I arrived.

You left your home in New York for college in Vermont.

Do you think that influenced you to want to move again?

Both my parents had relocated from their hometowns, I didn't have a model of someone who lived in one town their whole life.

After high school, it was expected that my friends and I would leave our homes for college. That was very common. What was uncommon was the school I chose; inspired by the teachings of John Dewey.

When I interviewed as a high school senior, the college had close to 200 students, but when I showed up in the fall of 1981, there were 39 students on campus, as the school was going through a serious financial crisis.

I'm glad I could be part of helping the school survive, and although the student body was small, it was diverse and vibrant, and we benefited from a dedicated, brave, and attentive faculty who believed strongly in progressive education.

My favorite teacher, Celia Houghton, was truly a mentor. Those of us studying education were put into the local public schools as volunteers right away. Celia taught us to identify the student we believed to be most at risk in each classroom and decide how we could be of benefit to that student in particular as well as to the group and the head teacher.

Nowadays it is very popular to relocate internationally, and it's highly encouraged. But in 1989, which is when you moved, it doesn't seem that it was that common.

What was the reaction of your family and friends upon hearing about your desire in relocating?

What advice did they give you?

My brothers and sisters are older than me, and they had all left home after high school.

My brothers traveled around the US extensively; hitchhiking, camping, mountain climbing, and doing odd jobs here and there to pay for their travel, one of my sisters went to Europe to work as an au pair and the other relocated for graduate school.

Traveling to Guadalajara where I had a teaching job waiting for me was actually a rather conservative plan, in my family.

My parents never let on if they had reservations.

Parents tend to be overprotective, here, in Mexico and pretty much everywhere, its pretty universal. How did they react?

Did they know anything about Mexico and its culture?

My parents were very supportive of all of their children's odd and adventurous plans.

I remember my dad being happy for me when I got the phone call from Dr. Argenziano offering me the position at ASFG. Our family had never been to Mexico before, and we didn't travel much while I was growing up, but once my siblings and I left home, my parents started traveling more internationally and seemed to enjoy learning more about the world first-hand.

They came to visit me for a wonderful trip to Oaxaca during my first year at the school.

My mother visited me right after my daughter was born, and then there was another visit from my family shortly after my son was born.

I felt my family saw and appreciated the beauty that had captivated me in Mexico on these visits.

Are both of your parents from New York?

My mother, Pam McDonald Carstensen was born in North Carolina and grew up in Florida.

My father, Edwin Carstensen was born in Nebraska.

They met at the Norfolk Navy Yard in Florida during World War II where my father was an engineer working on submarine technology, and my mother was a technician.

Rochester was about 88.2% Caucasian in 1989 according to the Census, the year that you moved.

It just so happens that I have been there and I had a very pleasant time, by the way. The people were so welcoming and so sweet.

Do you think that was a motivating factor in wanting to explore something else?

Having grown up in a surrounding like I just described, where people speak English, and for the most part look like you.

Because both my parents had come from different backgrounds within the US and felt slightly "foreign" in the Northeast, I was raised to be curious about and respectful of people's differences.

What was your perception of the rest of the world outside of your surroundings?

I was trusting, optimistic, and lucky to find myself cared for by the people I found in my journeys.

Your big move from New York to Guadalajara, Mexico, pre-internet, I suppose was more challenging than moving now.

What challenges did you encounter?

What did you pack with you?

Did you ship anything there?

Back then the school didn't have any allowance for extra baggage, so I brought only what I could pack in my allowed bags. I am amazed at how much stuff I've brought down to my home here over the years without ever once using a moving company.

I can imagine the hardest part of the journey was probably for my parents as they had to wait until I could find a public phone on a street corner to call them collect and let them know I had arrived safely.

What was going through your head once you arrived to the Guadalajara airport?

Was anyone there waiting for you?

What about your living situation, did the school help you find a place to live?

On the last leg of the flight, there were two other Canadian teachers on the plane with me who had been hired to work at ASFG, and their acquaintance made me feel more secure.

Both of these teachers would later become my close friends.

The school had arranged for volunteer parents to pick us up at the airport and put us up for one night in a hotel.

They picked us up the next morning and drove us to look at different apartments with the expectation that we all would settle in where we would live, by the end of the day.

I chose a house in Santa Tere, within walking distance of the school. I lived with two other foreign teachers in that first home.

Was there ever a time when you feared the decision you had made?

Many!!

When I arrived to my classroom there were no toys, no carpet for children to sit on for story time, only desks and tables and workbooks! There were no manipulatives in the classroom for children to freely explore.

I used my salary to go buy toys at *Gigante*, the local supermarket.

I had to sing a lot of songs and finger plays, make play-dough, and tell a lot of stories to keep my group of four-year-old's engaged for four-and-a-half hours a day.

When I first started working at the school, there was also a lot of unrest caused by a small group of parents trying to take over the school's administration.

That distraction made it hard to focus on teaching and students, and many staff members were unhappy. Neither of my two roommates the first year finished their contract, and I ended up living alone in that big house for a couple of months.

Because the social life in Guadalajara revolved very much around family, it was hard to find ways to meet other people my age, as they were often hanging out with their families. This was very different to how it had been for me in New York where there were many public meeting places for young people.

There have also been financial crises in Mexico, as well as security issues that sometimes make me nervous about my decision to live here, but I am in love with the country.

What about the food, did you get accustomed to it?

I've never been much of a cook, and I am happy with simple meals and snacks, so I made a lot of quesadillas with avocado.

I have always been able to appreciate a good meal, however, and I remember *pozole*, and *chilaquiles* becoming quick favorites when given a chance to eat at someone's house.

Did you know Spanish before moving to Guadalajara?

How did you learn it?

I had studied German in high school.

After graduating with my bachelors, I took a summer course in Spanish at the University of California in Santa Cruz along with an evening course at the University of Rochester.

Once I got the job offer at ASFG, I spent the following five months before the school year started traveling alone and studying at different language schools in Mexico and Guatemala.

I was doing my best to read Mexican classics and even audited a course on Mexican literature at the Autonoma University my first year at ASFG.

I also got a Mexican boyfriend the winter of my first year here, and he became my best teacher.

What did you find frustrating or annoying to live with, in Mexico?

For a long time, I was disappointed about how hard it was to find a good cup of brewed coffee in a restaurant, never having liked *café de olla* or Nescafe.

That's no longer a problem as it's possible to get great coffee here now.

The lack of job security at the school at the very start of my time at ASFG was hard. The climate at the school changed a lot when Janet Heinze became director general as she brought great stability and a climate of trust during her 13-year tenure which has continued with the current director general, David McGrath.

I am grateful to work with a great team of experienced educators who generously support each other while working for what we believe to be best for students.

Although you're currently a principal for the Early Childhood department at ASFG you initially began your career as a teacher.

Did you always know you wanted to be a teacher?

I always loved the way children see the world and so was attracted to children's literature and children's theater. It was meeting the professor Celia Houghton during my first semester at Goddard College that turned me onto the idea of how teaching was a noble and interesting career choice.

Its clear that when someone is truly where they belong in life and where they want to be, they will strive, and their passion will be one of the biggest factors for this.

It's evident that you are where you belong and that you are passionate.

You helped bring the Reggio Emilia approach as I stated earlier to the American School Foundation Guadalajara, A.C.

Why did you choose this approach?

What I love about education is how it offers our culture and society the chance to create a better world for others.

There's a lot in the field of education that gets in the way of those endeavors.

I'm saddened when I see educational programs that prescribe recipes or scripts for what and how teachers should approach their students because I think this misses what is probably most important about education and that is, the relationships.

The relationships between student and content, between students themselves, between students and teachers, and teachers and families and parents.

It's certainly important to be intentional, plan, and reflect, but there's no preplanned curriculum that can substitute what teachers do by being curious about and interested in their students, in setting a tone of respect, joy, and desire to learn in the classroom.

Reggio's philosophy of, "Nothing without joy," recognizes this.

What was the process that you had to take to bring that approach to your school?

I work at a school where parents believe in the importance of a good education from a very young age and come from a culture with a great respect and appreciation for children as important members of the family and society.

This has made it easy for our school community to embrace the ideas of Reggio such as the image of the child as a citizen of the world, with rights, and powerful interests that need to be fostered rather than redirected.

At the beginning of our shift toward a more Reggio inspired program there were just a couple misinformed parents critical about the amount of free play they saw replacing worksheet type activities but as our faculty became better at documenting and informing parents about the skills children were mastering through the play in the classroom, parents have become supportive of how we educate students.

Parents are grateful when they see their children look forward to coming to school every day and not wanting to leave.

During that time of your life, you were married and expecting a baby.

How did you meet your husband?

I married the boyfriend I had my first year at the school.

He is a saxophone player, and I kept going back to a local cafe to hear him play until I got brave enough to talk to him.

How was experiencing motherhood in a country you were slowly adapting to?

I had a very experienced well-known grandfatherly obstetrician and an energetic and incredibly supportive midwife friend attending both by children's births.

I learned as much as I could about how to get what I wanted at the hospital and to get home to my house as soon as possible.

My husband was a great father to his babies.

I was confident that my birthing experience would be lovely and it was.

What about parenting as an American to your Mexican-born children, how is that like?

Did you travel back to New York often?

Do you speak to them in English, Spanish, or both?

One of the reasons I love Mexico as much as I do and wanted to raise a family here is because of how much children are taken into consideration. They are seen at parties, restaurants, parks, churches, stores, and allowed to be themselves.

It is beautiful.

I think Mexico is very much like Italy and Reggio Emilia in this respect.

I also learned about parenting from observing and reflecting on the excellent parenting skills I saw in so many of my students' parents.

I typically spoke to my children in English, and their father spoke to them in Spanish, and we would go back and forth between languages when all four of us were together.

I traveled with my children to my parents' home every summer from when they were born until my father died only recently. My children felt at home in both New York and California where we would always be invited for Thanksgiving.

My daughter always planned to attend university in the States, and she chose Bard College in New York and now lives in Queens.

There is a famous quote that says something like, "You can take the person out from X place, but you cant take X place from that person."

You have been living in Mexico for 30 years, maybe even longer now, do you feel that quote suits you?

I have lived in Mexico for 30 years, longer than I lived in the States and the quote makes sense to me.

I can love it here with all my heart, but I'll never be from here.

I'll never fit in completely and that not fitting in has become a part of who I am.

I also don't fit in when visiting the States, I forget and speak Spanish to people, or I don't know how to use the phone there or fill a car with gasoline because here every gas station is full service.

Things like that.

Tell me about your favorites, like your favorite meal to eat?

I love to go to the market every Sunday morning and buy fresh fruits and vegetables.

Favorite meal to cook?

I like that I can afford to make a fresh fruit and veggie drink every morning for a fraction of what it would cost to do so in the US.

Favorite vacation spot?

While my parents were alive, our favorite vacation spot was with them, but over the last two years, my children and I have taken some amazing trips in Mexico.

We loved visiting Merida and the surrounding area of Chichen Itza and Celestum.

Our last vacation was in Mexico City visiting the incredible museums, ruins, and restaurants.

Favorite part of living in Mexico?

My family, friends, job, and my three dogs.

I know you are big on mindfulness, have you discovered an easier way to overcome the hard days we are sometimes faced with?

What would you encourage we do on those days?

I forever want to be a lifelong learner. Studying the Reggio approach brings meaning to my life because it combines a passion for children, democracy, the arts, and education.

I have a hobby in photography.

I am fascinated with the plants and pollinators in our school gardens.

Having things I'm interested in, gives meaning to my life.

About seven-years-ago, I began to practice meditation and found it helpful for my personal and professional life. When I saw how meditation helped me become more patient, a little nicer, and perhaps a little happier, I became interested in helping young children learn these skills through a secular mindfulness practice.

I am also part of a group encouraging educators how to use mindfulness practices in their own classrooms. I think the changes are subtle, but as teachers begin to learn more about it, our program is interacting with children in more respectful and empathetic manner and helping children to do that with each other.

Slowly but surely I think we are affecting a positive change in each other, our students, the parents, and the larger school community.

As a teacher, principal, and as an influential figure in the education scene in Mexico, I can imagine you have worked with a lot of different personalities.

Is there a repetitive trait you have seen, or anything worthy of comment that you think we should know?

Parenting is incredibly hard and rewarding. There is so much joy to be had, but it's a constant challenge to do better, be more patient, more present, less controlling. One, can never be a perfect parent, and so I see this challenge reflected in the parents I meet, and I have great compassion for them.

It's also hard to be a teacher and feel that you should always be doing more and reaching each child at a very personal and meaningful way while at the same time having the responsibility of knowing when to pack up and leave for the day, oftentimes, to go home to our own families.

The repetitive trait I see is, perseverance and dedication!

Life is so hard and so lovely.

What would you tell someone that wants to move to a place that is still unknown to them?

Tips, suggestions?

Working in a foreign place is a wonderful way to travel the world.

Make efforts to establish strong friendships with people from the area you are visiting and learn about their families, childhood, and experiences.

Read local literature, learn the local history, watch the local news, go to the museums.

You're still so young, but you have lived a lot. You have even revolutionized the Mexican Early Childhood education system. What can you tell us about life that perhaps you didn't know before and you do now?

Or perhaps something you feel like we need to know, or even advice you give to your own children.

I count my lucky stars I have always had a family that supports me in doing what I love, that values learning, and education and that love each other and enjoy spending time together.

That and the fact I have a job I look forward to going to every day and where I have enough autonomy to do what I think is best for children and teachers gives me a lot of satisfaction.

My advice is to eat healthy, get enough sleep and take your dogs out for daily walks, (smiles).

Although this book is intended for everyone, the theme of it is 30. Where were you at 30-years-old, what stage of your life were you in? And what would you recommend those of us turning 30 this year?

I had just had my son at 30, and my first daughter wasn't yet two-years-old, so I had two children in diapers, a double stroller, and a full-time job. I remember feeling, "If there was an earthquake or a fire I could grab one under each arm and try to keep them safe."

I think that shows a bit of how alone I felt with the responsibilities of parenthood and yet it was a really fun time, as children are so magical and spontaneous and ever-changing.

"Tips?"

Try to find a time to meditate even if it means you have to wake up early.

Appreciate and accept help from your friends and family.

Anything else you would like to add?

You are very flattering in the credit you give my influence on education in Mexico.

Thank you!!

JORGE MOTO
LONDON, UNITED KINGDOM

You have traveled to 29 countries and lived in 4. That's a lot of countries and a lot of flights taken.

How have you accomplished this?

When did it start?

I started with my first international trip back in 2012, when I traveled to Chile to represent Mexico in an international technology innovation contest. It was a 1-week trip that opened my eyes to the international culture and passion for travels.

After that, I just committed myself to at least one international trip each year.

I have this written resolution on my bedroom wall so I can see it every day; it has helped me to accomplish my travels by being reminded of this every day. Of course, there is planning and budget allocation for each travel.

Do you remember the first place you traveled to, where was it?

How old were you?

How did you choose that destination?

How do you normally choose a destination?

The first travel that I remember was a trip from Mexico City to Veracruz, a family trip. I was probably 6-years-old.

However, when I was a kid my family and I used to travel really frequently (twice-per-year) to Jalisco (Guadalajara and Los Altos region)to visit my mom's family and spend the summer and winter holidays there.

When I was a kid, the destination was chosen by my parents.

Now, I don't have a pattern in choosing a destination at all. I would say that currently, my choice is based on location. Since I am living in London, it is easy and cheap to travel within Europe.

However, I have chosen destinations based on another passion that I have, dancing. If there is a dancing festival or congress that I want to attend, then I choose that destination to travel and explore.

I know you were born in Mexico City, a melting pot for so many different ethnic groups. In fact, it is said that Mexico City houses a large amount of Argentines.

The Jewish community is also very dominant there.

And of course, there are a lot of other ethnicities living in Mexico City as well.

Do you think that influenced you, the diversity around you?

Maybe that sparked an interest in you to venture out of your comfort zone?

By the time I was living in Mexico City I was not close to that diversity, and also there wasn't that multicultural diversity that there is now.

However, later in my life when I was living in Guadalajara, I felt attracted to that multicultural experience. Mainly because I wanted to practice and improve my English language skills, I started to meet and hang out with foreign classmates at my university.

After this approach with foreigners, I definitely felt motivated and attracted to traveling abroad and experiencing diversity.

Tell me about your family. Are your parents from Mexico City?

How did they meet?

My mom is from a small town in Jalisco, but she moved to Mexico City when she was 15-years-old, living with her aunt, uncle, and cousins until she got married to my dad.

My dad is from Mexico City, and he used to travel a lot for work all over Mexico.

They met through my mom's uncle who worked with my dad.

I think the fact that my mom moved from a small-town to the biggest city in Mexico, while she was really young and, the fact that my dad traveled a lot for work somehow influenced me in my travels and adventures.

I have one older brother who moved from Mexico City to Guadalajara alone when he was 20-years-old.

Was traveling the norm in your family?

Did you travel often, as a child?

We normally traveled as a family when I was a kid. At least once-per-year. Although these travels were within Mexico and mainly from Mexico City to Guadalajara, I remember that those travels were really expected and full of great moments for me.

Later in life, you and your family relocated from Mexico City to Guadalajara. Guadalajara although still a very populated city—the 2nd in Mexico—is much smaller than Mexico City.

How did you adjust to the changes?

For me, it was a big adventure, everything was new, and I was open to exploring and having new experiences. Although I did not know anyone, I adapted to the new place and life really easily. I met fantastic people since the beginning, and always had my family's support.

I realized that I am *really* flexible, open to changes and good with being out of my comfort zone.

I know you are very passionate about dancing, you have done it for years now, and it has actually taken you abroad. I remember when you came back from a trip to Cuba, I think it was for a dancing contest. You talked about your experiences in Cuba—at a time when only certain countries were permitted entrance into their country.

When did dancing become a hobby of yours?

And where else has it taken you?

I started dancing when I was 8-years-old. My best friend's mom and sister taught my friend and me. Since then, I have danced at family parties, at high school parties, and on some sporadic occasions, but when I was at my university, I started to dance almost every day, and the passion started to grow.

Besides Cuba, I have traveled to Belgrade (Serbia), Odessa (Ukraine), Rovinj (Croatia), and Moscow (Russia) attending festivals and congresses. Also, I always try to dance in each city I am traveling to, which has helped me to meet a lot of local people; many of them now are good friends.

You're currently living in London, working with an American company. To many people this might sound like a dream they would like to achieve.

What were your steps for getting there?

And do you think you're living the "American Dream?"

And if so, is the "American Dream," still attainable?

I have always followed my dreams and passions; they are my priority over anything else.

After finishing university, I had the dream of having my own company. Therefore, I became an entrepreneur. Thanks to that, I was involved in the entrepreneurial environment in Guadalajara, where I met the founders and top Mexican executives of the U.S. company that I am working for.

When I closed my startup, I joined that company, and after a couple of years and some travels to the headquarters in California, I decided to keep traveling.

Then I requested the company to allow me one year to work from home. My plan was to travel all over Europe. However, the company offered me the option of relocation to the London office.

But I ended up in London by following my dream of continuing to travel all over Europe. I planned and asked for it until I attained it.

I do not think I am living the American Dream but my dream. It just so happens that I am working for an American company but this was my dream, and it would have happened any other way.

In fact, I do not believe in the American Dream, idea. Traveling has helped me to realize that this idea is also happening in other places too, this is just a reason for faith and for things to happen. For me, the American Dream is just cliché.

I do strongly believe that dreams can come true, it is just a matter of visualization, planning, hard work, patience, and perseverance.

Did you envision you would live in 4 different countries and travel as much as you have?

Or how did you envision your life would be?

At some point in my life, I envisioned traveling a lot but not as much as I have done, nor live in 4 different countries (so far). But as I mentioned before I visualized and planned for this life.

Tell me about life as an expat.

It's obvious to think of what the benefits can be but what are the difficulties that come with being an expat?

It is always hard but not impossible to start over again. You need to open a bank account, social healthcare, taxes and more registration of all official paperwork. You do not know anything. Therefore, you need to search and ask colleagues and call customer service. All of those are difficult since you are not familiar with them and you are moving out of your comfort zone.

Also, you need to learn where and how to buy groceries and food. Where to get a haircut and all those "small things" we do every day (or quite often). It seems to be unimportant, but at the end of the day, it is also a hardship—just for a while though.

The language, weather, and cultural differences also could be something to deal with, mostly at the beginning. This could endure for a while if you are not flexible and curious enough to get involved in the new culture and lifestyle of the new place.

When I think of you, I think of you as a very happy person, very friendly and a connecting force amongst diverse groups of people.

Were you always like this, or has this evolved throughout your travels?

I always have been a happy and positive person, but when I was kid and teenager I was really shy.

Dancing and traveling have helped me to grow and evolve these skills.

Through travels I have discovered and understood the importance of being connected with people; almost all of the time, I am traveling alone, and you need to be friendly, open and be able to connect with people to have a better journey.

You will never know if you need someone to assist you and also when you make friends all over the world, then you are not traveling alone anymore. Moreover, you will always find someone that can help you with an open heart.

Therefore, my main goal when I am traveling is to be friendly and open with all of the people that I meet.

A smile always breaks any barrier you could face.

There are so many different quotes that describe traveling, and those quotes are everywhere, on t-shirts, mugs, pencils, etc.

Do you have a favorite quote?

And what does traveling mean to you?

There are many that I like that I read frequently and identify with. Actually, I just recently read, "The world is a book and those who do not travel read only a page."

This represents a lot of what traveling means for me; you must keep learning and growing, and the best way to do it is by practicing (at least this is the way I like it), and I have chosen traveling to learn about life.

People have often said once they get a tattoo, they cant stop from getting another one, and it becomes repetitive.

It seems as if the same happens with traveling.

You have traveled to 29 countries; it seems as if, the same that happens when getting a tattoo happens with traveling, you just can't stop at one destination.

What is it about traveling that does this to a person?

Is there some type of urge to add stamps to a passport?

Is it the food that drives people to a country?

The unknown each country offers?

Or what is it?

Absolutely, I agree with this theory. You become addicted to the feelings and emotions when you are traveling; I would say this is one of the healthier addictions in life.

What drives these feelings and emotions depends on each person. It could be the food, the passport stamps, dance, the unknown, adventure, meeting people, etc.

For me, it has been a combination and also it has evolved through time. At the beginning, it was to have the experience of traveling and not just hear or read about it.

Later, I started to travel for the adrenaline of being in a completely different place.

Then, because of dance. Looking for dancing festivals and for being connected with myself.

More recently, traveling is part of my lifestyle; there is not a reason in particular but part of my routine.

Is there an adventure you would like to share?

There are many adventures and experiences that I have had while I have been traveling, but the one that's in my mind day-over-day is related to love.

By doing what I like most, traveling and dancing, I deeply fall in love.

What sensations do you feel when you fly into a new place?

Has fear, ever, been one of them?

I feel excitement; my heart is pumping hard when I am landing in a new place, but I have never felt fear.

You've traveled as I keep stating, to 29 countries, that has exposed you tremendously to a lot of the world. On those trips, you have met a lot of different people, some native to those places. You have tried their food, explored their culture, perhaps even spoken their language.

After having done all of that, what do you think of humanity?

Do you think, we have more in common than we think we do?

I think there are more good people than bad ones.

We normally are bombarded with news, full of bad things, and people. If you just hear that, you can believe that it is the end of the world and that people are the worst.

However, by traveling and meeting people from different nationalities and backgrounds, I have seen the good in people and the world, something that you do not expect nor imagine till you live it.

And, yes, we have more in common than what we think we do. Everywhere, no matter how developed the country is, there are same basic situations (good and bad) and behaviors.

I bet it's very hard to choose a favorite destination from everywhere you have visited. But if you had to choose, which one would it be?

Why is it your favorite?

Indeed, it is hard to choose one destination. Each place has its own charm.

But I have my top five places (not necessarily in this order):

Saint Petersburg was the first city that I visited of the ex-USSR. It is a beautiful city full of culture and history, the Orthodox churches and palaces are just amazing.

The Riviera Maya, Caribbean sea, white sand, warm weather and delicious food.

Iceland, unbelievable landscapes and wild nature.

Swiss Alps, fairy tale villages, surrounded by beautiful landscapes.

And Cuba, the people,and the dance culture is the best.

Tell me about a meal you ate that you still can't get over. Where was it and what as it?

Borscht is a sour soup, popular in several Eastern European cuisines. I tried it for the first time in Russian, but it's originally from Ukraine. I really love it so much that I even learned to cook it.

Where have you seen the happiest people?

Cuba and Mexico.

Is there anywhere you have been to where you have admired their way of doing things?

Maybe it's their education system, their labor laws, etc.

Germany. It is an educated country, not just in terms of university degrees but behavior in life.

While traveling the world I am sure people have asked you, about you, where you come from, what language you speak and all of that. Has that made you more patriotic towards your birth country (Mexico)?

Yes, definitely.

While you are abroad, you realize how your country is seen by other countries (good or bad).

Fortunately, Mexico is a country that almost all people from different nationalities like for different reasons. I have realized how lucky I am to be Mexican and I have appreciated more of what we have (even with our problems).

What about, you, towards other people, do you think traveling has made you more tolerant of those that are different from you?

And if so, in what ways has it made you more open to them?

Yes, of course. When you are traveling and in contact with different cultures and ways of thinking—not as a tourist, but as a local—you realize you are not the only one in this world.

You become humble.

I have been more tolerant and open to religion, traditions, criticism, and different point of views. Also, I have increased my level of patience.

Life is full of contrasts, we see them everyday. Sadness, happiness, hot days, cold days.

What contrasts have you encountered on your trips?

For example, possibly abundance in some, poverty in others.

Communism and democracy.

What has experiencing this taught you about life and the true importance of it?

Extreme poverty, versus extreme rich people, corruption versus legality, cold versus hot weather. Religious versus non-religious people and cities, developed versus non-developed cities, physical characteristics (like tall versus short people, white versus dark-skinned).

Educated versus uneducated people, soccer fans versus non-soccer fans cities, technological versus non-technological cities, wet versus dry cities, cold versus warm people, communism versus democracy, drinkable versus non-drinkable tap water, cheap versus expensive cities (in terms of food| stay|drinks).

Old versus new cities, among other things.

Experiencing this has taught me about differences, precisely. You need to learn and accept no one is like you and nothing is like you would like, almost in all the cases. By doing this, you become more tolerant and by not judging others, because they think different.

Being patient and open-minded help to build a better world.

We can not change others as we want to just because we think different, but we can change (and grow) ourselves by accepting and learning other points of views and of the contrasts of life.

Speaking of precisely that, of contrasts. What do you think of failure and how is it best to overcome it?

Failure is part of success.

We must learn to accept it and live with it. But must importantly be able to have failures in life. It is not to overcome it but to see failure as something positive and good. Failure gives you experience, knowledge and the possibility to grow.

If you are failing it is because you are trying, and this means you are looking and working towards your goals.

Sooner rather than later, failure after failure...if you keep trying, you will achieve anything you want. So, do not overcome it but embrace failure as something normal and positive.

Do not fear it.

It seems like a lot of aspects of life have become harder through the years. But with traveling it often seems that the contrary has happened, that it has actually become more attainable.

Do you think so?

Have you seen this over the course of your traveling?

If so, in what aspects have you seen the changes?

Yes, I agree. I think this is happening since you are exposed to different cultures and ways of life. Of course, you need to be open, have a positive mind, and try to live like a local.

You realize where in life you are standing and appreciate what you have and what you do not have by comparing yourself to people living in other countries.

A key aspect is to analyze your life towards your travel experiences in a positive and constructive way.

Even then with the accessibility, perhaps in travel, there are still some children and even some adults who haven't traveled abroad, or in general.

Maybe they are intimidated by the process, or don't know how to financially plan for a trip?

Are there any specific steps you take when you plan your trips?

What advice would you give someone who will be traveling for the first time?

First of all, I would like to encourage people to travel even if it seems crazy or even if they feel afraid. Never in life will we have all the images of what is going to happen. Therefore, you need to embrace the change and be flexible.

Second, I would like to say that traveling on the contrary to what many people may think, can be cheap and affordable. That being said, I recommend planning your travel in advance, not super detailedly but the big picture. This plan needs to have a general budget and things to do or that you would like you to do.

Consider commute time, traveling light (by all means) clothes, luggage, and attachments.

Make sure to let your bank know you are traveling; you do not want your credit card blocked.

Book your stay in advance. You can use, CouchSurfing, to exchange an experience, or a place to stay, or in exchange for teaching something. Or hostels or Airbnb.

Try to meet local people before getting there (if possible). This is always very helpful, especially to get the best tips of what to do in case of an emergency.

Try to not be a tourist if you want to have the full and real experience. Be open, patient, and flexible; do not carry stereotypes and prejudices with you. Do not have expectations, and if you do, then expect the unexpected.

Two big reasons I have heard why people aren't traveling are money and time. Although it is true that you need money and time to travel, you can have an amazing and unforgettable trip with a little bit of money. I recommend you read, *How to Travel the World on $50 a Day: Travel Cheaper, Longer, Smarter*, for more ideas of how to travel on a budget.

And having a plan will help you to maximize your time (note, never travel to a lot of countries in a short period) you will not enjoy the trip nor get to know the culture and place. And you will finish overwhelmed and really tired.

I have mentioned to plan a trip, several times. Well, the way I am doing it is by, first visualizing it in my mind (literally I dream day and night about it).

Then I start by creating a spreadsheet where I will be filling in flight information (I normally use Google flights to find good deals), lodging information and ideas on what I want to do. Having all of that information in place helps me to structure what I am visualizing and allows me to start deciding which flight to buy, where to stay and the to-do-list starts to have a shape and body.

Travel must-haves, recommendations, tips, suggestions?

Take your time to be at the airport.

Pack half the clothes and double the money of what you have thought. Travel light (as I mentioned above).

Buy a SIM card wherever you go (if your local data allowance is not useful where you go).

Be open, flexible and minimize your expectations.

Do not travel with a big towel, it takes a lot of luggage space, and you may end up traveling with a wet towel.

Always be alert and use common sense.

Try to learn basic words of the language even if English is spoken where you're traveling to (unless it is a native English country).

If you can choose between luggage and a backpack, choose a backpack.

Take care of your passport.

Do not worry and enjoy!

Have you mastered the art of packing and unpacking?

Yes!

I have traveled with a backpack that weighed 30 liters, for a 30-day-trip. If I am traveling for two weeks, I pack for one week and use lock laundry services to keep my clothes clean. Vacuum bags are a good option to save space. In my experience, rolling up your clothes helps to maximize your backpack space (yes, you need to iron your clothes later, if you want).

I have to ask you, has your luggage ever been lost?

Yes, just one time. Actually, it was on my first international flight. It arrived four days later. I learned with this to pack at least one complete outfit in my carry-on luggage.

Although this book is intended for everyone, the theme of it is 30. Where were you at 30-years-old, what stage of your life were you in? And what would you recommend those of us turning 30 this year?

I celebrated my 30th birthday in Chicago.

In my 30's, I started with my master plan of traveling the world and working remotely. Actually, by the time it was my 30th birthday, I was exercising this plan. I stayed in Chicago 1 week working from there.

My advice is to live your life as you want to. Do the things you want to do *now*. Be with the people you want to be with.

Do not postpone anymore! And of course...travel more!!

Anything else you would like to add about life?

Life is so beautiful to be wasted. Do, feel, say, go, try, and think all that you want (of course without harming others).

I would like to leave four principles that I read and follow in my life that I consider really useful during any situation of life taken from *The four agreements: A Practical Guide to Personal Freedom* by Don Miguel Ruiz:

"Be impeccable with your word."

"Don't take anything personally."

"Don't make assumptions."

"Always do your best."

Thank you!!

ARIYANNA O'NEAL
CALIFORNIA, USA

Ariyanna, I have a couple of questions that I want to ask you, let's start with the places where you have lived, can you name all of them?

Okay, so let's start!! I was born in Kansas, then I moved to North Carolina when I was four-years-old, after that I moved to Italy when I was eight-years-old.

Which one has been your favorite out of all of those?

My favorite place where I have been to is probably, Italy.

"Why?"

Well because there were all different types of food. Also, because the people there are so, so nice.

Tell me about the languages you speak and about your cultural background, you are so fortunate to be multicultural and to be able to represent so much of the world through your heritage.

All the languages I know are Japanese and English. The languages I have heard of are, German, and Italian.

My cultural background is a quarter Japanese, a quarter Caucasian and half Black.

What has been your favorite food from everything you have tried on your trips?

My favorite food from everything I have tried would probably be the pizza and pasta from Italy.

"Did you know that pizza was made in Napoli, Italy?"

I know you have moved because of your dad's job, can you tell me about his job?

Yes, I move so much because of my dad's job, but that is the good thing about it.

"Why?"

Well because if my dad wasn't in the Army, I wouldn't be doing this right now.

My dad is a military man. But I don't know what job in the military he does.

Are there any challenges that come with being 10? It's a pretty big number and an important age.

Yes, there are because if you knew that I have two sisters, I have to take care of both of them. When you're the oldest, it's so hard, because you can get in trouble for what your siblings do and then you get angry at your parents for not getting mad at them.

Like for example, your youngest sister breaks a lamp, and you were in the kitchen, cooking, then your mom smacks you for not watching her.

After that, you yell at your mom and tell her that you were in the kitchen cooking, but your sister doesn't get in trouble. See, now that is hard to work with.

Another challenge is to have to say, "bye" to your best friends and friends that are like family to you. Now that's hard because then you can't play with them anymore, you can't see them anymore, and you can't talk to them. But if they are like family to you, you should always stay in touch with them.

What should be know about kids?

Is there something that adults do, that is annoying?

Well being a kid is very hard especially when you have older brothers, or sisters, or younger brothers, or sisters.

It's hard because we have to listen to the rules that our family makes.

It's also easy because you don't have to do every single thing that adults do.

YES, there are things that are annoying that adults do. But I don't really know what it is. It's hard to explain, but there are things that are annoying to me that adults do.

You're ten-years-old, and I am sure you have heard this over and over again, but you can be anything you want to be in life. Anything.

Have you thought about what you want to be?

When I am older, I don't really know, what I want to be. But my mom always says, "You should be a doctor."

And I say, "Why?"

And she says, "Well because you can take care of everyone."

When I think about it, I would like to be a pediatric nurse because, I like to take care of people especially, infants.

Thank you!!

MELINA CHAVEZ BOBADILLA
JALISCO, MEXICO

I know you were on vacation, visiting your grandma in Mexico when you first met your husband. That was the first trip you had ever taken to Mexico by yourself. I am sure that since it was your very first trip alone, you had a lot of expectations.

Did you ever think you would meet your now husband on that trip?

It was odd because a week before taking my trip I was watching TV with my mother, we were watching a Pedro Infante movie, and he started singing the song *"Cien Años"* a song I had never heard before. I began to cry.

To my surprise the week I met Pepe we were at a restaurant, and the mariachi there started to sing that exact song. I told my now husband not to cry (I recognized the song), and Pepe said, "How did you know?" By then, he had already begun to cry. It's a special song…my mother-in-law's favorite.

I can say that I was so excited about going to Mexico, it was like I knew I had to go, I felt like there was something incredible about to happen.

Do you remember the day when you first met?

Where was it and how did it happen?

The *feria* was going on, and I went with my uncle Javier and my aunt, Ana.

We were at a bar when Pepe arrived at our table. He sat next to me and he said, "What do you think, that I can't take your drink away?" He was a complete stranger, so I just started laughing; to his surprise, I wasn't getting angry, and I had a good sense of humor.

We didn't speak to one another very much that day but the next day, my aunt and my uncle invited me to the rodeo and Pepe was also there.

Back then there weren't any cell phones, so Pepe had to look for us to find where we were. I called him telepathically, and he found us. Once he did, he immediately sat next to me. We talked until like 3 am or so.

A lot of people say that when they met the person they eventually married, they instantly felt something different, and they immediately knew they were the ones they'd marry.

Did that happen to you, or what was the first reaction you had of one another?

I felt like our skin bounded perfectly when I touched him, I had never felt that before. Also, it was odd to me because I had never allowed any of my past boyfriends to kiss me on the first date.

I didn't feel butterflies in my stomach but I felt like I was on top of the world and that the sunlight was brighter than ever before.

How old were you when you met?

I was 18 when I met him, when we got married I had just turned 20- years-old.

I was born in El Grullo, Jalisco but moved to Encinitas, California when I was 10-years-old. I was in college when Pepe and I met. After Pepe and I met, I went back to CSU San Marcos, and I continued there for a semester.

Now that I think back, I remember it was the most depressing period of my life when I was away from Pepe. I cried every day, and we would write to each other every day. Mail took a month to arrive, but it was the most incredible feeling when a letter from him would arrive.

The only solution was for us to get married and for me to move, he was not willing to move to the U.S.

During that period of your life that you just described, when you were back home in the U.S., and Pepe was back in Mexico. How did you make it work, it sounds pretty hard?

We would call each other on the phone, write to each other.

Receiving a phone call from him was the greatest feeling.

How was your love life before meeting one another? Were you actively dating?

Yes, I hate to say it, but I always had a boyfriend.

I wish I would have given myself the opportunity to have been alone and see life a different way, learn about myself, be myself without anyone else there.

How was the proposal like, did you have any idea it was coming? Had you talked about it? Where did you get proposed to you?

We had talked about it; it was not romantic. Pepe asked me over the phone, we both started to cry.

How long did it take you to plan your wedding?

It took us six months over the phone and one month before I moved to Mexico.

Where did you get married?

El Grullo, Jalisco.

Although you had visited Mexico on many occasions, prior to that trip you took by yourself. You had never actually lived there aside from when you were a child.

Did you find any challenges between you and your Mexican-born and raised boyfriend? And if so, what were they?

I was born in El Grullo, Jalisco and raised both in Mexico and in the U.S. I have a good sense of both cultures. But even though I have a good sense of both cultures, it was really hard for me when I moved back to Mexico. I missed my family, friends, the language, my life. I would cry a lot because I was homesick.

Were there any other challenges that you encountered?

Some of the other challenges were that I didn't know fluent Spanish, I missed my studies and the U.S.

Do you have any anecdotes that pertain to that time of your life?

I didn't talk too much to anyone because my Spanish was not great. I spoke Spanglish, I set myself a challenge to either only speak Spanish, or only speak in English but not mix the two. It was a great decision because now that I am a teacher it was necessary to do.

I read 11 Spanish books in one year and really pushed myself to only speak one or the other. I am so proud of myself because I made it.

Your 18-year-old son just left for college; he will now be living here in the States. Does this mean he speaks English fluently?

And how was raising him and your other son in Mexico? Did you speak to them in English ?

My son (Jose Luis Pozos) who is now 18-years-old had a hard time when he was a child because I spoke to him in English at home. He would cry but now, he thanks me because he speaks English.

My other son (Emilio Pozos) who is now 11-years-old, has always liked to practice English since he was a baby, now he is fluent and wants to learn Japanese too.

You've been married now for 20 years—that's a really long time. I am sure that there have been a lot of romantic things you and your husband have done for one another. Out of all of them, which one has been the most romantic?

We are not romantic to each other; we show appreciation, and our love in a different way.

I remember when I come back from New York he was waiting for me with a bouquet of flowers; it was so beautiful.

One day he brought the mariachi inside our house while I was sleeping and I was so surprised that I started crying.

Both you and Pepe, have seen the different types of love there are. Love between the two of you, love for your children, love for your extended families and so on.

What can you tell me about love, and what is love to you?

Love is a feeling I find in music, in a flower, and in a nice word, in a hug. I think it is everywhere you go, it is something that you cannot lie about, you either feel it or you don't.

Your love story is pretty interesting, have you ever thought about how different life could have been, had you not taken that trip that you took?

Yes, I have and I don't like to imagine myself in that situation. I think I would have continued to wear massive amounts of makeup, continued to wear the latest fashion trends. I probably wouldn't have such a wide variety of music, art and nature. I think I would have been caught in a consumerism, materialist world.

What do you think about your love story?

Our love story is so special that every time I think about it, it gives me chills. I love it and think it was meant to be.

You both took a risk in going forward with your relationship and believing in it; you have also experienced a lot throughout these 20 years of marriage.

Having experienced all of that, what is your perception of life?

Every experience helps you mature, it is hard at times but the only thing that can save a peaceful and pleasant life is love.

The only thing that can save a marriage is love.

Love is what makes the world go around.

Although this book is intended for everyone, the theme of it is 30. Where were you at 30-years-old, what stage of your life were you in? And what would you recommend those of us turning 30 this year?

I am now 39 when I was 30, I already had my two boys. I was waiting for my kids to grow up a little bit before I could start my bachelor's degree online. And it was so hard to do.

I finally finished a *Licenciatura en Docencia del Ingles como Lengua Extrañera*; I am so proud of my efforts.

So, I can tell you 30-year-old's that you shouldn't skip your studies. You should finish them first before thinking about doing anything else, I learned the hard way, and it was truly painful but rewarding at the end.

Is there anything you think we should know about love, dating, marriage, parenting, or life in general that you wish you knew, or that you think we can benefit from?

You are the owner of your life, and every decision will have benefits and other negative aspects that you will have to deal with.

Looking back at my life, I can say that I am truly satisfied with what I have done with my own, only because I have always looked for love in every aspect of my life.

Anything else you would like to add?

I told my older son about the opportunity I have of telling you, my love story and placing it in one of the chapters of your book; he asked me why you picked me to tell my story.

I said, "Because I think the writer thinks it was incredible to hear I gave everything I had in the U.S. to marry your father and it was all done because of the love I have for your father."

My son said, "Oohhh, I am the product of that love!"

He also told me he wants to buy your book, it was so neat to hear him say that. By the way, I called California to tell him about this.

Thank you!!

LINDA NEEL

CALIFORNIA, USA

Through your job, you get to work on cruise ships and travel around the world.

What exactly do you do, and when did you start your career?

Working on the cruise ship my only duty was to be an entertainer. However, as a crew member of the ship I had to go through rigorous safety training. This included knowing CPR, how to evacuate and properly handle a fire (if I needed to), crowd management, knowing the specific alarms (Code Bravo = fire, Code Oscar = man overboard, etc.), essentially anything basic any crew member would need to know in case of an emergency.

As far as shows went, we learned up to four mainstage shows. These were about forty-five minutes each and the themes varied per show. Mostly they were musical reviews, but sometimes they were established musicals (ninety-minute versions) from Broadway.

In addition to the mainstage shows, I had to perform cabarets in the lounge.

The workload for a performer on a ship depends on the length of the cruise. I mostly worked long cruises, up to twenty-one days, and the shortest I ever worked on was a seven-day cruise schedule.

I had wanted to do cruise ships because I felt it was a "rite of passage" as a performer. I auditioned in 2013 because a friend of mine was choreographing a new project on one of the ships. The project was a musical which meant I knew it was more "up my alley" versus the usual cruise ship style shows.

I was hired and then the funding fell through for the musical, so we ended up doing more traditional cruise ship reviews anyway.

I worked for the cruise line on and off for about four years.

You're very talented and are very connected to the arts, how old were you when you started performing?

I started performing at the young age of three. My mom enrolled me in ballet class not only because she was a dancer but also because I was "pigeon-toed" and the doctor suggested dance as an alternative to surgery.

I didn't start performing professionally until I was fifteen. At that age, I became an Equity Membership Candidate (EMC) which is part of the program that allows actors to work towards earning their Actor's Equity Union card.

Where was the first place you traveled to?

At seventeen I was part of a traveling kid's musical. We did a national tour with two mini-vans and one truck. We traveled around various regions in the U.S.

How many places have you traveled to while working?

Performing has allowed me to travel almost everywhere! I have toured in Canada with various shows. I went to Istanbul, Turkey for a month rehearsing and performing in a production of "Grease."

I lived in Hong Kong for about ten months while I worked at one of their theme parks.

With the cruise ship, I've been to both coasts of Mexico, parts of Central America, eastern and western Caribbean, the Baltics, Mediterranean, Middle East, India, Southeast Asia, Australia, and New Zealand.

Where have you spent the longest time in?

I spent the longest in Hong Kong. The hotel we were put up in was located on the outskirts of Hong Kong, close to the border of mainland China. Being out there definitely gave me a sense of common Hong Kong life.

What should we know about your occupation?

This occupation is a legitimate job, and I think a lot of times people forget that. So often I see notices for gigs that don't pay anything or small-town theaters that expect you to drop your life (day job, previous engagements) for their rehearsal schedules but don't expect to pay you a living wage.

Artists love what they do and would probably do it for free, but at the end of the day, we have to eat.

Not only does there have to be the passion for the artistry and the dedication to constantly be improving ourselves but you also need the discipline to take care of yourself. Our image is our business, and we have to be able to maintain it.

Don't forget being emotionally strong enough to be able to go in and out of work that requires you to go to dark places.

What we do requires great skill, and it should be compensated with a respectable wage in commercial and experimental avenues.

What is the biggest life lesson you have learned while working?

Be kind! It's very cliché, but it's one of the most important lessons I've learned.

Not only does it benefit you personally and professionally but then others around you will return the favor.

Of course, it doesn't mean, let people step all over you, but you can set your boundaries in a gentle way.

Be kind always!

What's your favorite part of your job?

My favorite aspect is when the audience comes in the equation. You rehearse acting moments, jokes, costume changes, songs, and dance steps for weeks on end but the best part is when you finally have an audience to see you work.

The best audiences are not passive; they're the ones that are engaged and right there with you. From moment to moment you can tell you have them eating out of the palm of your hand. Sometimes they're verbal and other times the moment is so profound you can hear a pin drop.

It varies with each show, but when the audience is great then it just adds to what I already love doing.

Your least favorite part?

The hardest part of my job is when I am not working. I audition as much as I can and sometimes there are months when nothing comes through. Self-doubt hits you hard, and you start to think you'll never work again.

What's difficult is that sometimes you have all the skills needed for the production, but you don't have the right look.

It's hard not to take all the rejection so personally because of that.

It's good to take classes or create your own work, but there's something about booking a job that gives you that excitement and outside validation.

There are a lot of people that would love to accomplish their dreams. Maybe their dream is to have a career like yours.

What would you tell them?

Make sure it's your passion because it's a long and hard road.

You have to not only be your own number one fan, but you have to be pro-active about your career.

This particular field is very competitive, and you have to willing to keep putting yourself out there to get ahead.

Do the work, stay persistent, find your strengths, and stay strong. One day you feel like you're at the top of your game and then the next day people could think you're only a "wannabe."

This is your chapter, what do you want people to take away from it?

Enjoy the journey.

I've had a goal in mind for as long as I can remember but I've also taken a lot of detours. These different paths have shaped me and exposed me to worlds I never thought I'd experience. It's been a fun ride, and I am continuing to enjoy it.

I am at a point now where I'd like to re-focus my path, and that's okay. I am still open to different opportunities because sometimes that side road will connect you back to where you wanted to go in the first place.

You just never know where life will take you.

Although this book is intended for everyone, the theme of it is 30. What stage of your life were you in at 30 and where were you living?

I am turning 30 next year. I think I'll still be living in LA navigating my way around the business while trying to stay afloat!

Do you have any advice for those of us turning 30 this year?

I'd like to tell myself that no matter where I am that's where I need to be.

It's hard not to compare your life to everyone else's, but you never know who's looking at my life and wishing they were in my shoes. Probably not many people but you never know!

Thank you!!

CARLOS IBARRA
NEW YORK, USA

I usually ask this question towards the end of an interview, but with you, I want it to be the first question that I ask you.

What do you want people to take away from your chapter?

I want to inspire people to go after the things they want in life. One of the biggest things we have in life is uncertainty, instead of running away from it, we should embrace it.

I know from personal experience that the person I've become is a result of all the risks I've taken in my life. For that reason, I continue to push myself and take risks, and do things that make me feel uncomfortable.

Risks are scary, but they are the foundation of growth and evolution.

I hope people will see that from my experiences and feel encouraged to take more risks.

I hope, I can motivate them to venture into the unknown so that they can be a step closer towards their dreams.

In 2015 you ran across America, your starting point was Brooklyn, New York, and your ending point was Costa Mesa, California.

You must have heard a lot of stories throughout your 3000-mile-run across America.

Did one stand out more than another?

There are a lot of stories that touched my heart; there were so many people that had amazing stories to share. It's hard to just pick one.

I fondly remember staying in Navajo Nation in Arizona.

We were invited by the Wings of America organization to go and share my story. I spent the night with members of their tribe and went on a 10-mile-run with Dustin Martin, the director of the organization.

The following morning, during our run, Dustin shared a brief portion of his tribe's history, and this was all happening as the sun was rising in beautiful Navajo Nation.

It felt surreal.

And Dustin's experience growing up in a bi-cultural environment-the constant hardship of balancing his Navajo and American identity, deeply resonated with me.

The history Native Americans have in this country, and the way we've pushed that part of our history aside, is horrible.

To get to see this first hand was beautiful.

Which states did you cross?

New York, New Jersey, Pennsylvania, West Virginia, Ohio, Illinois, Indiana, Missouri, Kansas, Arizona, New Mexico, Utah, Arizona, California.

How many miles did you run a day?

I would alternate between a short and long-day. My long-day would be between 40-45 miles a day, and my short-day was 36-40.

I would break into four legs of 13 miles, and rest in-between each leg.

Where were you sleeping at?

We were sleeping everywhere...we stayed in people's homes, hotels, and Airbnb's.

We camped out while in Navajo Nation, but for the most part, I was fortunate enough to have a bed every night.

You were able to film your entire run across America and therefore, had a film crew with you.

Did they drive next to you while you ran, or how did that work?

We had two cars. One van carried all of our film equipment and it was used for the production crew.

The second car was my follow car, and that was the vehicle that carried all my supplies. That was the car I would rest in and nap in, in-between legs.

For shooting, we coordinated with the logistics of the shoot, but luckily I had a fearless team that would follow me anywhere.

They would ride next to me, behind me, and in front of me. They, would send-up a drone and catch the scenery from a bird's-eye view.

They would hop out of the car, ride bikes, skateboards, essentially anything that was needed to make the shot possible.

You have been a runner ever since I've known you, and ever since then, you have participated in the most known marathons of the country, like the New York City Marathon and the Boston one.

What does running mean to you, and when did your passion for it start?

I've always been a runner ever since I can remember.

When I was in 6th grade, I won the Sonora Elementary "marathon" (2 laps around the giant field. I think it was like a mile and a half).

Running has always been an escape and a way to keep myself grounded. The minute I hit the ground and take off running, everything disappears. I'm able to connect with my breath, take everything in and let thoughts come in and out.

Running is my alone time.

Running, allows me to stay in shape, birth creativity, and maintain a deeply-rooted connection with myself.

Film and everything that surrounds it has also been a big interest for you. In fact, you have a degree in the Arts, and aside from *Run Carlos Run*, your latest work that documents your run across America. You are also the writer of *Botes al Amanecer*, your award-winning film.

Why do you love storytelling so much?

And when did your love for it begin?

I've always been a voracious reader. I can't remember exactly when I started reading, but I know I have always loved it.

As a child, I would sit in front of the TV, a *telenovela* was always playing in the background, and I would sit there, reading.

I love being a storyteller because it connects us. Stories bring people together and help form bonds.

Also, like theater, storytelling has always been a part of human life. Through stories, our history has been preserved, and I am glad to be a part of it.

I like the history, and I hope that through my stories I can create new perspectives for the world.

Your initial interest in wanting to run across the country was to see how people live, and to learn more about the country where you have been living since a 4-year-old boy. I am sure you experienced more than what you ever imagined you would.

What was the biggest life lesson that you learned on that trip?

Kansas is a very long state.

In all seriousness, goals are tough, and they take work.

If you want to accomplish anything, you have to be willing to put up with the good, and bad; the highs and lows, and push through the barriers every single day.

You were not only a dreamer like you have always seemed to be but also a DREAMer recipient during the time of that trip. And actually, at that time, you were waiting to hear if your permission to stay in this country would be renewed.

How did it feel to be running in the place where you have been living since you were 4-years-old, knowing that you could possibly be leaving, forever?

I consider America home and like I have said before, "I am American because, I feel American."

In the same way, that I'm Mexican because, I want to be Mexican.

When I was running, I never thought of leaving, that wasn't the purpose of this journey. This journey was to experience this land and take in all of its beauty.

I couldn't have negative thoughts. I had to stay positive, so, there was no room for thoughts that could hinder my mission.

Your journey took you across America which means that you got to experience, and see a little bit of everything that makes us, America.

You were able to see the changes in demographics, in climate, in lifestyles, and so on.

After having experienced that, what do you think life really is?

Life is about living. But it has to be dictated on your terms.

You can't be scared of what might happen, you just have to go for it.

Do you think your perspective on life changed after that trip?

Yes, I push myself even harder.

But at the same time, I'm easier with myself. I go after the things I want, but I try to keep myself in the present moment.

I know you mentioned that at the start of your journey across America, right after you left New York and entered New Jersey, you reminded yourself, it was time to either turn back, or go forth with your plans. You decided to go forth as we already know.

Why did you go forth with it, and did you ever along the way think that perhaps you would cut your trip short?

I had too many people that were rooting for me, and I couldn't fail them. Their belief in me, allowed me to believe in myself to a greater extent, even if it meant plowing through it.

I never thought I would cut my trip short, but Arizona with its mountainous range and 100+ degree weather made it feel impossible.

How are you capable of being so persistent with following and achieving your dreams?

I want to live the best life that I can, and if that means that I have to be persistent, then I will.

I want to make my dreams come true so that I can help others do the same.

There are moments when we encounter the most difficult of circumstances, or the most devastating and sometimes when we go to bed; we are left thinking of those.

Did you have a moment like that during your trip?

I thought I had lost my mind and I would constantly tell myself, "I made the dumbest decision by choosing to run."

But I would let it go.

I couldn't have negativity in my life, especially during the run but most importantly in my life.

When I had days like that, the best thing I could do was to think of the things that gave me joy.

I had to find the little things that brought me peace, and use them to move me forward.

Do you have a favorite place that you found on your voyage?

Missouri, the southern part is beautiful.

Do you remember your absolute favorite meal of the trip?

Everything.

Anything, that was food was delicious. I especially enjoyed pulled pork sandwiches (some of the best I have ever had).

America is known for a lot of things. Its innovation in technology, its pop culture, being built by immigrants—and to this day housing the most ethnic groups outside of their native countries.

It is known for caring for our human rights through not only our Constitution but with organizations like the United Nations.

It is known for its FREEDOM, for globally known brands and so on.

After having ran it, what are you most proud of?

I am proud to share my stories with others, and to hopefully, be creating a difference in the world.

You are very open about your immigration status, and of how you came to America as a 4-year-old boy.

In the last couple of years there have been a lot of opinions on that precise topic, and currently, there has been a lot of commotion on the Development, Relief, and Education for Alien Minors Act (Dream Act).

As I mentioned earlier you were a DREAMer recipient. Having been that, in your opinion, what do you think about the Dream Act, do you think our country benefits from it?

The country will benefit greatly from the Dream Act. And it's legislation that is way overdue.

We need to stop putting young lives on hold and give DREAMers an opportunity to reach their true potential, without fear of deportation.

It is impossible not to encounter an immigrant in this country, especially for someone like you that has lived in both California, New York, and has journeyed around the country.

Is there anything that you have learned from an immigrant that you would like to share?

We're all human, and if we can remember that, I think this world can become a better place.

There have been a lot of brilliant people that have changed our country that were also once immigrants here. Among those is Albert Einstein, the co-founder of Google, Larry Page, infinite designers like Carolina Herrera and Oscar de la Renta.

Journalists, like Joseph Pulitzer, film directors like Guillermo del Toro and of course many others.

Given your case, you are a great person to ask, which out of those that I mentioned and those that I did not mention, do you think has been the most important for our country and why?

I don't think any, one, immigrant merits more praise than the other.

We live in a world of constant comparison, and when we stop comparing each other, we'll be able to live rich and fuller lives.

I look at immigrants as a gift to this nation, and I draw a lot of my strength from hearing of those who've come before me.

I know, I can make it through hardships because I've heard of others who've experienced worse.

Also, "Why just recognize people that have reached some kind of fame?"

"Why, not honor the work and lives of immigrants in everyday life?"

There are plenty of those stories, and if we heard more of those, our perspectives could change.

Although this book is intended for everyone, the theme of the book is 30. Where were you living at 30 and what stage of your life were you in? What advice do you have for those of us turning 30 this year?

I was running across the country when I was 30, and spent the 2nd half traveling across the country, presenting the project.

So, turning 30 hasn't been so bad. I think the years leading up to 30 were scary.

I felt turning 30 signified the end of my youth, and that I was required to have my life in order.

But in reality, it's just a number, and it doesn't define you.

Embrace the number and directly live in the direction you want to take it.

Anything else you want to add?

Chase the life you want to have, and don't stop until you have it.

I want to end this interview with something that I took from the footage of your voyage.

Its a quote from you in reference to one of the many Americans you met on your journey. I am sure you will remember having said it.

"We are all on the same journey, but we all have different reasons."

Thank you!!

LUPE CARRILLO

CALIFORNIA, USA

Describe what it felt like when you received the acceptance letter from Stanford University for your doctoral degree.

I was at my parents' house in East San Jose when I first heard I was accepted into Stanford. I was an undergraduate at Berkeley at the time, and I would sometimes take the BART and local bus to visit my folks during the weekends.

It was a sunny day in February, which happens to be the month when you start hearing back from universities.

At that point, I had heard back from Berkeley and Yale that I had been accepted into their English PhD programs. I was still waiting to hear from Stanford—my top choice.

I was drawn to Stanford for many reasons. It had one of the best English departments in the country, but it was also a place that was known for producing an entire generation of Mexican-American scholars, writers, and intellectuals from many fields.

I wanted to be part of that history.

Also, since my family was now living in San Jose, ideally, I wanted to stay nearby.

So, you can imagine that when I saw the Palo Alto area code phone number pop up on my cell phone that Saturday morning I was excited that it might be Stanford.

I was sitting in the living room catching up with my parents, and then I quickly walked to the bedroom to answer the phone call, in private. It was Paula Moya, who is an English professor at Stanford. I knew who she was, since I had applied to work with her, so as soon as she said her name, I knew that it was happening.

I walked towards the window facing the backyard so that I could really listen to what was about to transpire over the phone. She said that the English department was excited to give me admission to its PhD program.

It was a dream come true!

I was at a loss for words but felt an overwhelming sense of joy and excitement that this amazing opportunity was coming my way. I blurted out something about being in San Jose with my family and that I couldn't wait to tell them.

She seemed equally excited to share with me the news and then provided details about an invitation for prospective students to visit the Stanford campus, so I could meet professors from the rest of the department.

Before the phone call ended, I thanked her again and told her that I was looking forward to meeting her and the other PhD prospective students.

She would later become my adviser.

I walked back to the living room and shared with my parents the great news. And of course, I immediately called my brother, *abuela, tios and tias* letting them know as well. It's surprising I didn't tell the whole neighborhood—I was that excited.

That was one of my happiest moments.

I know you and your family have a close relationship, what was it like for them to learn you were admitted into Stanford?

They were so happy to hear this amazing news!

You're right that I do come from a close-knit Mexican family. My dad is from Jalisco and my mom is from Durango, and while they did not have the chance to attend college here in the U.S., they did stress the importance of education while my brother and I grew up in Salinas, California. Education for us held the promise of a better life. So, when I told them that I was accepted into Stanford that felt like a big win for the entire family. I remember seeing the biggest smiles on their faces, and I think we did a little dance in the living room to celebrate before I started calling people.

I called my brother who was attending law school at Georgetown at the time. We've always been close—ever since we were young we shared a common interest in books, history, and college, and he was technically the first English major in the family, so he totally appreciated the nature of what I was about to pursue.

Soon after, I notified the rest of my extended Mexican family. I have the kind of family that likes to celebrate each other's big moments and successes. From First Communions to graduations. We show each other support, and a *carne asada* is almost always involved in the celebration.

I remember when I went off to college my aunts gave me a new piece of luggage and a winter coat because they were excited for me and the new stage in my life. I guess they also foresaw a lot of traveling, which they weren't wrong about.

Another moment that comes to mind is when my uncle helped me move into my first college apartment by transporting my mattress in his large white truck.

But my best memory of my family while at Stanford has to be when they came to my PhD graduation. They came from New York, Southern California, and San Jose to celebrate an achievement that I could have not done without their love and support.

I am sure that by applying to attend Stanford you must have believed in your qualifications enough to have actually applied.

But did you *really* think you would be accepted?

I didn't have the, "I have to get into Stanford," mentality.

As an undergraduate who already had the experience of applying to college, I knew that getting into a top graduate program was competitive. But I did feel confident about at least giving it a shot.

I also had the example of my older brother who went to law school to pursue his dreams. And though my parents were not familiar with the U.S. university system, they always supported our aspirations.

When I decided that I was going to apply to Stanford I really didn't know what my odds were. However, I did know that I felt prepared enough to apply and that there was something special about that campus that felt right to me.

When I visited the campus and walked around the arcades of the main quad or by the White Plaza fountain, I remember imagining myself sitting at one of the benches in front of Stanford's Old Union building and meeting with a professor to talk about an assignment or a book.

I could really see myself going there. Whether it was a gut instinct or me trying to motivate myself, I simply had a vision of what I wanted for myself.

I simply thought, "Maybe I could do this?"

I also credit my time at Berkeley for giving me that confidence to apply. I double majored in English and Political Science and was exposed to undergraduate research early on when I worked with a Sociology professor during my sophomore year.

It wasn't until I was accepted into the Ronald E. McNair scholars program—a federal TRIO program for underrepresented students interested in pursuing a PhD—that I started thinking about conducting research in literary studies.

Thanks to that program, and the English professors I worked with, I was able to dive into the field of American literature, Chicano literature, and theories of modernism and the avant-garde when I compared and analyzed the works of Mexican-American author Tomás Rivera and the Irish author James Joyce.

The McNair program also prepared me to apply to graduate school—from writing a personal statement to preparing a writing sample for the graduate school application. By the beginning of my senior year at Berkeley, I was meeting with my English professors to talk about my graduate school plans and senior thesis.

It's amazing to look back at how influential the McNair program was in my trajectory and in giving me the imagination to even consider a doctorate degree.

Oftentimes children have a clear idea of what they want to be in life and everything else that pertains to it. Some at a very young age even wear clothing with the name of a specific college.

Were you one of those kids?

Was it always your idea to attend Stanford?

I was definitely not one of those kids. While my parents talked about the importance of doing well in school, we never talked about universities and their rankings. I think that is very common for first-generation college students. In a way, this worked to my advantage because I didn't have that pressure of only imagining one specific school or pursuing one specific path.

I think that would have been too much pressure—to fixate on only elite colleges from a young age.

Not being groomed from the beginning for elite colleges gave me the liberty and self-motivation to eventually pursue this path on my own.

As a young girl, I only had a sense that I wanted to go to college because I wanted to explore the world outside of Salinas and also build a better future for myself and my family. My older brother, who was the first one to attend college at Berkeley, created that path towards higher education and upward mobility in our family and I continue to admire him for that pioneering sensibility.

When I was trying to figure out my own path towards college in the beginning of high school, I had told myself that the answer was somehow in reading books. I didn't think about the kinds of books or why that was a good strategy, but it just made sense to me that the more books I read, the better.

Not exactly the kind of college prep strategy that you would find in *The Princeton Review*, but I felt compelled nonetheless to read as many books that I could get my hands on. My specific plan was to try to read 100 pages a day. It was a big goal but I knew that I needed to challenge myself and go after, what seemed at the time, a far-reaching goal.

I started reading the canonical works, from Shakespeare and Herman Melville, to Harper Lee and Toni Morrison. I loved it. I also read anything else I found at the local library, including magazines like *Vanity Fair*, *Rolling Stone*, and *YM* (hey, I was still a teen!). I just wanted to read. And not surprisingly, my writing improved and I started to receive high marks on my English papers.

I also started doing well in my other classes. With literature, I had found something that I was passionate about, and it was the perfect outlet for me as a teen since reading had allowed me to see different worlds and learn about different life paths that I didn't get to see while growing up in Salinas.

I also loved that while I came from a background that was vastly different from those belonging to the characters I read about, I could sometimes relate and find shared experiences. Though I was certainly far from the English countryside, I appreciated reading about witty and brainy female characters, such as Jane Austen's Elizabeth Bennet, who continues to be one of my favorite heroines.

As for careers, I remember wanting to be a journalist because I thought it would be great to travel the world and interview people from all different walks of life. I had written to the local news station asking if I could meet and shadow KSBW news anchorwoman, Dina Ruiz. I never received a response.

She was my favorite after Barbara Walters, and I later found out that she eventually stopped working at the station because she ended up marrying the actor Clint Eastwood who lived in Carmel. So, that was a bummer.

I still thought about journalism when I attended Berkeley and wrote for the school newspaper about diversity issues in higher education and about what had happened to the UC university system, after the passing of Proposition 209. Writing those articles brought me closer to highly contested political debates, which I enjoyed, but my passion for literature returned when I started exploring undergraduate research as part of the McNair program.

After that, I decided that I would pursue my PhD and become an English professor.

I loved the idea that I could share with others my passion for books and also show them how much we can learn by reading about other people's experiences and stories and what they tell us about the general human experience.

My career plans started to shift toward the end of graduate school, however. In your twenties, you learn more about yourself and the kind of lifestyle that you'd want to lead. Additionally, my father had lost his battle with ALS (a terminal neurodegenerative disease, also known as Lou Gehrig's) during that time, and so that also made me reflect on what I wanted out of life.

I began to wonder if the tenure-track professor career was something that I wanted. I had missed the political activism that I enjoyed in college, and I was gravitating towards outreach and diversity work towards the end of my program.

Also, I would later learn that there was a general wave of graduate students in the humanities exploring alternative careers outside of academia during that time.

After graduating from Stanford and teaching as an adjunct lecturer at a local college, and also conducting multiple informational interviews in different fields, I decided to fully explore diversity and, inclusion, work in higher education.

I'm currently the director of a diversity undergraduate research program at Stanford, where I meet many wonderful students, and I continue to see the impact that such programs have on the career and lives of these young people.

What I have begun to learn in my thirties that I wish I knew in my twenties is that career paths are not linear; they take turns, and it is important to learn from each stage in your career.

I may return to teaching one day, but for now, I'd like to help make an impact in the field of diversity within higher education so that we can continue to bring the legacy of the civil rights movement well into the 21st century.

I think about 4.8% of applicants that apply are actually the ones admitted into Stanford University.

That's a very low number and a very big milestone for anyone who gets accepted.

Having experienced that, what do you recommend we should do to try to achieve our goals, even when they seem impossible to achieve?

I would focus less on how difficult or impossible it is to be admitted and more on what you need to do in order to achieve your goal.

I was not aware what the percentage amount was for students who received admission into Stanford—partly because the percentage rates for the graduate PhD program vary based on discipline and cohort size.

What I did know was that Stanford was one of the top three programs in English at the time and that I needed to excel in every way I could in order to have a chance to be considered.

I studied for the GRE, particularly the verbal section. I wrote at least ten drafts of my personal statement, I had my graduate student mentors read my writing sample, and I met with my recommenders to share with them my research interests and career aspirations.

It is important to learn how to talk to others about your goals and where you want to go. For me, as someone who doesn't love networking, I had to develop this skill. And it doesn't even have to be networking in the business kind of sense but more learning how to genuinely connect with people who would be open to helping you on your journey.

I remember as an undergraduate having a conversation with my Victorian Literature English professor at Berkeley about my desire to learn more about Mexican-American writers. Sharing this turned out to be serendipitous since his friend from his graduate school days at Yale was Ramón Saldívar, one of the pioneers of Mexican-American literary criticism.

He wrote a book on Chicano narrative and had been teaching at Stanford.

I mention this story because these are the types of conversations that I tell my students that they should be having with their professors to see how they can learn more about the research communities that they would like to enter.

Also, I recommend students talk with university student services staff—their job is to help them figure out any unknown written rules or processes of applying to graduate school.

For instance, I tell my students that on that fateful trip to Stanford (where I started to imagine myself there) it also included my first meeting with Ramón Saldívar, in which I expressed my interest in his research and also gave him a copy of my honors thesis.

One could say that it was "strategic," but it was just logical for me that if I really wanted to attend graduate school there, I needed to meet professors and learn more about them.

Overall, putting yourself out there and reaching out to folks that you'd like to potentially work with makes a difference.

And finally, just trust that you did everything that you could to work towards that goal and relax.

Let the rest unfold.

I tend to think that we move to the next stage in our life or achieve a goal when we are ready for it.

We can't control the outcome of anything, so the best thing we can do is to learn from the experience, whatever the outcome may be.

What was your favorite part about attending Stanford?

Least favorite part?

Do you have an anecdote of your time there that you want to share?

I have many great memories.

As much as I have stories of the challenges involved in getting through a PhD program, I have even more stories on why I continue to treasure this period of my life.

The graduate seminars in the Stanford English department were intellectually stimulating, and the mentorship and training that I received from my advisers and professors were priceless as it continues to impact the way I write and think.

I also have life-long friends who are equally nerdy about books as I am, so that's irreplaceable.

To give you an idea, I went to the Joyce Bloomsday festival one year in Dublin with another friend just because we loved *Ulysses* so much. Even the customs officer at the airport was surprised at our reason for travel.

Some of my favorite memories include spending an entire day deciphering a chapter from Hegel's *Phenomenology of Spirit* with my classmate at the time, who is now one of my best friends. We bonded over us wanting to understand such a difficult but brilliant text.

"Who knew that the Hegelian dialectic would lead to a long sisterhood?"

I also credit Stanford for opening up the world to me, as I had many opportunities to travel and present my work at academic conferences with my professors and classmates.

During my second year in grad school, I had the chance to travel to Europe for the first time. As part of the program, we were required to learn a second language, and our department provided funding to study abroad. I decided I would learn French, so I enrolled in a summer language program in Montpellier with a group of friends.

We lived in that southern French town for a month, and though that wasn't enough to learn a new language, I got to meet people from all over the world and live in a place outside of California.

That trip also sparked my love for travel and adventure.

But, I have to say, one of the best memories that continues to come to mind is move-in day. Arriving to the Rains graduate student housing complex as a 21-year-old, meeting other students, and having my parents there, helping me move in and start an exciting chapter in my life, is an image that I won't ever forget.

I'm really grateful for that memory and for the other great experiences I've had.

As an alumni, what do you think we should know about Stanford?

What were the best lessons that you learned at Stanford that weren't taught in a classroom?

I learned the best lessons outside the classroom.

Pursuing a PhD is a marathon and difficult for most students since research forces students to become producers of knowledge, which requires expertise and also a sense of ownership over that expertise.

It's a major shift from the undergraduate experience where students are expected to absorb and relay knowledge.

As a Latina, I was grateful to have worked with both Paula Moya and Michele Elam, both English professors at Stanford who modeled what it was like to be a woman of color, intellectual and a knowledge-producer.

Living in a world where we don't see a variety of representation of women of color depicted in mainstream media, it was important for me to have role models.

I also learned that it is important to be internally driven when you become a graduate student.

Looking back, I did well in high school and in college because I was a "good student" and did everything that the teacher or professor expected.

I received a lot of satisfaction from turning excellent work and receiving praise for it.

Perhaps this stems back to the day when I received high marks on my high school English papers, and my teacher had said I was a good writer.

That kind of validation propelled me to do even better.

I want to share this story with students because there is a point in graduate school or just in one's general maturation as an adult where relying on encouragement or positive feedback will no longer be productive. If the quest is to continue growing and learning—which is what becoming a good scholar and researcher is all about—then looking for validation from others for approval will stymie that process.

I learned that when writing a dissertation. The first drafts will most likely not be excellent, and you will come across challenges and failures when completing such a lofty project.

For this reason, internal motivation—wanting to do better for yourself and for your own growth—is the best type of guidance you can have while writing or attempting to achieve something difficult.

Graduate school (especially if you are in your twenties, like I was) should be about learning how to pursue your goals and overcome setbacks that will inevitably arise by using your own internal compass while also hearing feedback from others. Some questions that you could ask yourself are:

"Why is this work important to you?"

"Why do you want to accomplish it and for what purpose?"

"What steps do you need to take to reach your goal?"

"Did you put in the work and ask for help when you needed it?"

"Though it's not perfect, did you do your best?"

While it is great when our teachers and advisers can provide encouragement and express praise of our work (when we've done a good job) it is imperative that these external reasons are not the main motivator.

Having your own set of expectations, knowing when to ask for help, and being open to learning and growing as a way to achieve your goals have been a powerful concept for me that I learned in graduate school and that I continue to practice today.

Other advice, I would give young students about to pursue academia is to be more self-accepting of your own particular background, especially if you come from a background that doesn't "fit the mold" of what we think of as, intellectuals, scientists, researchers, professors, writers, etc. (even though we know that what we think of as "the mold" is a social construction).

During the first few years of graduate school, I was struggling with how to balance family responsibilities with academic obligations as my father was battling with ALS.

My parents had eventually moved from Salinas to San Jose, so when I started Stanford, I was only a short car ride away from visiting him.

I would be reading Immanuel Kant for a grad seminar, one day, and then visiting East San Jose during the weekends so I could go on walks with my father around Lake Cunningham.

Or, I would be setting up appointments with professors to visit them during office hours, while also setting up appointments to see doctors at UCSF.

During that time, my intellectual and emotional energies were very much split between two very disparate worlds.

I then became worried that because of my atypical graduate school experience I wasn't quite fitting in and would be at a disadvantage for not being completely immersed in the world of literature and literary theory.

But then, I quickly realized, that I didn't have to see those experiences of not completely fitting in, that were probably common to many people, in a negative light.

As my friend once told me, I didn't have to "knock-it."

No one really has a typical educational track or career track anyways.

Additionally, I also felt empowered when I started looking for the advantages that do come from learning how to be resilient and resourceful in the face of challenges. And I learned how to engage with different communities and social spaces.

Whether you're a daughter of immigrants, first-gen student or hail from another diverse background, you're in a position to contribute to these academic, intellectual spaces in very unique ways since these points of views are often underrepresented.

Also, realizing that I am part of a small percentage of Latinas who have a PhD motivates me to share the knowledge that I learned while in graduate school and to continue to create opportunities for the next generation.

The more self-accepting I became of my own path, the easier it was for me to focus on the goals that I wanted to achieve and to think about how I wanted to make an impact in the world.

This book although intended for everyone, the theme of it is 30. Where were you at 30-years-old, where were you living and what stage of your life were you in?

What advice do you have for those of us turning 30 this year?

At 30 I had my PhD in tow and was teaching an Asian-American literature course at a local community college and also working in outreach and diversity.

I was in the midst of shaping the next phase of my career and deciding what I was going to do with my degree. You think that by then you have everything figured out, but really you only continue to learn and grow.

What I did "know for sure," as Oprah would say, is that I was going to enjoy my 30's. I had been a very studious person in my 20's so I was looking forward to taking a step back and enjoy myself and what life has given me so far.

Now, I have more of a work-life balance, and I also travel for fun. I even started a travel blog to document my adventures.

If I were to give advice to my younger self (or someone turning 30), I think I would tell her that, she's going to be fine.

Relax, enjoy, love, be grateful, and embrace what life throws your way so you can make something great out of it.

You got this.

Thank you!!

STAFF SERGEANT NELSON BENAVIDES
STAFF SERGEANT JEEANDY MORALES
STAFF SERGEANT JOSEPH NINO

CALIFORNIA, USA

---

*Staff Sergeant Nelson Benavides is author's brother.

*Staff Sergeants often mention, Abitu, Real and TG. They are referring to colleagues/friends of theirs.

All 3 of you are veterans of the Iraq War.

Did you ever think you would become soldiers and possibly even veterans?

When did you get your orders?

N.Benavides: We got orders to deploy from 2007-2008.

N.Benavides: I always liked discipline and structure, but I never thought about becoming a soldier much less a veteran.

N.Benavides: It started with my parents and grandparents instilling in us, respect for our elders. Then joining the Boy Scouts and learning a sense of patriotism for our country and finally, joining the Police Explorers where I learned discipline and structure.

J. Morales: Yes, since I was little I always knew I would join some branch of service. I initially wanted to join the Marines.

J.Nino: No, I never thought I would become a veteran.

Sacrifice, Selflessness, Courage.

Those are some words that are often accompanied by the word, soldier.

What does being a soldier, mean to you?

N.Benavides: Unlike our past troops from past wars, we weren't drafted. So, being a soldier was our choice. To me being a soldier is no different than choosing to do any other job. It obviously has a different job description but it is still, a job.

N.Benavides: However, I hold a lot of pride in having been a soldier because not every job requires you to raise your right hand and pledge an oath. ("I, Nelson Benavides, do solemnly swear that I will support and defend the Constitution of the United States and against all enemies, foreign and domestic; that I will bear true faith and allegiance to the same; and that I will obey all orders of the President of the United States and the orders of the officers appointed over me, according to the regulations and the Uniform Code of Military Justice. So help me God!")

N.Benavides: It's an oath that I take very seriously. Especially because it asks God for help.

N.Benavides: It's a hard and humble job. One does not join the military because of the money, because military personnel do not get paid a lot. I like it, because of the brotherhood that exists in the military. It really sounds cliché and something everyone says, but I find it to be true. Being a soldier means you represent the U.S. as a whole.

J. Morales: Someone who is willing to go above and beyond. A regular citizen that has a love for service, that is willing to do anything for their country, their community and even for people they don't know. They would be willing to leave their family and friends and go to the unknown.

J. Morales: The word solider to me, means a lot of different things.

J.Nino: Protecting the freedom of my fellow countrymen.

You could have been anything you wanted to be, other than a solider. A couple of you were in college before you enlisted, which meant you might have been on the road to a perhaps safer profession.

And some of you enlisted right out of high school, also with the possibility of choosing a safer, more traditional career.

But instead, you chose to be apart of our military.

There must have been a strong desire that inclined you towards this.

What was it?

N.Benavides: I joined the military while I was attending community college. College was fun, but I wanted to do a little more than just that. It was kind of boring to me. I have never been someone who can just sit in a classroom for many hours at a time. The military sounded a bit fun and challenging.

J. Morales: The urge was to serve my country. When I was a young boy along with Nelson, I served my community as a Police Explorer and volunteered within my community. I went to college, I graduated from Orange Coast College with an associates degree, then I transferred to Cal State Fullerton and received my bachelors—I have since started my masters degree.

J.Morales: Being a solider and being in the military was always on my mind. Whether 9/11 and everything else that happened, had happened or not, I would have still joined the military.

J.Nino: Well, several factors inclined me to join. Since high school, I knew that I wanted to enter the career field of law enforcement. I looked at many options at getting me ready for the field. One, of course, was going to college. But unfortunately, we grew up poor, so money for college was hard to come by. I worked but didn't make enough to pay for tuition.

J.Nino: Joining the military was always an option for me since 9/11. So, I decided to join. I knew by joining, it would instill discipline in me, strengthen my values, prepare me for a career in law enforcement, and of course pay for college.

You don't just have that in common (having chosen the military as your career of choice) but you also chose the Army as your military of choice.

There are other choices within the armed forces of our country like the Marines, National Guard, Air Force, Navy and Coast Guard.

Why did you feel, you belonged in the Army?

N.Benavides: I was first interested in the Marines and tested with them. I wanted the military police job with them but they wouldn't promise me that I would get it.

N.Benavides: I had a few friends who were already in the Marines, and they advised me not to join because it wasn't all that it was led-up to be. I also knew a Police Explorer adviser who was in the Army; he gave me his advice too. All those incidents helped me decide on joining the Army instead.

J. Morales: Originally, I always wanted to join the Marine Corps. I was going to join the Marines but while I was there talking to the recruiter, he wasn't being completely honest with my job choice. The next office over was the Army's, I guess it was meant to be because I then joined the Army right away.

J.Nino: I believe the best answer to this is fate. Fate led me to join the Army. Law enforcement for me has always been a career choice (well since my senior year).

J.Nino: I actually went to talk to a Marine Corps recruiter and told them I wanted to be a military police officer with them. They told me I was *too* young to be an MP and that it would be best for me to join the infantry and when I turned 21, I could become an MP. Of course, that's not what I wanted, so I respectfully declined.

J.Nino: The funny thing is that when I went to talk to an Army recruiter; I told them I wanted to join the infantry. The recruiter knew I wanted to be a law enforcement officer and suggested I become an MP with the Army. So, I joined the Army instead of the Marine Corps because I felt that the Marine Corps wanted to give me a job that *they* wanted instead of what I wanted. The Army off the bat gave me the job I wanted.

At the moment of your enlistment, our country was at war with Afghanistan. This was the first war that our generations, yours and mine—children born in the late 80's had ever experienced in our lifetime.

War, recession, extreme, terrorist attacks in our own territory, were new to us. We had heard about all about that in our history class, but we had never actually experienced it ourselves.

Even then, you chose to join the Army, knowing you could be sent to war and most likely would be sent.

That's a pretty big deal and a fact that would detour many of us from deciding to go forth with a decision like that.

But you, on the contrary, continued with your enlistment.

Why?

N.Benavides: I enlisted at 20-years-old. I was out of high school and a bit less prone to peer pressure from recruiters. I knew, sooner, or later, I may be sent to war. But that wasn't a top issue on my mind.

N.Benavides: If, and, when that time came, I would deal with it.

J. Morales: I already had it set in my mind that I was going to join the military of some sort of branch, regardless. Despite knowing that it was a possibility (a very high possibility) of going to war since it was already in my mind, I was prepared in that sense. It wasn't a big deal to me.

J. Morales: What is funny is that when everyone got their orders to go to Iraq I was actually non-deployable. I was in college at Cal State Fullerton and I was in the Reserve Officers' Training Corps program (ROTC). A program that helps develop soldiers into officers in the military. But when I found out Nelson was going to be sent to Iraq, I actually quit school and volunteered to go to Iraq even though I didn't have to go. Just because Nelson was going to be sent, I felt that I had to go. We both were Police Explorers together and we both joined the Army together. I felt that since we joined together, I had to go.

J.Nino: I wanted to serve my country. And after seeing the attacks, it motivated me to join.

J.Nino: During the Afghan War, I watched the news every day, I watched the progress the military was doing in the invasion of Afghanistan. Watching it made me want to be there and take part of that campaign. So when I joined, I knew that being sent to war would happen. People that join the military should expect to go to war, it's like becoming a chef and expecting to never cook (laughs).

Little boys and girls, little boys in particular, grow up watching superheroes that have a certain type of superpower and with that superpower, they go around saving the world.

Veterans sound like superheroes to me, except better because they don't have superpowers.

Do you think that influenced you, superheroes?

N.Benavides: No, that never influenced me. Like you said, "That's just little kid stuff." After a while, you realize those types of superheroes don't really exist.

N.Benavides: Life is much different from TV superheroes.

J.Morales: Personally I never watched cartoons, I was a strange kid (laughs). I was never into cartoons, or superheroes or anything like that. I have always been into comedies and just regular movies. But I can imagine superheroes and video games, now-a-days, is a somewhat of an influence for kids. But personally it was never the case for me.

J.Nino: Yes, movies like *Lord of the Rings* inspired me, as well as *Batman*. Good people fighting evil to protect humanity.

Do you have a favorite superhero?

If so, which one is your favorite and why?

N.Benavides: I like Batman because he doesn't have "powers."

N.Benavides: He's a guy who saw his community going south and took it upon himself to do something about it. A lot of people see their community plagued with violence, and crime but stay back and don't do anything to fix the problem. They just talk and complain but offer no real solution to fix it.

N.Benavides: Batman took the initiative and used his resources to make his community better.

J.Morales: I never grew up with superheros, at all. But my son loves Batman, so now all of a sudden I am a Batman fan, because my son likes him. But I never grew up liking any superhero.

J.Nino: It's between Batman and Iron Man. If you look at them, they're both the same—billionaire playboy's who help fight against evil and protect the public rather than enjoy being billionaires and spend their money.

The start of the Afghanistan War was also the era when a lot of us truly first experienced patriotism. It seems like in many ways we had never stopped being patriotic, but when we were at war, that's when we heard phrases like, "Support our troops" and similar ones to that, more than ever.

What does patriotism mean to you?

And, why is it important for our country to be patriotic?

N.Benavides: Patriotism is always supporting your country and letting the world know you do. Other nations like Japan, Germany, Mexico, Italy, etc., show a lot of patriotism to their respective countries.

N.Benavides: Every country has its issues but the US is probably the one with the least, or the one with the issues that people will deal with. I never understand protesters burning the American flag or saying, "This country is horrible." Yet, they still live here. It's not that hard, or expensive to denounce your American citizenship but those people won't do it.

N.Benavides: It's super important for our country to show patriotism because we can show our younger generations. "Imagine what our World War II generation would think of, of all this nonsense going on now?" If we stop being patriots our younger generation will truly feel and think this country isn't the greatest.

J.Morales: Being patriotic to me means that you literally would die for your country. I personally am EXTREMELY, extremely patriotic. I am the type of person that has American flags on my truck. I have a 9 foot American flag in front of my door. I teach my kids every time they see the flag, they should salute it. Its a sign of respect.

J.Morales: A lot of people die for our freedom.

J.Morales: If you are willing to die for your country, if you're willing to support the people who die for your country, that's what being patriotic means to me. You don't have to join the military to be patriotic, just support it.

J.Nino: Having pride in your country and your flag. Respecting the flag and national anthem. Loving the colors of the flag.

J.Nino: Defending your country as well.

J.Nino: It's important to have patriotism because we're the best country in the world. People who have never been to a Third World country or a country where their citizens are oppressed will never know the true definition of freedom.

As I just mentioned, war was new to our generations. I still remember the start to it. To really put things into perspective, I'll mention that, I was in 8th grade when war was declared by our then 43rd president—George W. Bush.

After that, it seemed like we had actually stepped back into the past and into what we had read in our textbooks.

During a time when we were experiencing so much uncertainty, how did you find the courage to tell your loved ones, like your mothers, fathers, siblings and even girlfriends, you were joining the Army?

N.Benavides: I remember telling my mom that I was going to join and that the recruiter was going to come to our house. When the recruiter came, he also spoke to my dad. I think I did that out of respect because I was already an adult and I didn't need their consent to join.

N.Benavides: At the point, I had already decided that I was going to join, so, my mind was already made-up.

J.Morales: I have always been very independent. I have been working since I was 14-years-old, at 15, I worked at McDonald's. I have always been very independent and that was something my mom was scared of because she has always known that if I set my mind on something, I will do it. And when I was 17-years-old, I told my mom I was going to join the military. She didn't completely understand me.

J.Morales: She was a Cuban refugee when she came over here. She didn't understand why I wanted to join the Army. But years later, when she saw how important it was for me and what it meant to me, she learned to understand me and support me.

J.Nino: It was hard, especially being the only son. When I signed the contract, I was gone all day. I remember calling my family and telling them that I wanted a family meeting when I got home. When I got home I remember placing my contract on the table and telling my family, "I joined the Army, and I leave for basic training in two weeks."

J.Nino: I knew it would crush their hearts, but they needed to understand it was something I wanted to do and something that would benefit me in the future.

Some of you are the only males in your family—other than your fathers.

How did your family react?

N.Benavides: I think they didn't want me to join and they were nervous. I don't remember. But being that we are Mexican they probably thought it was a horrible idea and that they would never see me again.

J. Morales: My family has two boys, my older brother and myself. But at that time, my older brother was just starting his family in Louisiana. So, I was the only boy at home with my mom. I actually never, ever, told my mom that I volunteered until after I came back from Iraq. Just in case something would have happened (while I was away), I wanted her to be confident, thinking I hadn't had a choice. If something would have happened, she would have been okay with that.

J. Morales: Essentially we all volunteered to join the Army but as far as the deployment goes, I volunteered. But I didn't tell anyone that I volunteered. I didn't want anyone to be upset or be sad.

J. Morales: But my mom was very sad and she couldn't sleep. It was tough on her. One of the lady's that went to church with us, her son—I cant remember his name—was also in the Army. My mom told her that I was leaving to Iraq and that same week that we were leaving to Iraq her son was supposed to be coming home to visit. But at that time the lady found out her son had passed, he had died. So, my mom freaked out.

J.Nino: They were sad, but they supported me. The one who took it the hardest was my mom. She fell into a depression when I left for basic training.

Eventually, the time came when you were given orders of your deployment to war. By then it wasn't the Afghanistan War but the Iraq War.

Do you remember the day when you received your orders?

N.Benavides: Yes, I was at work, and I received a phone call from a Sergeant saying he was with the, "56th Military Police Company," and he was about to read me the orders. He read my orders to go to Iraq.

N.Benavides: At first, I got excited and nervous. I told my boss, and I called my girlfriend. Then I thought about my parents, and I got really sad and nervous to tell them. I couldn't find the way to let them know. So, my big sister Beatrice (we call her Betty) offered to tell them for me.

J.Morales: I actually remember being in Costa Mesa, on Harbor and Newport, right were Triangle Square is, I was at a shoe store. I got a phone call, I think it was from Nelson telling me he got the orders and that's when I decided I was going too. I was 22-years-old.

J.Nino: I remember like if it were yesterday (laughs). I remember your brother and Abitu telling me that the unit had called them informing them of their orders.

J.Nino: I guess they were going by alphabetical order. Of course, me being impatient, contacted the unit to see if I was on the list and sure thing I was. A few minutes after calling, I received, "the call." And shortly after, I called my sister Maciel and broke the news to her first. I asked her to help me tell the rest of the family because I knew they wouldn't take it so lightly.

It seems to me that fear isn't your thing. But ultimately you are human beings and not fictional superheroes like I keep referring to you as, which means you aren't excluded from feeling rational emotions like fear and worry...etc.

Did you ever feel any of those?

N.Benavides: Yes. I had never been to war, or knew what to expect. Fear was there but having my buddies next to me and knowing they too, had never been to war and knowing this was the first time for all of us, made me feel better.

N.Benavides: I think none of us let fear take over our emotions, or let fear obstruct us from doing our jobs. Fear was there but in the back of our heads.

J.Morales: To be completely honest, I was never scared or worried. We had such a tight support system and we were all there for each other. I always felt comfortable and I always accepted the possibility that anything could happen.

J.Morales: I never experienced those feelings until after I came back. Now I think back and I think, "Wow, this could have happened." And now I get scared but when I was there it didn't bother me.

J.Nino: Of course, I did. Like you said, "I'm a human being." Any person that denies feeling fear or worry is a liar. Everyone feels fear and worry. There have been plenty of times when I have felt those feelings. "And in Iraq? Absolutely!"

J.Nino: In the military we have a term called, "pucker effect." The best way to describe it is when you're so scared, your buttocks tighten, you get this weird feeling in your stomach, and you feel like you have to go, "number 2." In other words you're scared, shitless!

J.Nino: I felt like that one day when we were tasked to visit an Iraqi Police Station far from our usual zones we would be in. We were going into the unknown, and that caused fear because anything could have gone wrong.

How old were you when you received orders of your deployment to Iraq?

N.Benavides: I believe I was 23-years-old.

J.Morales: I was 22-years-old.

J.Nino: I was 21 when I received my orders.

Up until then, the 3 of you, had pretty ordinary, "normal lives." Aside from working for the Army either as active duty members, or as reserved. Just like everyone else, you enjoyed what most of us do, watch movies, go out to dinner, spend time with loved ones and so forth.

But all of that would be paused for you.

Even the simplest of them, like waking up at home with your family.

How did you prepare for that?

N.Benavides: I don't think I prepared for that, I just went with it day-by-day.

N.Benavides: During the day we did our jobs and when we had downtime we would hang out with our buddies and talk (mostly joke around). We called home when we could and would get news, then.

J.Morales: I don't think its possible to prepare for it. I just think you have to understand that you're going to have do it. You just have to do it and assimilate to the situation of wherever you're at. I don't think you can mentality prepare for something like that, especially if you have never experienced something like that.

When we watch movies based on war/soldiers, everything happens so fast. It seems as if the orders are given, and then you are sent to war.

It also seems as if, you are provided with very little training, and truthfully, it seems alarming. I am assuming it isn't that fast, considering

movies have about 2 hours to tell their story. And more importantly, considering the U.S. Military is known for being one of the most competent in the world.

Can you tell me how much training is actually provided?

N.Benavides: We had a lot of training, 12+ hours of it, almost every day. It was at places that the military creates that allow us to feel as if we were in Iraq.

N.Benavides: If the military is not at war, they're training. So, training is your job until you get sent off to war.

J.Morales: When we found out we got orders we actually went from Orange County (California) to Mesa, Arizona. In Mesa, Arizona we were there for about 3 weeks. From Mesa, Arizona, we went to Fort Dix, New Jersey, we spent months there (about 3 months). We were just training and training.

J.Morales: Once we finally landed in Iraq we were very well-trained and very prepared.

J.Nino: A lot of training was provided. Before getting to Iraq, we have to do what is called, "Mobilization Training." It's basically training that will mentally and physically prepare us for what's ahead; in other words, war. I believe we spent 2-3 months training in Fort Dix getting ready for Iraq.

How is packing for a trip like that?

Are you allowed to pack anything you need?

N.Benavides: The Army gave us all the gear we needed, and we could pack some personal items too—laptops, DVD players—stuff like that. A lot of us didn't pack a lot of personal items. We either had them mailed to us, or brought some stuff over with us.

J.Morales: Besides all of our uniforms and gear, some of us brought computers, movies, hard drives…etc. I pretty much took whatever I wanted.

J.Nino: It's a stressful task!

J.Nino: I've learned to be a good packer and also hate it at the same time. The number one thing to take, of course, is all of your military gear. The rest are, of course, toiletry items, a laptop with a hard drive loaded with movies, music, pictures, etc.

J.Nino: And snacks. Snacks, or as we refer to it as, "pogey bait," is a must, as well.

What did you pack that was special to you?

N.Benavides: I had a rosary and other religious items my family had given me. I took a religious necklace my mom took off and gave to me at the airport.

N.Benavides: 10-years-later, I still have it on.

J.Morales: Pictures.

J.Nino: A picture of my family and my religious items like a rosary, novenas, etc.

You finally landed in Iraq, after how many hours?

N.Benavides: I don't recall; I believe it was like 16 hours.

J.Morales: We were traveling for days, from New Jersey we had to fly to Kuwait and that took forever. From Kuwait we stayed there a few days, or a week, I cant really remember (it was over a decade ago). But then from Kuwait we landed in Iraq.

J.Nino: I believe it was a 2-hour flight from Kuwait to Iraq.

The 3 of you, were in the same unit, did you get to fly together?

N.Benavides: No, I was sent separately because I had surgery while on leave. So, I was sent back while the others were in Kuwait.

J.Morales: We were mainly together in the beginning, then we got separated. TG, Real and I were together. Nino and Nelson were in the same base, together.

J.Nino: No, we didn't fly-in together. I don't know if your brother told you, but he and I stayed back due to medical reasons. We met with the rest of the unit in Iraq about a month after they left.

Does the military have its own airplanes?

And does this mean, you fly to the destinations where you are needed, in military-owned and operated planes?

N.Benavides: Yes, the military has its own planes. Mostly owned by the Air Force. The other branches have aircraft's too but different types and for different jobs. The military fly all over the world and land in its territories, or where allied countries allow us to.

J.Morales: I remember flying in a separate commercial airplane to our trip to New Jersey. But from New Jersey to Kuwait we flew in Air Force airplanes.

J.Nino: The military does have its own planes. As a matter of fact, the Air Force is the branch that gave us "a ride" to Iraq from Kuwait. However, the military does contract commercial airlines to fly us from the U.S. to other bases in Europe.

You finally arrived to Iraq—for the first-time for all 3 of you. Not only for the first-time to Iraq but to the Middle East as well.

You were coming from cities like Anaheim, Costa Mesa and Santa Clarita. For the most part, safe, diverse, and all-American cities of Southern California.

I am sure you had studied the geography heavily before relocating there but how different was the reality from what you had envisioned?

N.Benavides: I didn't study it *that* much. I imagined the Middle East looked like it did in movies, with dunes, and camels everywhere.

N.Benavides: Tikrit, Iraq was not like that. It looked like the deserts of California and Mexico. To me it looked like driving through Mexico with all the food stands, and people off the highway.

J.Morales: We would always look at a lot of pictures of it.

J.Morales: I would compare it a lot to Mexico, that's pretty much how it looked—well some parts of Mexico—like the poorer parts of Mexico. It was more like that. But I had a good idea of how it looked like.

J.Nino: So, it's quite funny you ask. I thought it was going to be different, but in reality it looked a bit like Mexico (laughs), it reminded me of Mexico. The small *pueblos*.

California is known to have great weather. Even when temperatures are not *that* hot, or *that* cold, for us Californians, it is.

How was the climate assimilation for you while being stationed in Iraq?

How hot/cold does it get?

N.Benavides: During the winter it got really cold for me. A few times a small layer of frost and even snow were on the ground.

N.Benavides: And during the summer it did get pretty hot, like California desert heat, 100+.

N.Benavides: During the winter we layered-up with body thermals. In the summer we couldn't take off gear so we just rolled-up our sleeves, a bit.

J.Morales: Its pretty much a desert, so everything is extreme. It would get *really* hot, like 120-130 degrees but its dry heat so its a lot different from how it is here (California). When it would get cold, it would be freezing cold. I have never been to Afghanistan but I heard it snows there. It also snows in some parts of Iraq.

J.Morales: It gets really cold and extremely hot.

J.Morales: With human beings its really funny, sometimes you could sit there and think you couldn't do that but if you're put into a position where you don't have a choice, as human beings, we assimilate to our surroundings and we are able to do anything, its all in the mind.

J.Nino: It was hot!

J.Nino: If I remember correctly, it was like 120-ish-130-ish. So, it was hot. When it got cold, it got cold as well. It snowed while we were there and I guess they said, it was the first time in 100 years it had snowed.

Aside from the obvious challenges a war zone can have. What are simpler ones, you faced?

Like maybe the shower situation, the beds you slept in, the food?

N.Benavides: About half of us stayed in a big base, and the others stayed in a small outpost. I stayed at a base where we had little, trailer-style-rooms. It was 3-per-room. We had showers, but sometimes the water was turned off, or it only poured out freezing, cold water.

N.Benavides: Food was regular military chow hall food. Stuff, a lot of us had eaten since basic training. So, it gets boring right away. We would either cook our own meals or find something else.

J.Morales: Other than the obvious ones like you said, our food wasn't that great. We did work a lot but there was a lot of down time, if you didn't go to the gym, you would just be sitting there watching a movie.

J.Morales: The communication with our family was very difficult. If someone would die or get hurt, they would shut down all communication for a few hours, until the family would find out, they didn't want us to call anyone and tell anyone before the family of that person found out.

J.Morales: But other than that, people getting hurt, people getting injured.

J.Nino: The living situation was not bad at all. Being in the Army, allows you to adapt to any living conditions. We had these trailers that housed 2-3 soldiers-per-room.

J.Nino: The food was good. The dining facility was open four times a day and had a variety of options from salads, healthy food, a sandwich bar, ice cream bar, fried food, and regular food.

A lot of us that witnessed your journey, saw your relationship go from colleagues to friends, to eventually, like brothers. You were even groomsmen at each other's weddings.

How did it start?

And what was the first reaction you had of one another?

N.Benavides: A few of us already knew each other before Iraq. And me and my buddy (Jeeandy) were in the Police Explorers together (before joining the military).

N.Benavides: We all have friendly attitudes, and we all had one goal in mind, to come back home alive.

N.Benavides: We also, all had, great support group back home. Our siblings and parents were also there for us. And, I believe that's what helped us get closer together. And it helped us while we were there, knowing that our families were also going through a lot but also had each other's backs, like we did in Iraq.

J.Morales: Its funny, I don't exactly remember how we all ended up hanging out together. Nelson and I know each other since before the military, we sort of stuck together.

J.Morales: I remember meeting Nino (Joseph) at the unit but we weren't very close. I think what got me close to Nino, TG and Real was the deployment because I wasn't close to them before that.

J.Nino: Well, it all started when Jeeandy (Morales) first got to the unit, after he graduated. I knew how it felt to be, "the new guy," at the unit. So, I kind of helped him out.

J.Nino: After that, your brother showed up, and the three of us kind of started hanging out. Soon after Abitu showed up and we started hanging out with him too. I believe Real and Torres, we met when we started Mobilizing to Iraq.

J.Nino: "First reaction?" Well to me they seemed, "pretty chill." We were new to the unit and the Army so we kind of hung out together and depended on each other.

Part of the little reunions you had while life on base were your *Menudito* Monday's. But for *Menudito* Monday's to actually happen, you had to be supplied with cans of *menudo*, which meant care packages were really meaningful to you—I am assuming.

Tell me more about that.

Out of the bits and pieces I know of your time there, *Menudito* Monday's really stood out to me.

N.Benavides: Receiving any care package was great because we received stuff that we couldn't get there and it was our little taste of back home. I remember during the Christmas season, my buddy's mom (Nino's) even sent him *tamales*. We all shared food. So, he gave me some.

J.Morales: I was actually separated from them, I wasn't in a big base like Nelson and Nino were. TG, Real and I, were in a really small base, we didn't have a store to buy anything from. We didn't get mail until we went to the big base where everyone was—once a month.

J.Morales: We never had "*Menudo* Monday" or those amenities, we never had the opportunity to have anything like that until we would go visit them

J.Morales: But what I do remember is Real and I had DVDs of the show *Martin* (the Martin Lawrence sitcom) and we would literally watch that all of the time. That's what I remember. I would also workout, we had a little "bunker." A bunker is a place that is underground that we had just in case we got bombed, we had a little gym built there. I would go to the gym after work, take a shower and then go watch *Martin*.

J.Nino: For me, I felt like a little kid getting a Christmas gift every time I received a care package. It was a good feeling

J.Nino: *Menudo* Mondays were great! I loved them! It made you feel like home and miss home (laughs). It's funny because one time my mom sent me corn *tortillas*, oregano, *chile*, and limes. The *tortillas* made a 1-week shipping journey and let me tell you, they were, "soo good."

When I heard there was a Subway restaurant at your base in Iraq, I was surprised.

For people like me that are also learning about your occupation, can you please tell me, what a base is and what your Iraq base had on location, aside from Subway?

N.Benavides: The base I was at used to be an old Iraq airbase, so it was actually a military base. They had Subway, Burger King and I believe, Pizza Hut.

J.Morales: Where I was at, there was nothing. It was a compound in the middle of three cities that surrounded us from different sides. It was literally just a building with dirt all around it. We didn't have anything, anything. But as far as the base where Nelson and Nino were there was a Subway, a pizza place, cafeterias, ice cream, gyms, there was everything. I would only go there once a month.

J.Nino: Well, I guess you can say, "A military base is a functioning city within a fence."

J.Nino: Just think of a city but everyone is in uniform. You have a big store called a "PX" or Post Exchange. It's almost like a big Walmart but for the military. Usually, there are smaller stores on the outside to make it feel like a mall.

J.Nino: There's a food court as well. There's a movie theater, bowling alley, gym, military barracks, tract homes for military members and their families, a big open land where training is conducted, and... much more.

J.Nino: The great thing about the military is that they'll try to make you feel like home in a war zone. The military has a department called, MWR (Morale, Welfare, and Recreation). They're in charge of operating the gyms, movie theaters and of hosting events.

J.Nino: The base in Iraq had a gym, a small PX, Subway, Green Beans Coffee, Pizza Hut, Cinnabon, and Burger King. Of course, the food at those restaurants wasn't the same as the restaurants here in the US, it had a different taste and sometimes a different texture.

What food chain did you miss the most?

N.Benavides: I missed small Mexican food stores. *El Toro Bravo* definitely. And out of the bigger chains, I missed McDonald's.

J.Morales: I missed any type of Mexican food, I love Mexican food, its my favorite type of food. That's the only food that I missed. I missed tacos, I missed burritos...

J.Nino: I didn't miss any food chains. I missed my mother's cooking, I missed home-cooked meals. Well okay, I missed Mexican food too!

What about your work schedule. Ultimately we know your job isn't like a 9-5 job. But it is, however, a job in the sense that you are on a payroll system.

How does the schedule work, are you handed a physical sheet of paper, with your hours for the week?

N.Benavides: Our schedule changed every day. It was mostly about a 10, or so, hour day. We never left, or came back at the same time because we wouldn't want the "bad guys," to know our schedule. Sometimes, we would go out during the day and then come back to refuel, eat, and go back out for a night mission.

N.Benavides: I liked night missions because a lot of times we would drive without headlights and use all those cool "toys," I would see in the movies—like night vision goggles.

N.Benavides: We would get one day during the week to service our vehicles and whatever other equipment needed to be serviced. Those were our "days off."

J.Morales: If you're in the military, you're working 24-hours a day, 7 days a week. When you're a solider you're a military member 24-7, 7 days a week, 365 days of the year, until your contract is over. There is no time-and-a-half or overtime. They were times when we worked 72-hours straight.

J:Morales: During combat, just assume you're going to be working, every single day. Sometimes, its very rare, but you'll get a day off. But its very rare. From my experience, I worked almost every single day.

J.Nino: A schedule in the military is different. There are no set hours. When you're deployed you're on call 24-7. Of course, they let you rest in-between, and have days off, but they're really not days off because you can be recalled at any moment. You can work up to 20-hours a day.

Speaking of precisely that, of how your job wasn't a 9-5 job. It was also new to me, to learn the different careers that are offered within the Army and within the military.

For example, you went as military police, there are also nurses, cooks, and just about everything we would have here in the States.

Is that determined upon entering the Army, or how does that work?

N.Benavides: You first take a test to see what jobs you're qualified for. Once, you take that test; they let you know what jobs you qualify for and what jobs are available because sometimes the military might not be in need of nurses, or cooks, etc. So, even though you might want a nurse job, if the military branch doesn't need nurses, you mostly likely won't get that job. But the recruiter can help you find another job in that field, if, you're still interested.

J.Morales: You take an exam, whatever score you get, is how you are able to qualify for the different type of jobs that are offered. They give you a list of the jobs you qualify for, you then go to basic training and then you go to a job course where you learn to do that job.

J.Nino: Yes, it's determined before signing your contract. You have to take the Armed Services Vocational Aptitude Battery (ASVAB) test. Depending on what score you achieve, will determine what jobs in the military, you qualify for.

J.Nino: Once you choose a MOS (Military Occupational Specialty) or career, you'll attend basic training (Army Basic Combat Training, also known as boot camp). After you successfully graduate "basic," you'll attend Advanced Individual Training (AIT) which is training for the career you chose. In our case for our MOS/AIT, we attended Military Police School.

How were your days off in Iraq spent?

N.Benavides: We technically had no days off.

N.Benavides: But usually one day a week we would have, a day, we wouldn't go on missions. Those days were used to fix our vehicle (if something was broken). Or service it, like change the oil, etc. On days like that we were just in our living areas wearing sandals and Army shorts, chit-chatting.

N.Benavides: When my buddies (from the other base) would come, we would sometimes have a little, *carne asada*. There was a store on base that sometimes sold frozen meat, we would buy meat there and all hang out together.

J.Morales: I would wash my clothes, maybe go to the gym, make sure all my gear was ready for the next day, watch TV, call home—if I could. That's pretty much how I spent them, you couldn't really do much.

J.Nino: Sleeping, calling my family, going to the gym, watching movies, listening to music, going to the store and stocking up on junk food— and eating whatever fast-food they had like Pizza Hut, or Burger King— nothing close to the real thing (laughs). If any of the other guys were off at the same time, then hang out with them as well.

What about holidays like Christmas and/or, birthdays?

N.Benavides: We went on missions every holiday except Christmas. On Christmas night a few of us went to Midnight Mass.

N.Benavides: One of my buddies turned 21 while in Iraq, we found some non-alcoholic beer that had been in the hot sun for about one month, and we made him drink it. I turned 24 in Iraq; I think we had a little barbecue.

J.Morales: I remember Halloween, Thanksgiving and Christmas were spent in Iraq. I remember my birthday actually passed and I didn't even realize it was my birthday until days later. I didn't even remember it was my birthday.

J.Morales: For Christmas we went to the big base and we spent it together, we had coffee and we were just hanging out, we didn't really do much.

J.Nino: Christmas and birthdays were like any other day. Well, Christmas and Thanksgiving were cool because at the dining facility they had an amazingly delicious dinner prepared for us. Prime rib, turkey, ham and all the goodies that come with it.

J.Nino: We actually sat together and ate like a family. Birthdays and the other holidays were spent like any other normal day. I remember, New Year's Day, I was on a mission. As soon as midnight hit, I was like, "Huh, it's a new year?"

How was your faith before going to war, were you religious?

What about after and currently?

N:Benavides: I grew up Catholic, and I still am.

N:Benavides: I prayed to God daily and asked him for protection. In times when things got tough I always prayed to him and *la Virgin*. In my vehicle I wrote on a piece of tape, a quote that always motivated me to do my job. It was a quote I used from one of Tupac's song's, "My only fear is God." I taped that in front of me so, I saw it all the time.

N:Benavides: To this day, I thank God and *la Virgin* for bringing me home. My family back home also prayed for me and for my buddies.

J.Morales: I have always gone to church since a very young age. My faith has always been the same, before I joined, and now.

J.Nino: Before war, my faith was not strong at all. After war, it got a lot stronger, and it remains strong. Not a day goes by that I don't thank God for all the blessings he's given me.

Despite what a war zone could bring, the 3 of you, are very positive, happy people and tried to make the most of your experience there.

You had to for your own sanity as humans.

What were some of those things you did to distract yourself and in a way allow yourself to feel a little bit like you did before Iraq?

N.Benavides: I think all of us just being there for one another and always joking around. Playing pranks on other people, or on one another, helped me.

N.Benavides: I love music so listening to music also helped.

J.Morales: Workout, watch TV, watch *Martin*, that's about it. We didn't really get to do much.

Do you have an anecdote you would like to share?

N.Benavides: There are many good ones. One, I like was when we had a barbecue. We were all sitting next to a fire pit talking and looking at the fire when all of a sudden we heard a, "pop," like if it were a gunshot near us.

N.Benavides: So, we all jumped and each went in a different direction without hesitation, to find cover. All except, one idiot. That idiot was the one who threw a little bottle of gunpowder into the fire, which is why it sounded like a, "pop." He was there laughing and we laughed afterwards.

N.Benavides: Another one was when we knew we were all a week or so, from coming home, we had a small baseball game.

Getting back to the "deeper stuff."
At times we have really rough days at work, but then we realize there are only a couple of hours left of that workday and that cheers us back up and that thought allows us to finish the day.

We can go home and bathe, eat pizza, watch our favorite shows, or do whatever it is, we want.

Your work, however, is very different. You happen to live where you work, and for you, it wasn't about the hours in a workday but the length of time.

How did you keep going, knowing it was day 60 of a maybe 300- day-mission?

N.Benavides: I didn't focus on the last day of the mission—that was too far. I just focused on the job and getting home later that day.

N.Benavides: It was really important to stay focused and do your job and not be thinking about other stuff.

J.Morales: You just cant think about that. You just have to live it and realize that is your life. You cant be counting the days, you cant be counting the time, because if you do, you will drive yourself crazy. You just have to accept where you are at and just live your life.

J.Morales: It got to the point that I actually forgot how it was like to live in the United States, it was weird (laughs).

J.Nino: You just adapt to it—it's hard to explain. The military teaches you how to adapt to any environment. There is no point in counting down the days either. You just have to live day by day—keep yourself busy.

You have seen a lot. You have experienced a lot. You have heard a lot. And you have also traveled a lot (for work and for pleasure) even to places that might be unknown to us.

Having experienced that, what can you tell us about life?

What is the meaning of life to you?

N.Benavides: Life is the most important thing God has given us, and we must respect life. If we were to respect our lives and of our common human being's life, in the same way, I think less hate, and violence, and suffrage, would exist.

J.Morales: "What is life?" Life is extremely beautiful. Its not until we go through something significant that we realize how important life is especially at a young age we always tend to take everything for granted.

J.Morales: There is a lot to experience and a lot to learn from. I feel like, I am a life leaner, no matter how old you are, you are always going to learn something new.

J.Nino: Life is a beautiful gift from God that shouldn't be wasted or taken for granted.

What about democracy? Many people even today (2018) have not been abroad, or have left the city in which they live in. They might assume democracy, is the same everywhere, or that in fact, every country governs in that way.

You know this isn't the case, sometimes it takes wars to get this way, and our history has shown us it always takes men and women like you, soldiers, to keep a democracy alive.

What does that word, democracy, mean to you?

N.Benavides: The word democracy to me is America. The whole world knows we have it, and that is why they choose to come to the U.S.

J.Morales: Democracy to me means, equality. It means to me, opportunity. My family come from a communist country (Cuba), where we don't have the opportunity to do anything. Democracy to us is extremely important, that's pretty much what I fight for, to be able to say whatever I want and feel however I want to feel.

J.Morales: In our country, its so nice, whether you agree or disagree with whatever politics that are going on, you have the right to express, the way you feel. There are some countries that if you even dare to express how you feel, you get beaten or even killed.

Do you think war is really necessary?

N.Benavides: Unfortunately, yes. War is nothing new.

N.Benavides: War is what shaped the US and almost every major nation.

N.Benavides: Wars have happened and will continue to happen. And thankfully because of technology, less and less troops, have died in wars because of it.

J.Morales: I do think wars are necessary. I wish we would all get along and wouldn't have to go to war but that's not the case. There are countries out there that want to take over. There are countries out there that want to be ahead of the game. If we allow that to happen, what is going to happen is, those bad guys are going to come here to the United States and do everything over here and kill our families and put roadside bombs on our streets and on our freeways.

J.Morales: "How would you feel, if you're coming down the 55 Freeway, and you're hit by a roadside bomb?"

J.Morales: Yes, I do think we have to send our soldiers elsewhere and have war and be able to stop those people from coming here and doing that to us. Everyone wants to be stronger than the other person. There have been wars as far as I can remember, as far as humans have been alive, there have always been wars.

J.Nino: One of my favorite quotes is, "The only thing necessary for the triumph of evil is for good men to do nothing," by Edmund Burke.

J.Nino: To me, it means that sometimes war is necessary. From World War II, to the Afghan War, to the War Against Terrorism; we can't let evil try to take over the world. So, to answer your question, yes, war sometimes is necessary.

If we look at the history of the presidents of our country, most have served in our military. In fact, George Washington was the first president and therefore the 1st commander in chief of the Army.

However, it isn't a mandatory requirement to run for office, and there have been many presidents, including our current president (Trump) and our prior president (Obama) who have never served.

It seems as though having served could be beneficial for a president, after all, he essentially governs our entire country and has the final say when it comes to our troops.

What do you think about this?

Does that bother you, or how do you feel about this?

N.Benavides: It would be nice if the president served. He is the commander in chief—he leads the military. But serving in the military doesn't make you a great leader, or a better leader. A lot of presidents have served great terms and never served in the military.

N.Benavides: The ones that didn't serve could bring a new perspective, and different ideas. However, if the ones that didn't serve try to change the military into something they want to see it can be dangerous. Trying to change a military of over 200 years in customs and traditions, is dangerous.

J.Morales: To be honest with you, I have never thought about this, until now that you ask me. But its obviously not necessary to be a great leader or to be a great president. But if it were me, I would love for it to be mandatory. But if you think about it everyone has different walks of life, and their very own calling.

J.Morales: "If it wasn't their calling when they were 18-years-old, and now they're older, now they cant be president because they didn't join?" We would be missing out on a good president.

J.Nino: No, it doesn't bother me at all. Trump wasn't in the military, and he's doing a mighty fine job so far running this country.

America is known for a lot of things. Its innovation in technology, its pop culture, being built by immigrants and to this day housing the most ethnic groups outside of their native countries, caring for our human rights through not only our Constitution but by organizations like the United Nations.

For its FREEDOM...and so on.

What are you most proud of America for?

N.Benavides: It's freedom. Other nations kill or imprison its citizens for protesting, or for speaking up. But in the US you can burn the flag and talk bad about its leaders and, still, live happily.

J.Morales: How we stick together. Everything we do, we do together. We help out worldwide. And everything you mentioned—you just hit it right on the door nail.

J.Morales: I am extremely proud of this country and that's why I always call myself an American, I fly American flags everywhere I go. I come from Cuban descent but I consider myself an American, *I am* an American.

J.Morales: I always say, "I am an American," because I am so proud from where I come from.

J.Nino: I am proud of America for its freedom! Being in Iraq shows you, what it is like to live in poverty and have no rights. It's sad to think people here think they are oppressed by the government but in reality, they don't know the true meaning of oppression.

I just had dinner with a little nephew of mine who is 6-years-old. All of dinner, he talked about wanting to be a soldier when he grows up (he was wearing a camouflage sweater).

There are a lot of little boys and girls who just like him want to be soldiers when they grow up.

What would you tell them?

N.Benavides: To first go to school, and get a degree. Research exactly what you want and if you don't end up joining, still keep that patriotism.

J.Morales: If it comes from the heart and that's something that they really want to do, then go for it. My son is 1-years-old and I dress him up in little Army onesies, Army uniforms, and stuff like that. I also have a stepson that is 8-years-old and one that is 6-years-old. They're dad and their mom were in the Military too. Their dad was in the Army, *I am* in the Army and their mom was in the Marine Corps for 9 years. They have a lot of influence, they always talk about joining the military. I would be very supportive.

J.Morales: Its up to them (it depends on their personalities) but if I could go back and do it all over again, I would have probably graduated from college before I joined, so I could have been an officer. I would have definitely joined as an officer just because you have more opportunities. But either way, it would have been the best. The only advice I have is that, it would be a great opportunity for everyone.

J.Nino: I would just tell him, how cool it is to be a soldier (laughs).

J.Nino: It's cute when little kids are inspired to be a soldier. My nephew tells me the same thing. He's very patriotic too—I love it!

Is there anything you want all of us to know, not just Americans, but everyone about the military?

Or, wish we knew about the military/war?

N.Benavides: Don't believe everything Hollywood or the media, tell you.

N.Benavides: And every soldier has a story, they're all different and won't be the same. What one troop experienced can be different from another.

J.Morales: Right now we're fortunate that we have so much support because during the Vietnam War Era the soldiers (Marines, the Airmen..etc.) didn't have the support we have today. They were treated very badly, they were even called "killers."

J.Morales: I just want everyone to know worldwide how appreciative I am of the support. My generation has been extremely supportive.

J.Morales: We're proud of our service and it has a lot to do with everyone's support.

J.Nino: Support our troops.

J.Nino: Our troops don't decide what wars we go into, we just follow orders. Sometimes troops are against war, but we follow orders.

As veterans, what do you think is a respectful way that we can honor our troops?

N.Benavides: By not forgetting them.

N.Benavides: If they need medical support, always help them, they shouldn't have to wait this long. Have a day to appreciate veterans. But also I think veterans aren't entitled to any special treatment. Especially post 9/11 veterans.

N.Benavides: Like I said before, "We all volunteered to do this job." We shouldn't walk around thinking the world owes us everything for having volunteered.

J.Morales: If you see a veteran, thank them for their service, that's extremely nice. I think everyone appreciates that.

J.Nino: Show support by thanking them. It's not necessary but a simple, "thank you," means a lot to us. Supporting us means a lot to us.

In every job, we will have those that love what we do, and we will also have critics.

We know this is the case for you too, what has been the worst thing said to you about your job?

Or what is something perhaps, you, yourself don't like about it?

N:Benavides: Waking up, very early, and just standing in formation for a long time, until people figure out whats going on.

J.Morales: The worst thing that has ever been said was, "You're probably going to die." Which was a possibility but that was probably the worst thing said to me. But it didn't stop me from what I wanted to do.

J.Nino: Nothing really bad has ever been said to me. But there have been things said that really boils my blood like protesters at a military members funeral, holding up signs that read, "Thank God for a dead soldier," etc.

There have also been people (a lot of them strangers) that have been very supportive of you. One of those strangers that I am referring to, gave you tickets to a baseball game.

Tell me more about gestures like that.

What have they meant to you?

N.Benavides: People buy meals for us—and the military is known for drinking— a lot of people will buy us drinks or ask to have a beer with us.

J.Morales: I wasn't there for the baseball game but I have experienced going to a restaurant and when I go to pay the bill, the bill has already been paid. That is amazing, that makes me feel extremely good. And because that has happened to me, I have done it to others. When I've encountered older Vietnam vets, I have paid for their meal and then walked away. Not expecting a thank you, or anything, just because I know how good that feels.

J.Morales: It feels amazing and I am very appreciative of that.

J.Nino: It's a great feeling but in all honesty, I don't like to receive gifts from people. Like previously said a simple, "thank you," is perfect.

J.Nino: It shows people really care and it makes us feel really good about what we have done and what we are doing.

What about the holidays that are devoted to all of our military like Veterans Day, Memorial Day, 4th of July...?

How should we observe those days without forgetting their significance?

N.Benavides: Have fun! Be with your loved ones and family. But take time to notice people died for us to enjoy our time.

N.Benavides: And realize that there are still people overseas fighting while we are enjoying our days off.

J.Morales: My family and I (my wife,kids and I), for Veterans Day we like to go to the veteran cemeteries. We put flags on all of the veterans gravesites. We like to go to parades and just be involved. I think its extremely import ant not just because we were in the military but to also celebrate people who are still serving and those who passed away.

J.Morales: I always make it about all of us spending time together and celebrating.

J.Nino: Enjoy the day as if it were any other day. But not only those days, enjoy every day, because we live in a country that's given us the right to live freely.

It seemed to be that last year (2017) there was a sudden uproar of boycotting the national anthem by not standing for it. Those that did, felt they were simply doing what America has always taught us to do when we don't believe in something—revolutionize through protest. Those that protested in that way, also, stand firm in believing they are simply exercising their First Amendment, the right to freedom of speech, religion, and press. And feel that by being looked badly upon for doing this, it contradicts what America is all about.

Americans, however, have been paying homage to our country by standing for the national anthem since the start of it. According to *The Hill*, we do this to salute our military that fight for our freedom, to show the unity we share for our flag that unites us as Americans, to honor the fact that we don't have reigning monarchy in power but in fact a president that, we, ourselves, as citizens of our country elect, to honor the justice system that has been put in place ever since our founding fathers. And lastly, we stand to show the future generations the respect we believe our country deserves.

Do you want to comment on this?

What's your perspective?

N.Benavides: It is absolutely their right. However, just because it's their right, it doesn't make it right. The anthem represents American and also the troops.

N.Benavides: They were protesting police brutally. Although police officers also say an oath and are very patriotic, it is more known that the anthem represents the troops more than it does the police.

N.Benavides: By choosing to pretest the anthem they are showing a great disrespect to the troops and anthem. I believe it is wrong. Those protesters have the right to protest but should choose a different subject to protest.

J.Morales: I personally think its extremely offensive. People died for our flag and for our country. I completely agree that we have our Fist Amendment right and everyone deserves the right to do whatever they want to do and speak of whatever they want to speak of. But as far as burning the flag and stomping on it, that is disrespectful.

J.Morales: Its one of those things that even if I am in a different country and they are saying their anthem or saluting their flag, I respect them enough to stand up and even if I don't want to participate, I will stand up, quietly. I wont disrespect their country.

J.Morales: I just find it extremely offensive because if you need this country's help whether its for disability, or welfare—this country is right there to help you, right away. When you're disrespecting the flag—I never have liked that at all.

J.Nino: I think it's stupid and ignorant to not stand for the national anthem, and to relate racism to the national anthem and the flag. But that's what the First Amendment is there for, and that's why, soldier's like myself risk our lives for.

Tell me something that you admire from each other?

N.Benavides: We are all different. I admire every one of my brothers for being great men. They are funny, sarcastic and humble.

J.Morales: Their loyalty and their friendship—period.

J.Morales: I have friends that I have known longer, than I have known any of these guys, but my bond is nothing close to my bond with my buddies that I deployed with.

J.Morales: How loyal they are, how respectful they are—that is what I admire from them.

J.Nino: They're the brothers, I never had.

J.Nino: We've been through so much—good and bad. And they have always been there for me.

J.Nino: We may argue, we may disagree with things, talk crap to one another, but at the end of the day, they're *still* my brothers, and I love them with all of my heart.

Although this book is intended for everyone, the theme of it is 30. What stage of your life were you in, at 30, and where were you living?

Do you have any advice for those of us turning 30 this year?

N.Benavides: I was with my family—I had a little daughter and was enjoying life.

N.Benavides: For 30-year-old's, I would say, "Enjoy life."

N.Benavides: You aren't in your 20's anymore, so you shouldn't act that dumb but still enjoy life and focus on living a good life for yourself and for your community.

J.Morales: At 30, I think it was a turning point in my life. At 30-years-old, I ended up getting married, buying a house, my wife and I were expecting a baby, we started our family. I traveled, I worked...

J.Morales: I feel that at 30-years-old, its kind of like the time of your life when you should be settled in. Your 20's can be your experimental years (maybe you changed jobs, you looked for different opportunities). But I think that as 30-years-old, its the time when all of us as adults, need to settle down and do what we need to do, as adults.

J.Morales: At that age a lot of the younger kids in their early twenties look at you. Be a hard worker, always think of others before you think of yourself, always be respectful. At that age (30) you need to think differently and act differently from when you were in your twenties.

How can we live a better life?

N.Benavides: Help when you can.

N.Benavides: Respect everyone.

N.Benavides: And be firm and proud of your beliefs, and values.

J.Morales:Just love each other, help each other out, as best as you can. There are a lot of people who are extremely selfish and its all about, themselves, over other people.

J.Morales: I think that once we start thinking of others instead of ourselves by donating our time and efforts, this world will be a better place.

J.Nino: Live your life however you want to live it. Humans aren't good at taking advice.

J.Nino: It's not until we're in a life-or-death situation where they really find the true meaning of life.

Anything else you want to add?

N.Benavides: I would like to thank my brothers for still keeping in touch after ten years.

N.Benavides: Also, my family for always supporting me while I was deployed. And my wife, and children for putting up with me.

N.Benavides: And the *Chiva* community (C.D. Guadalajara) for also showing their support while I was in Iraq.

I want the pages of this book, or at least of your chapter, to be a tribute to every single military person of our country. Alive and deceased. Veterans that fought wars before I was born to soldiers that are fighting current ones for our country, today, right now.

Having said that, can you please name one person who is either serving or who has served that you want to thank (other than the 3 of you)?

J.Morales: Definitely. I want to thank my Police Explorer adviser, Rob Dimel, he is a police officer for the Costa Mesa Police Department. He was actually also in the Army. My whole life, like I mentioned earlier in the interview, I always wanted to join the military. But it was him that made me say to myself, "Hey, I look up to this man and want to do everything that he ever did."

J.Morales: I want to thank Rob Dimel for always being there for me and for always giving me great advice, and for being such a great support system. From the age of 17 until now—on Wednesday I'll be 33-years-old—he still keeps in touch and he is still always there for whenever I need good advice.

J.Morales: He's my mentor, he's my friend, he's my brother. If it wasn't for him giving me the opportunity to be in the Police Explorer program, I think I would have ended up a lot different than how I did.

Thank you!!

ACKNOWLEDGMENTS

I talked about how hard this project was in my Introduction but I also want to mention how much fun I had, I really did have a lot of fun, this has been my favorite project of my life. I am extremely thankful for everyone's help, participation and the flexibility you had with me. There are days when random thoughts, words, and phrases pop up in my head from what I heard during the interviews. And a lot of those thoughts have helped me in so many great ways.

Thank you, to all of you for that!!

Mr. José Hernández, your participation in this book is very special to me. I have grown up listening to your music and have enjoyed it for many years. I could probably say all of my life. But I still remember the day when one of your performances changed my life. It was on a summer day, about 10-years-ago, my mother and I were surrounded by a crowd that felt just like we did, amazed at how wonderful your concert was. We like the rest of the people there were enjoying the music, the happiness, the professionalism you transmit while you're on stage. And the beautiful way in which you introduce our culture through your music to those that are just beginning to learn about it.

It was that day at the Orange County Fair when I was about 20-years-old that I realized it wasn't just my parent's influence that made me like you and Mariachi Sol de Mexico but it was actually myself who did. And like I told you already, I went home and Googled you because I knew you from afar but I wanted to know more about your story. And that night, after the concert while I Googled you and read all about you and your wife, Teresa, I became even more fascinated with you, your family and Sol de Mexico.

But even then I never thought that one day, I would send you an email that asked you for your participation in what at that moment was just an idea, a thought, and a hope. And even though you have your Mariachi Heritage Society foundation and help a lot throughout our community—I know how busy you are—I never actually thought I would receive a response from you or from your team. Much less, a "Yes." But I received both— a response and a "Yes."

And my favorite part about it all were your actions and your simplicity throughout the process. Even though you didn't know me, you treated me as if we were cousins or friends. And in the interview, you said, "I'll tell you this," and then you mentioned something profound you felt in your life. Well, I'll tell *you* this, you have touched my entire heart Mr. Hernández.

Thank you from my entire heart!!

Enrique A. Gutierrez, I still see you as the winner of Univision's contest but you have become even more than that, and you have become even more than the young boy who you describe in your chapter.

You have become a talented journalist—serious but also approachable. You have become an inspiration to me through all of the philanthropy work you do. And for the passion you have for your job.

I never thought I would receive a response from you either but I was happy I did, because I knew you had a great story to share—a story that is full of perseverance, hard work, and dedication.

Thank you!!

To everyone else that also participated in this book and that I have met throughout my life—30 years of it. Thank you!! It was hard choosing who

I wanted in this book, and it was even harder to narrow it down to 30 chapters, 36 people, but I knew you were the indicated ones and the ones that have stories—journeys—and personality traits we could all learn from.

I enjoyed learning even more than I already knew about you!!

Thank you!!

Alexander Yu

Andrea Maradiaga

Angie and Jorge Garcia

Angie C. Seagren

Araceli Torres Padilla

Ariyanna O'Neal

Baoyiruole

Carlos Ibarra

Chato

Christina McFaul

Ginamarie and Annamarie Russo

Gloria Barrera

Jorge Moto

Linda Neel

Lupe Carrillo

Mario Alberto Guzmán Jaime

Marisol Ugues

Melina Chavez Bobadilla

Michele and Keith Green

Nadia Adose

Polen Pulluoğlu

Rodrigo Navarro-Ramirez, M.D., M.S

Ruth and Marco Argueta

Sonia Masters

Staff Sergeant Nelson Benavides

Staff Sergeant Jeeandy Morales

Staff Sergeant Joseph Nino

Stefhania Mejia

Tina Carstensen

Yasmin Siqueira Dahás

I also want to thank my parents, I think I have made it clear in this book how much I love them and the enormous meaning they have in my life. But just in case I haven't made it clear here or in my 30 years of life, mom and dad, I love you!!

Thank you for everything you do for me, and have done for me!!

And to the rest that don't fall too far behind...

My big sister, Beatrice. She is the first writer of the family.

I was a child when "Betty," would recount stories for me late at night that led to my bedtime. I believe it was those stories that allowed me to dream beautifully at night and allowed me to wake up feeling as if I could make those dreams come alive.

She's never stopped telling me stories—just like our dad—I think she inherited that gene too. And not only has she shared stories with me that have expanded my mind—she has also always provided me with the tools that have allowed me to create my very own stories. And with many hours of usage on her many laptops. Somehow I always break mine (internally) and somehow she always has laptops to share.

She's also manged to learn how to tune me out without me noticing...that takes a lot of skills.

Thank you, I love you!!

My middle sister, Lorena. Lis, as we call her. She's the relaxed one but secretly super brilliant! Beware.

I was just a 5-year-old kindergartner when I ran to tell her that I had written a song. A song I told her I had written for our dad. Without any laughter and without asking any questions—she believed me. I don't know what she was thinking in her head, probably the obvious, "Okay that is *so* not a song."

But she believed me—and that motivated me.

She also made all the fuss that a 5-year-old nourishes from. I still strongly believe that day, helped shape my life—it allowed me to feel as if I could really do anything I wanted—simply because my sister believed me.

She's been doing that ever since.

Thank you, I love you!!

My brother, Nelson. The self-proclaimed, "Man of the House."

Nelson and I would wrestle together when we were little! I didn't know that wasn't necessarily "normal" behavior for a little girl—until I was in the 3rd grade. I still clearly remember the day when I walked up to Ms.Crockey and asked her how to spell the world, "wrestle." I was writing about what I loved to do, and wrestling with my brother made it to my list.

Suddenly, as I had just finished my sentence to Mrs.Crockey—the two cutest boys of the 3rd grade and of my classroom looked at one another, giggled, and then they asked me, " You wrestle with your brother??"

That's the day I realized wrestling with a brother isn't *that* normal, when you're a little girl. But, hey, it was fun and ultimately I share this story because those days have helped me even today! What Nelson taught me back then has helped me on days when I need to break boxes here in New York City. And on days when I need to be "tough," I think of those days with my brother, and suddenly I am.

Thank you!! I love you!

Lorena, my sister-in-law.

Thank you for sharing your girls with us and for incorporating to our family so well.

Love you!!

Shannon, my brother-in-law.

You are selfless in every way possible. Thank you for loving my family, for always being there to help us.

Love you and your band Rumble King!!

To everyone else who made my childhood special and who has provided me with the "little things" that have actually turned into very big things in my life.

Saint Joachim Catholic Church

Saint Joachim Youth Group

Saint Justin Martyr Young Adult Group

Girl Scouts of America

Mr. and Mrs. Hasbrouck

Mr. and Mrs. Grantham and the entire Grantham family!

All of my friends and extended family...I LOVE you!!

I also want to thank everyone who donates their time and money to support the causes that need us most.

Thank you to everyone who helped with this book, and provided a service.

To everyone who purchased this book and is reading this, thank you!!

Thank you Jesus Christ for helping me every single day of my life! I love you!

From my entire heart,

Griselda Benavides

Q&A SESSION
BETWEEN YOU AND I

---

1. What interview did you enjoy the most?

Why?

2. What is your favorite piece of advice that was offered?

3. What is something new that you learned from reading this book?

4. Most of the participants of this book talk about a goal they've had. Can you name a goal you have?

5. How do you plan to reach that goal?

What is the first step you plan to take to reach your goal?

When do you want to reach it by?

6. Many of the participants also mention they had to let go of something to move forward, perhaps even forgive someone, or forget about something that was haunting them.

What do you plan to forget (that is haunting you), or who do you plan to forgive to allow yourself to move forward with your life?

7. What quality do you love most about yourself?

How can you use that quality of yours to help serve those in your community?

8. If you could do ANYTHING that you wanted to do, what would it be?

9. After reading about the different issues that exist around us, what cause would you like to contribute to?

And how will you contribute?

When will you contribute?

10. If you could thank anyone that you wanted to, or tell someone that you loved them, who would it be?

When will it be?

Thank you!!

www.ingramcontent.com/pod-product-compliance
Lightning Source LLC
LaVergne TN
LVHW041606070426
835507LV00008B/160